Enrico Finazzer
Ralph Riccio

Italian Artillery
of the Second Word War

STRATUS

Published in Poland in 2015
by STRATUS s.c.
Po. Box 123,
27-600 Sandomierz 1, Poland
e-mail: office@mmpbooks.biz
for
Mushroom Model Publica-
tions,
e-mail: rogerw@mmpbooks.biz
© 2015 Mushroom Model
Publications.
http://www.mmpbooks.biz

ISBN
978-83-63678-61-6

Editor in chief
Roger Wallsgrove

Editorial Team
Bartłomiej Belcarz
Robert Pęczkowski
Artur Juszczak

Scale Plans
Dariusz Karnas
based on
Rodolfo Ciuffoletti,
Nicola Pignato
drawings

DTP
Artur Juszczak

Printed by
Drukarnia Diecezjalna,
ul. Żeromskiego 4,
27-600 Sandomierz
tel. +48 (15) 832 31 92;
fax +48 (15) 832 77 87
www.wds.pl
marketing@wds.pl

PRINTED IN POLAND

Table of contents

To my wife who always encourages this passion of mine for military history and to my wonderful boys, Alessandro and Massimiliano, who have followed daily the progress of my work. (Enrico Finazzer)

For my part, this book is dedicated to the memory of Nicola Pignato who was Italy's preeminent military historian, a prolific writer, and who acted as a mentor to me for many years prior to his untimely passing in July 2010. Although no longer with us, Nicola has left an enduring legacy in the field of Italian military history.

Acknowledgements

Many people, organizations and institutions have offered their co-operation for this book, providing material and advice.

First of all, I would thank my friends Luca and Paolo, who have supported me since the beginning of my adventure.

A special thanks to Claudio Pergher and to the Gruppo Modellistico Trentino, who have generously opened their archives, as well as to Andrea and Antonio Tallillo. Other contributors whose help is particularly appreciated have been Gianna Olivero, Paolo Zanlucchi, Daniele Ravenna, Fabio Temeroli and Daniele Guglielmi.

Rodolfo Ciuffoletti deserves a special mention for his ground-breaking work with the scale drawings that have added much to this book.

We would also like to thank Roger Wallsgrove, our editor in England, and Robert Pęczkowski and the staff of Stratus in Poland for their willingness to take on this project and their enthusiasm and encouragement as the work progressed.

This work would not have been possible without the contributions of USSME, Rome; Istituto Piemontese per la Storia della Resistenza, Torino; Istituto Panzarasa, Trieste; Sacrario dei Caduti d'Oltremare, Bari; Fondazione Ansaldo, Genova; Centro Storico FIAT, Torino; Museo Storico Nazionale dell'Artiglieria, Torino; Museo Storico della Guerra, Rovereto; Gordon Blakely and Jon Bernstein of the US Army Artillery Museum, Fort Sill, Oklahoma.

As co-author of this book, duty compels me to acknowledge the role that Nicola Pignato played in my ability to contribute to this book. Nicola ("Nick") and I were working together on a book very similar to this one at the time of his passing in July 2010, but I lost all interest in the project when Nick was no longer there to offer advice, encouragement, and information. Some three years later when I was contacted by Enrico Finazzer who asked if I would be interested in working with him on an expanded English-language version of a book he had published in Italy on the subject I readily agreed, sensing an opportunity to renew work in an area that I believe would very much have pleased Nick, who had coached me through my earlier research and work on the subject. (Ralph Riccio)

List of abbreviations

ARMIR	*Armata Italiana in Russia* – Italian Army in Russia; code name of the 8th Army formed in spring 1942 by sending the II Army Corps and the Alpine Troops Army Corps to the Eastern Front to join the XXXV Army Corps already in Russia.
CSIR	*Corpo di Spedizione Italiano in Russia* – Italian Army Corps in Russia; code name of the XXXV Army Corps sent to the Eastern Front in summer 1941 to fight alongside the *Wehrmacht*
DSSTAM	*Direzione Superiore del Servizio Tecnico Armi e Munizioni* – Weapon and Ammunition Technical Service Command
ENR	*Esercito Nazionale Repubblicano* – National Republican Army; the army levied by the RSI after the Italian Armistice
GaF	*Guardia alla Frontiera* – Frontier Guard; branch of the *Regio Esercito* entrusted with the fixed military emplacements and fortifications along Italian borders
GNR	*Guardia Nazionale Repubblicana* – National Republican Guard; military organization formed by the reconstituted Fascist party in the RSI territory, charged with territorial defence.
MACA	*Milizia Artiglieria Contraerei* – Anti-Aircraft Militia; branch of the MVSN responsible for territorial air defence
MILMART	*Milizia Marittima* – Maritime Militia; branch of the MVSN charged with the defence of the coasts and responsible for coastal artillery
MVSN	*Milizia Volontaria per la Sicurezza Nazionale* – National Security Voluntary Militia; military organization levied on a voluntary basis by the Fascist party. During the war this organization was entrusted with territorial defence, but several units (*legioni* – legions) saw front line action
RSI	*Repubblica Sociale Italiana* – Italian Social Republic; the state established by Benito Mussolini in the centre and north of Italy in autumn 1943, after the Armistice of the Kingdom of Italy with the Allies. It fell in April 1945.

Introduction

Historical framework

In 1918 Italy came out of WWI as a victorious but very destabilized country. After a few years of ferocious struggle among opposing factions, in October 1922 the Fascist Party of Benito Mussolini, supported by its para-military organization, the Blackshirts *(Camicie Nere)*, imposed its dictatorship on the country.

In the following years the Italian government promoted an adventurous foreign policy, devised to obtain prestige and territories, even if this meant openly challenging France and Great Britain. It was in this context that war was waged against the Kingdom of Ethiopia, between autumn 1935 and spring 1936, ending with the conquest of the country which became an Italian colony, forming along with the former Italian colonies of Eritrea and Somalia the territory known as *Africa Orientale Italiana* (Italian East Africa). Italian forces also participated In the Spanish civil war, from 1936 to 1939, aiding General Francisco Franco and his coup against the legitimate government.

These moves finally put an end to friendly relationships with France and Great Britain and pushed Italy into the arms of the new Third Reich, with the signature of a first pact in 1936, called *Asse Roma Berlino* (Rome Berlin Axis) and, in 1939, of the *Patto d'acciaio* (Iron Pact).

When in September 1939 Germany invaded Poland, thus starting WWII, Italy, whose army was not at all ready for a new war, remained neutral, finally entering the war in June 1940. The first months of the war were a real disaster for the Italian Army, which lost Italian East Africa, almost lost its entire North African colony of Libya and was at risk of being defeated by the Greek army. It was only the intervention of the German army that saved the day.

In 1943, after almost three years of war, the situation appeared desperate for the Axis forces, with North Africa almost lost to the Anglo-American forces, the German army completely absorbed on the Eastern Front, Italian cities exposed to continuous bombing and the Allied landing in Sicily. With this scenario facing him, in July the Italian King, Vittorio Emanuele III, decided to get rid of the Fascist government and ordered the arrest of Mussolini. A new government, led by General Pietro Badoglio, negotiated an armistice with the Allies and in September Italy surrendered.

In the few confused days following the surrender, the Germans took over most of Italy's territory, capturing hundreds of thousands of Italian soldiers; the King and the government left the capital city of Rome and took refuge in the south, in Brindisi, an area free of German troops. In the north Benito Mussolini, in the meantime liberated by the Germans, formed a new government and proclaimed the republic, called the *Repubblica Sociale Italiana*.

The war in Italy continued until 1945, waged by the Germans and the armed forces of the *RSI*, mainly the *Esercito Nazionale Repubblicano* but by other units as well, like the volunteer X^a *MAS*, against the Allies and the small army raised by the legitimate government in the south, the *I Raggruppamento Motorizzato* (1st Motorised Group) and later the *Corpo Italiano di Liberazione* (Italian Liberation Corps). Irregular units, known as partisan units, had operated behind German lines since the armistice was signed.

The war in Italy ended on 2 May 1945, when the surrender of the German and *RSI* forces, signed previously on 29 April, became effective.

Italian artillery between the wars

During WWII the Italian army suffered a severe lack of good artillery. In fact, when Italy entered the war in June 1940, its army, the *Regio Esercito*, was equipped with pieces of artillery that were not very dissimilar to those of the other belligerents, apart from the German army, but during the next three years until the surrender to the Allies in September 1943, the inferiority became more and more evident.

This situation depended mainly on three circumstances. First of all, Italy had acquired hundreds of pieces of artillery of various calibers from the former Austro-Hungarian Empire at the end of WWI, either captured in the field or obtained as war reparations. Since these pieces were of good quality, being produced by some of the best factories in Europe such as Škoda and Böhler, the Italian army did not feel the need to develop and adopt anything new for many years.

Secondly, the financial situation of Italy between the wars was not such as to permit an extensive program of renovation of the artillery, nor, for that matter, of any other military equipment, since the country lacked both the money and the industrial capability to carry it out[1]. Furthermore, the few resources at hand were dispersed in a series of adventurous actions, the more notorious being the above mentioned conquest of Abyssinia and the intervention in the Spanish Civil War, which added some prestige to the Fascist regime that held power in Italy, but at a heavy cost.

Finally, the Italian army itself made some mistakes in the evaluation of its own needs, wasting time and resources on artillery types that favoured lightness and agility but which sacrificed power and range. The *Regio Esercito* was indeed convinced that the theatre of the next war in which it would be engaged would be the Alps, leaving aside other options that were obviously at hand, like the vast deserts of North Africa where the Italian colony of Libya was surrounded by potentially hostile French Tunisia and British Egypt. As a consequence, the main effort went into the development of new 75mm divisional artillery while other armies were already focused for the same purpose on pieces of larger caliber that ranged from 88mm, like the British 25 pdr, to 105mm pieces.

With the situation as described, until the early 1930s, the best efforts were dedicated to the improvement of the old material, by developing more effective ammunition and by adapting it to a certain degree of mechanization.

On the first point, the major pre-war innovation was the introduction of the *modello 32* ammunition, which added some range. Later, during the war, new hollow charge rounds went into production, called *EP* (i.e *Effetto Pronto*) and *EPS*, which enhanced the anti-tank capability of Italian artillery.

Concerning the latter point, heavier artillery was in principle based on mechanical towing since the middle of WWI, basically due to a shortage of animals to assign to this duty, although at a slow pace, while the divisional artillery, equipped, as seen, with WWI guns and howitzers with wooden wheels, was until the 1930s based almost entirely on animal traction. Eventually, the Italian army tried to adapt its artillery pieces to powered traction at higher speed, by mounting them on special bogies, called *carrelli elastici*, that had metal wheels with semi-pneumatic tires and which were towed by artillery tractors.

Later on, as the war approached, they began a program to replace the original wheels with new metal wheels, first in elektron[2] and later in pressed steel, that allowed direct towing of the pieces by artillery tractors, but the process was slow and at the outbreak of WWII only few dozen pieces were ready.

As for prime movers, historically, the Italian army, like many other armies, used purpose-built tractors to tow artillery pieces but made relatively little use of general purpose or general service cargo trucks, to tow anything other than light artillery pieces. The late 1920s and early 1930s saw an important and successful effort to upgrade the heavy artillery tractors, with the introduction of new vehicles that gave a good account of themselves during the war. For field artillery, however, the shift from animal traction to mechanical traction was more difficult, because the production of the new vehicles started late and Italian industry could not keep up with the requests, so that at the outset of the war, much of the Italian artillery was still towed by horses, not unlike the German

---

1   According to C. Favagrossa, responsible for the military production in the years preceding the war and during the war itself, in 1939 the production capacity of the Italian industry did not exceed 70 pieces per month, and the forecast was to reach 300 per month in 1941. See Perchè perdemmo la Guerra, page 48.

2   Elektron was an alloy of magnesium, copper and zinc.

army which, despite its renown as a mechanized force, still used huge numbers of horses to tow its artillery.

For those new designs that were considered, in 1929 the army put forward specific requests for new and more effective artillery pieces, that in the next few years gave rise to some very good prototypes that were produced in small numbers. However, it was not until a few months before the outbreak of WWII, in spring 1938, that Italy launched a vast program of total renovation of its artillery inventory (*Primo Programma*). That program involved the production of several hundred pieces, followed in spring 1940 by another program, which added more orders (*Secondo Programma*)[3]. Both of these programs were drastically scaled back shortly thereafter, in December 1940, due to the lack of raw materials that already affected Italian industry. By February 1941 the *Secondo Programma* was abandoned altogether in order to concentrate resources on the reduced first program. Priority was given to more powerful anti-aircraft guns, which were badly needed.

Collar flash: Field artillery; horse-drawn artillery; heavy field artillery; heavy anti-aircraft artillery.

Collar flash: Mountain artillery.

Collar flash: Armoured artillery (self-propelled).

Collar flash: Airborne artillery.

See also back cover.

Collar flashes or insignia denoted a soldier's branch of service. There were four types of collar flash used by the artillery. The basic insignia consisted of an irregularly shaped badge with one straight long side, a straight short side at a right angle to the long side, another straight short side parallel to the long side, and a concave curve connecting the ends of the two parallel straight sides; the field of this badge was black, with an orange border, and within the black field, close to the short side or end was a five-pointed silver star. The basic artillery insignia was worn by field artillery, heavy field artillery, heavy anti-aircraft artillery, and horse-drawn artillery personnel. Mountain artillery personnel wore an insignia rectangular in shape superimposing the basic insignia on a green background; similarly, armoured artillery personnel wore a rectangular insignia formed by superimposing the basic insignia on a blue background; finally, airborne (parachute) artillery personnel wore a rectangular insignia which had the basic artillery badge superimposed on a blue background that had a white parachute and golden wing in the blue field.

With respect to the organization of the army, and of the artillery in particular, Italy entered the war with the army organized on divisions based on two infantry regiments and one *reggimento d'artiglieria divisionale* (divisional artillery regiment), which was the new designation for the old *artiglieria campale* (field artillery), changed in the mid 1930s. The artillery regiment consisted of three *gruppi* (battalions) generally equipped with 75mm guns of various types and 100mm howitzers. Later during the war front line artillery regiments were sometimes reinforced with 105mm guns.

Two or more divisions formed an army corps (*corpo d'armata*) that had its own artillery grouped in a *raggruppamento d'artiglieria di corpo d'armata*, (army corps artillery grouping), a designation that in the same period replaced the traditional one of *artiglieria pesante campale* (heavy field artillery), consisting of several battalions, that ranged from 105mm guns to 149mm howitzers.

Two or more army corps formed an army (*armata*), equipped with the heavier artillery, e.g. 149mm guns and a variety of howitzers and bombards, assigned to a *raggruppamento di artiglieria d'armata* (army artillery grouping), the designation that had replaced *artiglieria pesante*[4].

There were as well pieces of light artillery, either 47mm or 65mm, assigned to direct infantry support within the infantry regiments.

---

3   The Primo Programma entailed the production of over 3,500 pieces of artillery, from 47mm to 210mm; the Secondo Programma added over 4,600 pieces more.

4   According to documents issued by the Italian High Command, in June 1940 there were an average of four battalions for each army corps artillery grouping and nine battalions for each army artillery grouping, with a total of 139 operational battalions. See Stato di efficienza dell'esercito al 1° giugno 1940 – XVIII, in M. Montanari, L'esercito italiano alla vigilia della Seconda Guerra Mondiale, page 526.

At each level there was also an anti-aircraft component, which, until well into the war, was based on 20mm cannon and 75mm guns. It was not until 1942 that the field units received a few batteries of 90mm guns, the excellent 90/53, which was a dual-purpose gun useful also as an anti-tank weapon, and the famous German *8.8 cm FlaK*.

In summary, Italy entered WWII in June 1940 equipped with about 10,000 cannons, but only about 1,300 produced in the 1930s; among them, about 1,000 were small 47mm guns while about 300 other pieces were of various calibers. The remaining pieces were produced before and during WWI, and a good share of them had not seen any significant renovation between the wars. Wartime production, unfortunately, could not meet in any way the mounting demand for new and better material.

In addition to the categories of artillery used by Italy during WWII that are examined in detail in this volume, several hundred additional pieces of various types, normally older pieces or war booty guns and howitzers, were assigned to static or coastal artillery duties along Italy's borders as well as in occupied territories and are not within the scope of this book. These guns were manned by special units of the *GaF* and MILMART which was a special branch of the Blackshirts. A large number of these guns were former Austro-Hungarian pieces; these included the 305/8 siege mortar, 305/10 siege howitzer, 380/15 siege howitzer, and the monstrous 420/12 coastal howitzer which was the largest piece of artillery ever to be included in the Italian artillery inventory. Italian-origin siege artillery included the 210/8 DS, the 260/9, and the 305/17G siege howitzers. The *Regio Esercito* also fielded very limited numbers of the antiquated 70/15 gun, the 75/27 AV (*anti-velivolo*, anti-aircraft) gun, the 76/30 RM (*Regia Marina*, Royal Navy, naval gun adapted to the ground role) system, the 76/40 AA gun, the British-origin 152/13 howitzer (the 6-inch 26 cwt howitzer), the 152/45 gun, which was another naval gun adapted to the ground role, and the 155/25 gun. A number of prototypes were either planned or built, including the 75/17, 75/20, 75/36, 75/45, 105/20, 105/23, 105/40, 210/16, and 210/21 pieces.

Indeed, Italy made some important progress in late 1941 and 1942, with the design of a number of self-propelled guns, based on the chassis of tanks, which mounted guns and howitzers ranging from 47mm to 149mm, some of which were first-rate items of equipment. However, they could never be issued to front line units in time and in such numbers to make any difference on the battlefield in the long term

The Italian army also used some pieces captured on the battlefield, mainly in Yugoslavia or in Greece, but also in small numbers in North Africa, while other pieces were acquired from their German ally.

Italian gun and howitzer designation

The normal Italian method to designate guns and howitzers is by using two numbers divided by an oblique. The first number designates the caliber expressed in millimetres, the second number the length of the barrel, expressed as a multiple of the bore diameter.

For example, taking the 47/32 gun, the number 47 indicates that the caliber is 47 millimetres (mm), which, multiplied by 32, results in a barrel length of 1,504 millimetres.

MODERN GUNS

20/65 Breda mod. 35 and mod. 39 anti-aircraft gun

One of the outstanding Italian achievements in weapons design and production during the 1930s was the Breda Model 35 (and its derivative Model 39) dual-purpose cannon. Designed as an anti-aircraft weapon, it also saw extensive use as an anti-tank weapon, and was mounted on several Italian armoured and non-armoured vehicles as main or heavy armament. The Breda 35 was designed in response to an early 1930s Italian Army requirement for a light anti-aircraft gun to provide a low altitude air defence capability. Initially, the 20mm Solothurn was considered for the role, but stability problems were a negative consideration, and in 1932 Breda entered its proposal into competition against several other contenders, including those from Scotti, Oerlikon, Madsen, and Lübbe. In 1935, following extensive testing, the Breda was judged the winner. By 1938 some modifications were made to correct sighting problems caused by vibration transmitted to the frame. Development of a fixed mounting for use by territorial units was completed in 1939. The Italian Navy also adopted the 20/65 in both a single and double-mount as a replacement for its 13.2mm heavy machine guns.

The Breda was a gas operated weapon. Ammunition was fed by a twelve-round charger plate that collected the spent cartridge cases. The Model 35 mount consisted of a three-legged platform that was carried on a two-wheel trailer; it had a counterbalance system and parallelogram sights that enabled the gunner to stand behind the gun while tracking and firing. As with most Italian light guns, the Breda could be broken down, into four loads in this case, for transport by pack animal in mountain terrain. Normally it was either towed by a light truck or mounted in the bed of a truck for mobility.

The Breda was first employed by the Italians during the civil war in Spain in 1936, where 138 of the Model 35 guns were sent to support the Italian troop contingent there. Although its effectiveness against enemy aircraft flying at altitudes above 2,000 meters was judged unsatisfactory, as might be expected for a low-level air defence gun, its performance against tanks, armoured vehicles, and other ground targets was deemed to be very satisfactory, thus establishing the parameters for future use in the ground role.

The 20mm Breda Model 35 cannon mounted on its three-trail field carriage. In an anti-tank role it could penetrate 30mm of armour plate at 400 metres. (Ralph Riccio files)

In October 1939 the Army had 786 Breda 20/65s in the inventory, that by 1 June 1940, just before Italy entered the war, had risen to 1,088, with 1,198 ordered; to these must be added a further 116 pieces of the MACA, with 1,542 ordered. The production of the Breda 20/65 increased from 50 in September 1939 to 80 in September 1940 and 160 in November 1941, with 1,640 of the guns having been delivered during the first eleven months of 1941. In September 1942 the *Regio Esercito* had a total of 2,442 Model 35s on hand, and the MACA had 326 of the Model 39. In mid-1943 the pieces available to the Army dropped to 1655. The peak of production was reached in March 1943, with 320 pieces of the various models. In addition to being produced by Breda in its Brescia and Rome plants, the 20/65 may also have been produced by Fabbrica d'Armi di Terni, but there seems to be no firm documented evidence of Terni production. It should be noted that an undetermined number of Bredas had also been purchased by Italian industries to protect their factories from air attack.

The ease with which the Breda 35 could be displaced rapidly is demonstrated by this crew on the Russian front. (USSME – Ufficio Storico dello Stato Maggiore dell'Esercito/ Army Staff Historical Office)

A 20mm Breda Model 39 mounted on a Canadian Military Pattern Ford F-15 light truck. The vehicle has been repainted in Italian colours; camouflage netting is strapped to the sand channel. (Ralph Riccio files)

The breech mechanism of the Breda Model 39 has been shrouded to guard against the desert environment. Note the ammunition lockers behind the driver. This vehicle was from a section commanded by Sergeant (later Lieutenant) Francesco Tumiati, who was awarded the Gold Medal for Military Valor. (Tumiati/Ravenna Archives, courtesy Daniele Ravenna)

Organizationally, during the early period of WWII, one battery of eight Breda 20/65 guns was assigned to the artillery regiments of Italian infantry divisions, while the armoured, motorised, and cavalry divisions, as well as the Libyan and Militia divisions and the corps-level artillery regiments each had two similar eight gun batteries. As the war continued and as more of the Breda guns became available some batteries were replaced by companies, notably in the armoured and motorised divisions in North Africa. Some GaF units also received the Bredas for defence of important fixed installations.

The Breda was also mounted in a number of armoured vehicles; interestingly, the first use of the Model 35 in an armoured vehicle was in 1937, during the Spanish Civil War, when four German PzKpfw light tanks were locally modified in Seville to mount the Breda. The Breda later was standard armament on the Italian L 6/40 light tank and the SPA armoured cars, as well as AS42 and AS43 light desert trucks.

Both the Breda Model 35 and Model 39 were mounted aboard captured 15 cwt Ford and Chevrolet Canadian Military Pattern (CMP) trucks in North Africa and formed part of the *batterie*

Breda Model 35 mounted on an AS 37 light desert truck; the gun is manned by a native Saharan crew. (Claudio Pergher Archive)

An interesting photograph of a modified A.S. 37 light truck mounting both a 20mm Breda Model 35 as well as an 8mm Breda Model 37 machine gun. The driver and machine gunner are Italian, while the 20mm gun crew consists of native Saharan troops. (Ralph Riccio files)

volanti (flying batteries) that wrote a special chapter in the annals of Italian operations in the desert. The Model 39 stationary mount was preferred over the Model 35 for mounting on wheeled vehicles. Allied fighter pilots soon came to respect the capabilities of the Bredas that routinely provided protection for Italian mobile columns in the desert.

British and Commonwealth forces eagerly put to use as many captured Bredas as possible, as they were far superior to the machine guns normally used by the British for air defence, and were also much more convenient than the 40mm Bofors in Commonwealth service.

Following 8 September 1943, upon liberation of Corsica by the Allies, 73 guns were handed over to the Free French Forces. Later, the Italian co-belligerent *I Raggruppamento Motorizzato* was equipped with the Breda 20/65 as its only anti-aircraft weapon.

Production of the Breda continued in the area of Italy under German control, for issue to German *Luftwaffe* and RSI units. In January 1945 the *Luftwaffe* had 469 of the Breda 20/65s in its inventory, known as the *2cm FlaK 282 (i)*. Following the war, the Breda remained in Italian service for a brief period, with some improvements in the sighting system; some were mounted on Dodge WC 51 ¾ ton trucks.

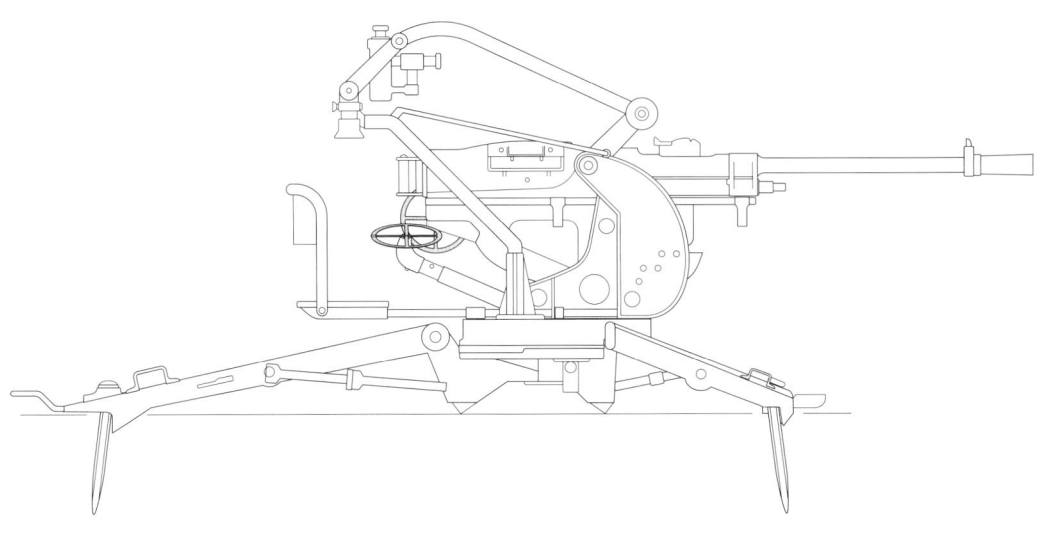

Breda mod. 35 20/65 gun.

Specifications:

Designation:	cannone-mitragliera Breda da 20/65 (mod. 35 and mod. 39)
Originator:	Società Italiana Ernesto Breda, Brescia
Producer:	Breda Meccanica Bresciana (Brescia and Rome); Fabbrica D'Armi Terni
Caliber:	20mm (0.787 inches)
Length of barrel:	1.87m (73.6 inches)
Overall length:	3.303m (130.03 inches)
Overall height:	1.12m (in firing position) (44.09 inches)
Weight in action:	330 kg (726 lb)
Wheel track:	1.00m (39.4 inches)
Wheel type/diameter:	Steel spokes or pressed steel disc wheels with solid tires/600mm (23.62 inches)
Breech type:	gas-operated recoil
Recuperator type:	gas operated
Elevation:	-10° to +80°
Traverse:	360°
Muzzle velocity:	840 m/s (2756 fps)
Maximum range:	5,500 metres (6,015 yards) ground targets; 2,700 metres (8,858 feet) anti-aircraft role
Rate of fire:	240 rounds per minute
Ammunition types:	AA, AP
Shell weight:	(135) grams (0.297 lb)
Armour penetration:	30mm (1.18 inches) at 500 metres (547 yards)

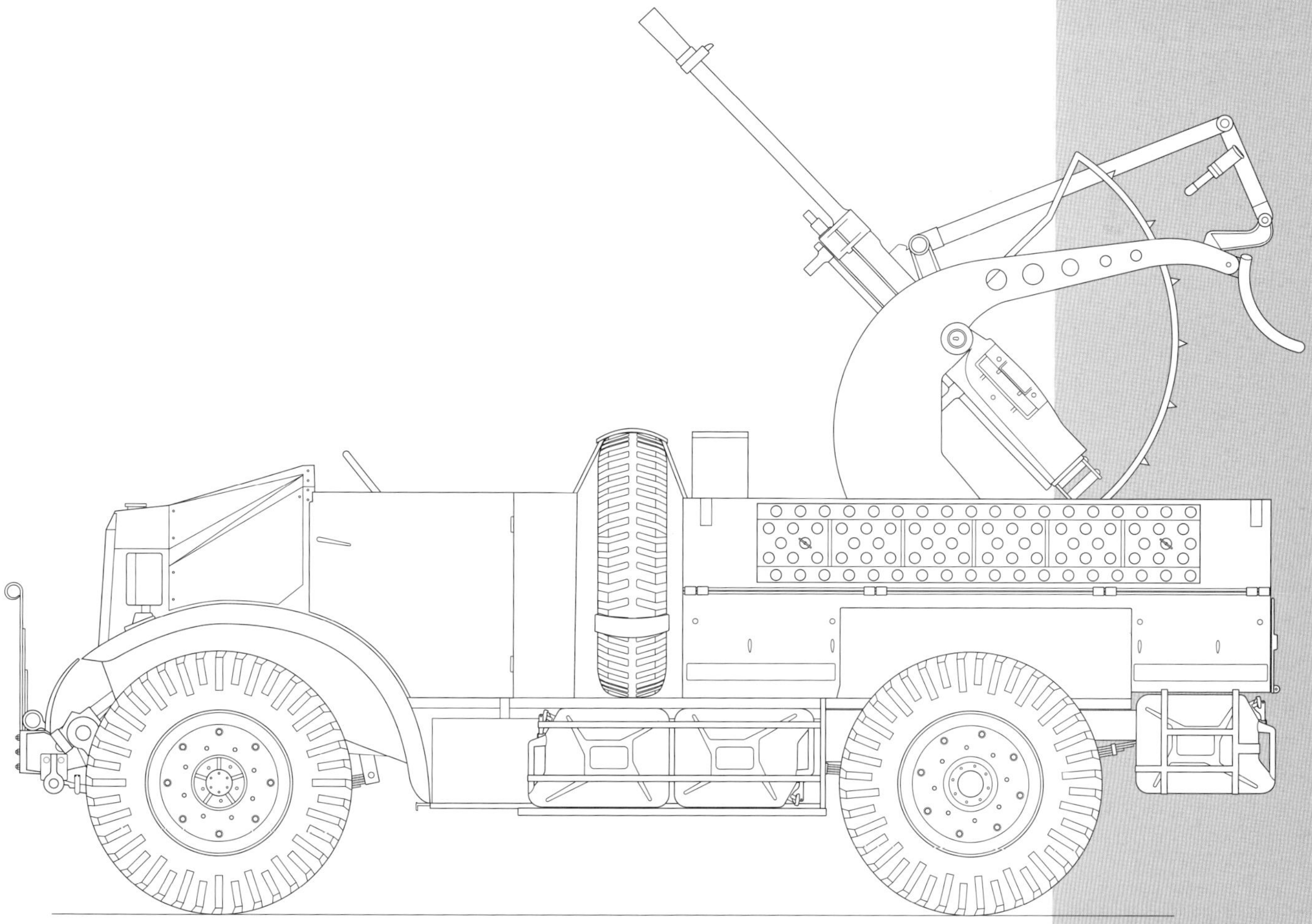

Breda mod. 39 20/65 gun on a Canadian Military Pattern Ford F15.

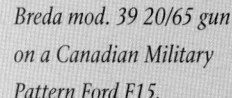

20/70 Scotti - Isotta Fraschini — OM anti-aircraft gun

The 20mm Scotti cannon, designed by Alfredo Scotti in 1932, was a contemporary of the 20mm Breda Model 35. Despite the fact that the Scotti was a simpler weapon than the Breda and its barrel was longer, which in theory would give it a greater range, overall the Scotti's performance did not match that of the Breda and consequently it never approached the numbers of the Breda in Italian service.

Initial production was by Oerlikon in Switzerland, which had acquired the license from Scotti, apart from the Italian market, and used a 60-round Oerlikon type drum magazine. Developments in Italy continued with Isotta Fraschini, a luxury car manufacturer known for its high quality machines, which acquired the license for the Italian market, changing the Oerlikon drum magazine to the Italian system that used a 12-round tray as a magazine. Because of this, the Scotti is sometimes referred to by Italian sources as the Isotta Fraschini. This 20mm weapon did not find favour with the Italian armed forces, which continued to prefer the Breda competitor. Until 1941, when it was finally adopted, only small orders were placed by the *Regio Esercito* and the *Regia Marina*. From 1941 the gun was produced also by OM (Officine Meccaniche, a FIAT subsidiary).

20/70 Scotti in action in North Africa. (Museo Storico della Guerra di Rovereto)

The Scotti was used in a prototype quad-mounted anti-aircraft system mounted on an M15 medium tank chassis. (Centro Studi ed Esperienze della Motorizzazione)

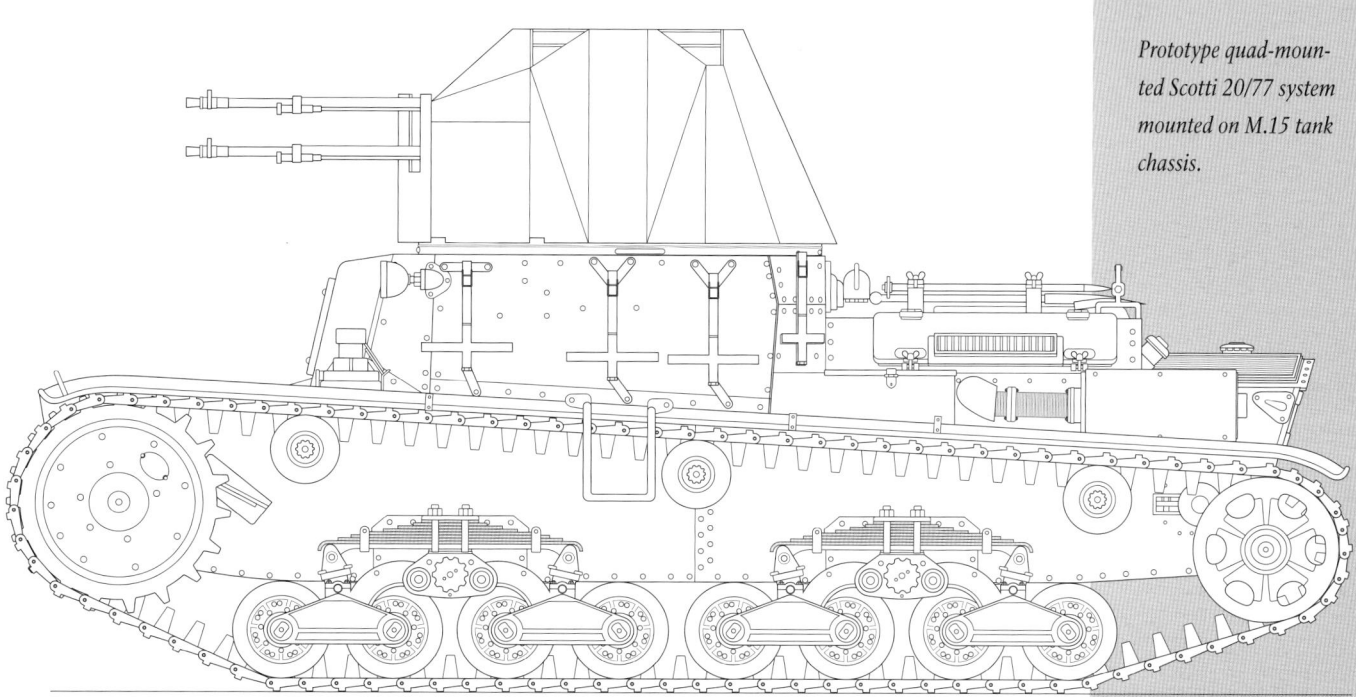

Two versions of the Scotti were produced; the first version was semi-mobile and was transported on trucks, but was dismounted for use, and the second version was a static mount on a fixed pedestal. The semi-mobile version had a two-wheel carriage and once off the truck could be man-handled into position by its crew, which would then remove the wheels so that the gun rested flat on a three-legged mount for action.

Although a certain number were produced from 1941 onwards, continuing through the end of the war, the 20/70 Scotti failed to achieve the status of the Breda Model 35 in Italian service, serving mainly for airfield defence, with crews supplied by the *Regio Esercito* and weapons supplied by the *Regia Aeronautica*, and with the *Regia Marina*. The gun did achieve some success in the export market, with copies being sold to China and several South American countries. German troops in North Africa also used the Scotti, which they designated as the *2 cm Scotti (i)*, and following September 1943, many Scottis were incorporated into the German inventory and were used by the armed forces of the RSI.

The Italians attempted to develop a tracked self-propelled anti-aircraft system using the Scotti. Due to disruption caused by the September 1943 events, only one prototype of the system was built in March 1943. The system consisted of four Scottis mounted in an open turret on the chassis of an M.15 tank, and was very similar to the later German *Flakpanzer IV/3*. The Germans confiscated it following the Italian surrender, and reportedly it was used in action against Soviet troops in Teupitz, Austria.

Specifications:

Designation:	cannone-mitragliera da 20/70 (Scotti)
Originator:	Alfredo Scotti
Producer:	Oerlikon, Zurich, Switzerland; Isotta Fraschini, Torino
Caliber:	20mm (0.787 inches)
Length of barrel:	1.54m (60.6 inches
Overall length:	2.278m (89.7 inches); 2.03m (79.9 inches) in travel position
Overall width:	radius 1.805m (weapon at 0°) (71.06 inches)
Overall height:	2.01m (79.13 inches)
Weight in action:	386 kg (851 lb)
Wheel type/diameter:	ten-spoke elektron wheels with *Celerflex* tires/600mm (23.62 inches)
Breech type:	recoil
Recuperator type:	gas operated
Elevation:	-10° to + 85°

Traverse:	360°
Muzzle velocity:	830 m/s (2723 fps)
Maximum range:	2,135 metres (7005 feet) effective ceiling
Rate of fire:	250 round per minute cyclic; 120 rounds per minute practical
Ammunition types:	AA, AP
Shell weight:	135 grams (0.298 lb)

Solothurn S-18/1000 anti-tank gun

Although technically the Solothurn was a Swiss weapon, as it was produced in Switzerland by a Swiss company, in reality the weapon was a German Rheinmetall design manufactured in Switzerland by a Rheinmetall front company (Waffenfabrik Solothurn) to circumvent restrictions on German weapon production following WWI. Its developmental origin dates back to an early 1930s design by Fritz Herlach and Theodor Rakula. The early version of the gun was tested in Italy, in competition with the 20mm Breda and Oerlikon guns. The gun thus tested was designated the S18/100 mod. 35 and received an Italian patent on 17 February 1934. It was a semiautomatic weapon. The S18/100 was soon adopted by Hungary and Finland, but a number of years were to pass before an improved heavier version, the S18/1000, which had a longer barrel and higher muzzle velocity, would be adopted by the *Regio Esercito* in 1939. In 1942 it was assigned the official designation of *fucile anticarro tipo S*. The S18/1100 version, capable of full automatic fire, was also acquired later on, and began to be distributed in July 1942.

Left side view of the Solothurn S 18/1000 20mm anti-tank rifle. (Enrico Finazzer)

Right side view of the Solothurn S 18/1000 20mm anti-tank rifle. (Enrico Finazzer)

The Italians adopted the Solothurn to fill the need for a support weapon that was capable of defeating armoured cars, light tracked vehicles, and light tanks. At the time of its selection, the Solothurn was an effective weapon for its size and was capable of defeating the types of light armour likely to be encountered in many contemporary situations. The cannon was recoil operated

and was fed by a 10-round box magazine mounted on the left-hand side of the weapon. The weapon used the Italian manufactured Breda mod. 35 20mm armour piercing explosive round whose penetration was comparable to that of the Rheinmetall or Solothurn rounds. The Solothurn could be fitted with different pattern muzzle brakes depending on the type of ammunition used; armour piercing projectiles required the use of a 5-hole muzzle brake.

The Solothurn was a crew-served weapon with a crew of four and could be carried on and fired from the SO-9 two-wheel cart that could be pulled by the crew; in addition to the gun, the cart carried two ammunition cases, each holding three 10-round magazines for a total of 60 rounds available. The gun could also be fitted with a bipod for firing when not on the cart. The fully automatic version of the Solothurn could be mounted on the SO-11 universal mount that had three legs and removable wheels and could be used either in the anti-tank mode, in which case it was fitted with a shield, or in the anti-aircraft mode with appropriate sights. Deliveries to the *Regio Esercito* began in the summer of 1940, and by September the first 100 had been shipped to Libya. In December 1940, Germany supplied 63 Dutch war booty Solothurns to Italy. Further orders followed, but the total number of Solothurns delivered to Italy is open to question, and information concerning

numbers is at times conflicting. The most credible information indicates that in early 1942 the requirement was for 1,131 weapons of this type, and that 578 were on hand, 350 of which were in North Africa. In February 1943 114 were still available with the 1st Army in Tunisia.

In 1940, in North Africa, the weapon was planned to be assigned on the scale of two weapons per standard infantry, *bersaglieri,* and Libyan battalions. The *divisione tipo AS* (North Africa Type Division) formed in 1941 had a platoon in each company, amounting to 12 per battalion, plus a regimental company of undetermined size; the later *tipo AS 42* (North Africa Type 42) divisions were issued 12 per battalion, for a total of 72 per division. *Bersaglieri* battalions of the armoured and motorised divisions in North Africa also had 12 per battalion plus a regimental company with eight more guns. The *Superga, Friuli* and *Livorno* divisions each had a company of 12 Solothurns incorporated into the divisional anti-tank battalion. The company consisted of a Headquarters Squad and three Solothurn platoons of two squads, each with two Solothurns. The *Folgore* Parachute Division had assigned an anti-tank squad with two Solothurns per battalion plus six more weapons in the divisional *guastatori* (sapper) company, and the two battalions of *Giovani Fascisti* had one platoon of two squads per company, for a total number of 12 per battalion. These numbers reflected requirements specified in organizational tables, but to what extent the Solothurn's were actually issued varied according to unit and timeframe.

Some Solothurns were mounted on pickup trucks, on L.3 tankettes, or later, on captured British Universal Carriers and the AS42 light desert truck. In 1943 the *Nembo* Parachute Division replaced its Polish wz 35 Maroszek anti-tank rifles with two Solothurns per company. An undetermined number of Solothurns were used until 1945 by RSI units.

Specifications:

Designation:	fucile anticarro tipo S
Originator:	Rheinmetall-Borsig AG, Düsseldorf
Producer:	Waffenfabrik Solothurn, Zurich
User countries:	Germany, Italy
Caliber:	20mm (0.79 inches)
Length of barrel:	1.42m (55.9 inches) with flash hider; 1.3m (51.2 inches) without flash hider/muzzle brake
Overall length:	2.16m (85 inches)
Overall width:	180mm (7 inches)
Overall height:	413mm (16.3 inches) on bipod
Weight in action:	54.7 kg (120.6 lb) without bipod; 58.7 kg (129.4 lb) with bipod; 127 kg (280 lb) with cart
Wheel track:	NA/bipod mounted
Wheel type/diameter:	for SO-9 cart, pressed steel/400mm (15.75 inches)
Breech type:	positively locked on firing by rotation of locking lugs.
Recuperator type:	spring
Elevation:	0° to +10°
Traverse:	50°
Muzzle velocity:	832 m/s (2730 fps)
Maximum range:	3,000 metres (3,281 yards) maximum; 500 metres (547 yards) effective
Rate of fire:	10-20 rounds per minute
Ammunition types:	armour piercing tracer (AP-T); high explosive tracer (HE-T); AP training; HE training
Shell weight:	320 grams (0.7 lb) for both AP-T and HE-T
Armour penetration:	20-22mm (0.79-0.86 inches) at 100 metres (109 yards)

47/32 mod. 35 and mod. 39 gun

The Breda/Böhler 47/32 mod. 35 gun was the most widely used anti-tank and infantry support gun in the Italian Army during WWII. The gun was originally designed and developed by the Austrian firm of Böhler and was adopted by the Italian Army in 1935 to replace the WWI vintage 65/17 infantry support gun. It met the need felt by the *Regio Esercito* to have a modern piece for direct infantry support and anti-tank use, a role that in the 1930s was gaining increasing importance as a consequence of the new theories concerning the use of tanks in modern warfare. The Böhler gun was an ideal anti-tank gun for the times – it was small, light, easily transportable, highly accurate, and was able to penetrate the armour of most contemporary tanks. It used a variety of ammunition, from explosive to armour piercing, and during the war it used hollow charge ammunition (so called *EP* and *EPS*) developed by the Italians.

Soon after adoption the gun was licensed to Italian industry and produced locally in several thousand copies. With respect to the original Austrian gun, the Italian model underwent a number of modifications including improvements designed to make replacing the barrel easier, and was given a stronger suspension system. The 47/32 gun had a split trail carriage; the trails could be positioned separately according to conditions of the ground, to permit fire on virtually all types of terrain. While in the firing position, the wheels could be removed, giving the gun a very low silhouette. It had a mono-bloc steel barrel, with a sliding wedge breech mechanism. The gun could be carried by five pack mules, or could be towed by draft animals or by its crew as well as by truck.

North Africa: A 47/32 gun being towed by its crew in March 1942. (USSME)

A dug-in 47/32 gun manned by a Libyan crew while an Italian officer looks for targets, May 1942. (USSME)

19

A 47/32 gun position in Tunisia. The gun's low silhouette enabled it to be dug in and concealed easily. (USSME)

A group of Giovani Fascisti with their 47/32 guns in North Africa, March 1942. A battery of 20mm Breda Model 39 guns mounted on captured light trucks is in the background. (USSME)

For transport by pack animal, the lightest component weighed 25 kg (55 lb) and the heaviest 78 kg (172 lb).

The gun was slightly improved in the Model 39 variant for motorised units, with new spoked wheels replacing the disc wheels, reinforced suspension, and a new optical sight for anti-tank fire. Different types of shields designed for both versions were not standardized. A final variant of the gun, 48 calibers long, was built in 1941 by Ansaldo Genova (with shield and new wheeled carriage with pneumatic tires) but after testing never entered production.

The 47/32 was produced by a number of different government arsenals and private companies in Italy. The production rose steadily during the war, and by end 1941 had reached an average of 200 pieces per month of both 47/32 and 47/40, the version for the M15/42 tank turret, that was kept until the Armistice with a peak of 229 in February 1943.

In October 1939 there were 773 47/32 guns in the Italian inventory, that by June 1940 had risen to 928, with orders to the producers for 3,150 field pieces and 373 pieces for tank turrets. In October the same year the number had already risen to 1,318, with 550,000 rounds of ammunition. By 30 September 1942 the *Regio Esercito* had 3,150 field pieces and 373 pieces for tanks and self-propelled artillery, with orders placed respectively for 2,406 and 53 pieces. In addition to the guns produced in Italy, the *Regio Esercito* received a batch of 276 47/32s supplied by Germany; these were a mix of Austrian Böhlers and Dutch K.n. 36 versions. The Dutch version was marked by a pepperbox muzzle brake and a modified carriage with pneumatic tires.

Thirty of the 47/32 guns were sent to Spain in 1938 during the civil war for tests and evaluation. Although accuracy was deemed excellent, the time to place the gun in battery was a somewhat negative note for anti-tank employment, and ammunition performance was not totally satisfactory. The lack of a shield for crew protection was also judged to be a negative factor, but this was offset by the fact that the gun without the shield was easy to camouflage.

March 1943: A patrol consisting of Spa-Viberti Mod. 42 "Sahariana" light desert trucks in action. The truck in the foreground is armed with a Breda 20mm cannon, while the truck in the background is armed with a 47/32 gun. (USSME)

A 47/32 mounted on a modified A.S. 37 light desert truck in North Africa. (Ralph Riccio files)

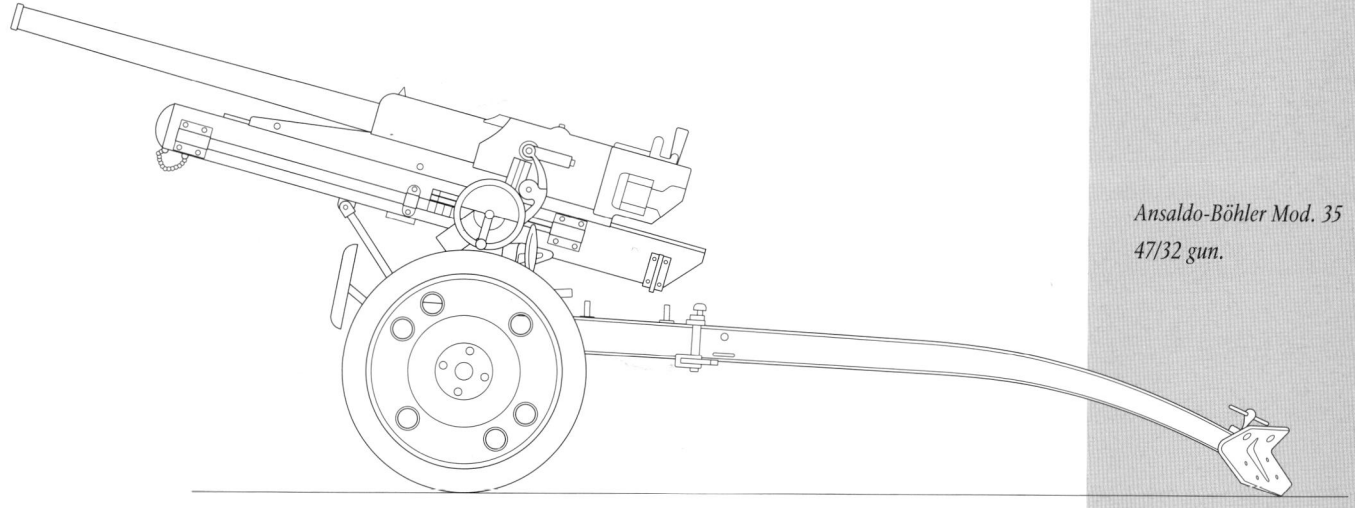

Ansaldo-Böhler Mod. 35 47/32 gun.

According to tables of organization, in June 1940 each infantry regiment was supposed to have eight 47/32 guns for close support fire, and each infantry division likewise was supposed to have an additional divisional company with eight guns as an anti-tank unit. In 1941 the army began to constitute independent anti-tank battalions, based on 24 pieces, for assignment at the corps and divisional level. Four of these battalions (the 101st through the 104th) were equipped with ex-Dutch K.n 36 guns, and another three were equipped with guns taken from the GaF. Between 1941 and 1942 the infantry battalions of the motorised divisions and *bersaglieri* and *Giovani Fascisti* battalions of the armoured and motorised divisions, as well as selected infantry divisions (*Livorno* and *Superga*, trained for the invasion of Malta, and the *La Spezia* Air Transportable division), were reinforced by the addition of one, two, or three platoons of four 47/32 guns. From January 1943 the ordinary infantry divisions were supposed to receive two platoons, with four guns in total, per battalion, but implementation may have been problematic. The 47/32 was also the heaviest weapon assigned to the parachute divisions. Each of the three parachute infantry regiments in the *Folgore* and *Nembo* divisions had a company with six of the 47/32 guns, and the divisional artillery regiments had three battalions with two batteries equipped with the 47/32.

It is interesting to note that for three years the gun remained virtually the only anti-tank weapon in the Italian inventory, even when the development of armoured vehicles made it clear that, at least from mid-1941 onwards, the 47mm caliber was almost useless in that role. The hollow charge ammunition that could have enhanced its anti-tank capability was always in too short supply to really make a difference on the battlefield.

In North Africa the gun was mounted on specially designed rotating platforms on trucks such as the Lancia 3 Ro, as well as on the AS 37, AS 42 light desert trucks and on the later AS 43. The 47/32 was also, in the Ansaldo modified version 47/32 *per carro*, the main armament on the Italian M.13 and M.14 medium tanks as well as on the L40 light self-propelled gun (see separate entry); the M.15 medium tank used a modified gun, a 47/40. Although by 1942 the 47/32 was inadequate as a first-line anti-tank weapon, it nevertheless had acquitted itself well during the initial years of the conflict, outclassing other anti-tank weapons of the time such as the British 2-pdr and the German 3.7cm Pak 35/36 anti-tank gun described later.

No data about total production (continued by the German Army after the Italian surrender in 1943) are available, but total numbers are on the order of at least 4,000.

Following September 1943, the 47/32 guns seized by the Germans were redesignated as the *4.7cm Pak 177 (i)*.

Specifications:

Designation:	cannone anticarro e d'accompagnamento 47/32 mod. 35 and mod. 39
Adopted by Italy:	1935
Inventory 10/06/1940:	928
Subsequent production:	about 3,000
Originator:	Böhler, Kapfenberg, Austria
Producer:	Breda; Cogne; Ansaldo (Pozzuoli); Arsenali *Regio Esercito* (Piacenza, Napoli and Torino)
User countries:	Italy, Germany (after September 1943)
Caliber:	47mm (1.85 inches)
Crew:	5
Length of barrel:	1.68m (66.1 inches)
Overall length:	3.92m (154.3 inches)
Overall width:	1.02m (40.1 inches)
Overall height:	744mm (29.3 inches)
Weight in action:	277 kg (611 lb)
Carriage:	Split trail
Wheel track:	880mm (34.6 inches)
Wheel type/diameter:	Model 39 elektron alloy with seven spokes; semi-pneumatic *Celerflex* tires/600mm (23.62 inches); Model 35 were fitted with disc wheels instead

Breech type:	Horizontal sliding wedge
Recuperator type:	Spring
Elevation:	-10°to +56°
Traverse:	60°
Muzzle velocity:	630 m/s (2067 fps) AP; 250 m/s (820 fps) HE
Maximum range:	7,000 metres (7,655 yards) maximum; 3,500 metres (3,828 yards) effective
Rate of fire:	7-8 rounds per minute
Ammunition types:	AP, HE, hollow charge
Shell weight:	AP 1.5 kg (3.3 lb); HE 2.45 kg (5.4 lb)
Armour penetration:	40mm at 650 m (1.6 inches at 711 yards)

75/18 mod. 34 howitzer

When the Italians decided to modernize their artillery inventory in 1929, their positive experience with the 75mm Škoda mountain howitzer, numbers of which had been captured or taken as war booty from Austria-Hungary (in Italian service designated the *obice da 75/13*, see separate entry) led them to develop their own design based on the Škoda. Requirements were drawn up including a high degree of mobility, the ability to be broken down into several loads for transport by pack animal, and a wide traverse arc. The new gun was needed to replace the 75/13 howitzer for mountain troops as well as the even older 75/27 gun that still equipped the regular infantry divisions and represented the bulk of divisional artillery. The requirement for a 75mm gun was based largely on the consideration that Italy had huge stocks of 75mm ammunition available at the time. In 1932 Ansaldo offered a prototype with a 17-caliber long barrel, but the DSSTAM presented another version with an 18-caliber long barrel which, following extensive trials, was adopted in 1934 as the *obice da 75/18 mod. 34*. However, when the 75/18 mod. 34 was adopted in 1934, it was already at a disadvantage compared to guns roughly in the 100mm category, such as the British 25-pdr (87.6mm) and the US M2 howitzer (105mm).

The 75/18 mod. 34 howitzer, as shown in a 1938 Ansaldo brochure. (Fondazione Ansaldo)

The mod. 34 was an updated mountain howitzer designed expressly for mountain service. It presented a very distinctive appearance, with the barrel enveloped by a circular cradle that had elongated cutouts along the sides; it also had a muzzle brake. The split-trail carriage allowed a wide traverse (a total of 50°). The trails themselves were in sections so that, depending on the terrain, they could be set up as either long or short trails; if the terrain so demanded, the howitzer could also be fired with one long and one short trail. It mounted two small diameter 700mm, 10-spoke wheels in elektron with semi-pneumatic tires, and the wheel track was variable to enable the gun to be moved along narrow mountain trails. The mod. 34 could be easily disassembled and assembled; the breechblock could be removed from the barrel to facilitate pack transport, and the gun could be broken down into eight separate pack loads weighing between 100 to 115 kg. It was equipped with a shield 4.4mm thick. The gun could be put in battery in five to ten minutes. A very interesting feature, which was extended to every piece designed in Italy from that time on, was the barrel made of an inner and an outer tube which could be separated cold even with the howitzer in firing position. This allowed a maintenance unit to replace a worn out inner tube on the spot with a new one without withdrawing the piece from the front line.

The 75/18 mod. 34 had its first public exposure during the large scale exercise in southern Italy's mountainous Irpinia region from 24 to 29 August 1936. By then, 40 pieces were available and three batteries had been formed; the guns had been issued to the *Volturno* Division's 10th Artillery Regiment only 20 days previous to the exercise[1]. Its initial operational debut was during the civil war in Spain where two guns were sent on a test basis. Production that should have started in 1936 at a very high pace was instead very slow, mainly due to financial problems. Furthermore, some mod. 34s were exported to some South American countries and to Portugal. Therefore in June 1940 the Italian army entered the war with only 114 model 1934s. During subsequent years, due to the severe shortage of raw materials and the diversion of materials to other equipment, the number of pieces produced was very small and they could be assigned to only a limited number of divisions. By September 1942 there were 230 in service, with further 380 on order, and in June 1943 19 divisional artillery battalions were equipped with the 75/18 mod. 34

During WWII, the howitzer saw action during the Greek campaign where, in October 1940, the artillery regiments of the *Venezia* and *Ferrara* divisions had a battalion each. By March 1941

---

1   Sources differ as to whether all three batteries were towed by FIAT OCI 708 CM light tracked tractors or if two batteries were towed by the OCI 708 CM and one battery was a pack battery.

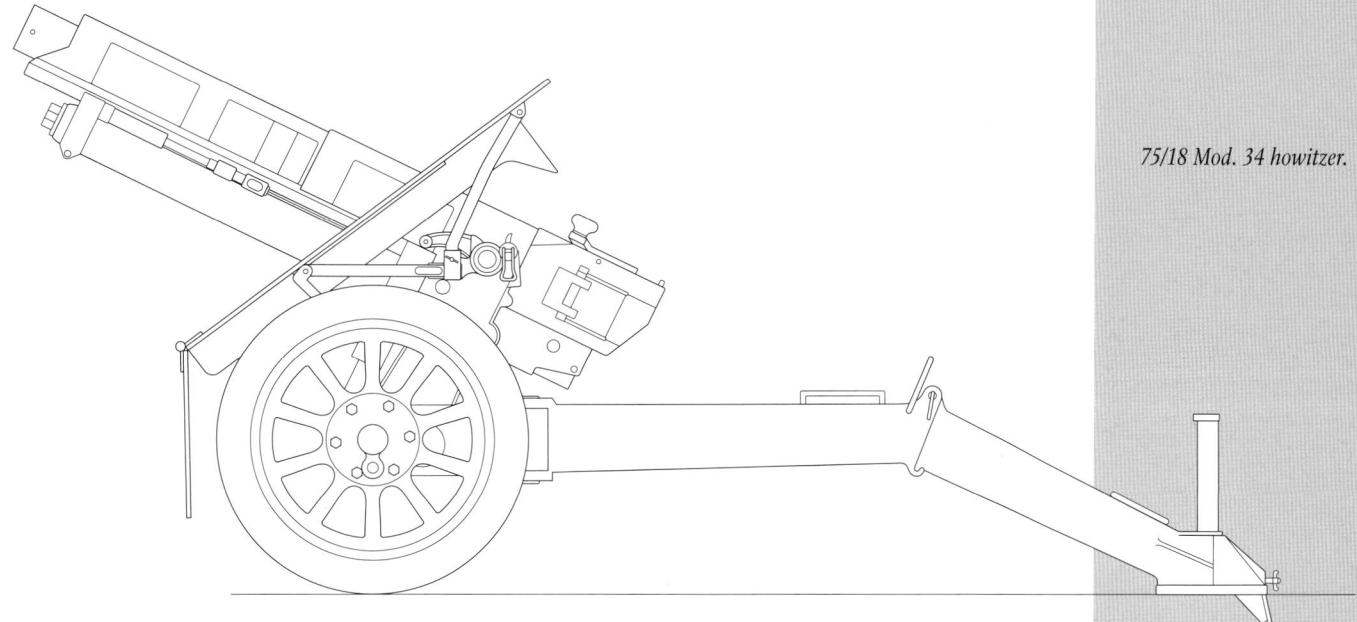

96 pieces were deployed on that front. Following the September 1943 events, two mod. 34 battalions of the *Friuli* Division stationed in Corsica fought against the Germans; both of these groups subsequently relinquished their guns to French forces. On the continent, the Germans took over all of the 75/18 howitzers that they could find; production of the mod. 34 continued in northern Italy after September 1943 for use by German forces. The 75/18 was used by the Germans as the *7.5 cm GebH 254(i)*.

A modified version of the 75/18 mod. 34 (the *obice da 75/18 mod. 35*) was developed for use in the field artillery role (see following entry). Another modified version of the howitzer mounted in a ball mount and fitted with a distinctive pepperbox muzzle brake was used as the principal armament on various versions of the Italian 75/18 self-propelled gun, or *semovente*, which proved to be an extremely effective weapon system, comparable to the German *Sturmgeschütz* assault guns (see separate entry for the *semovente*). Following the war the 75mm field guns in the Italian inventory were replaced by 105mm M2 howitzers and 25-pdrs furnished by the US and Britain, respectively.

Specifications:

Designation:	obice da 75/18 mod. 34
Adopted:	1934
Inventory 10/06/1940:	114
Subsequent production:	300*
Originator:	Ansaldo-DSSTAM
Producer:	Arsenale Regio Esercito Piacenza; Arsenale Regio Esercito Napoli; Odero Terni Orlando (OTO); Ansaldo (Pozzuoli)
User countries:	Italy, Bolivia, Portugal, San Salvador, Venezuela, Germany (after September 1943)
Caliber:	75mm (2.95 inches)
Length of barrel:	1.557m (61.3 inches)
Overall length:	2.345m (92.3 inches)
Overall width:	1.470m (58.87 inches)
Weight in action:	780 kg (1720 lb) without shield
Carriage:	Split trail
Wheel track:	984-1284mm (38.7 – 50.6 inches)
Wheel type/diameter:	Semi-pneumatic tires on elektron wheels/700mm (27.5 inches)
Breech type:	Horizontal wedge
Recuperator type:	telescoping springs
Recoil length:	1,000mm maximum; 400mm minimum
Elevation:	-10° to +65°

Traverse:	50°
Muzzle velocity:	430 m/s (1411 fps)
Maximum range:	9,500 metres (10,390 yards)
Rate of fire:	10 rounds per minute
Ammunition types:	HE, AP, hollow charge
Shell weight (HE)	HE 6.4 kg (14.1 lb)

* The numbers are controversial and different sources disagree about the precise number of pieces produced, especially during the final months of the war. According to L. Ceva, *Storia delle Forze Armate in Italia*, based on figures released by Ansaldo (production until 30 June 1943) and OTO (production until 31 December 1942) the number is 418, without distinction between the two models. According to N. Pignato, *L'ultimo 75 dell'artiglieria italiana*, until 31 December 1942 Ansaldo produced 60 mod. 35, while OTO produced 300 pieces, but does not report the model. *Storia dell'artiglieria italiana*, book XV, reports instead 64 mod. 35 produced by Ansaldo by the same date, and 54 more by June 1943. It also adds that as of 30 November 1942 there were 230 mod 34 and 68 mod. 35 in service.

75/18 mod. 35 howitzer

The *obice da 75/18 mod. 35* was derived directly from the earlier *obice da 75/18 mod. 34* described above. In the interests of standardization, in order to issue the piece as the light howitzer component of field artillery batteries, the Italians modified the design of the mountain howitzer, mainly by adopting a conventional carriage to replace the mountain howitzer carriage, while maintaining the same barrel. The new carriage mounted a torsion bar that allowed relatively high speed towing by an appropriate tractor, and three types of semi-pneumatic tired wheels were mounted through the years (a 10-spoke metal, an elektron model and finally a third model with 9 spokes made of stamped steel plate); in the mountains the howitzer was divided into two loads each towed by a horse, the shield was removed and the track reduced to its narrowest width. A subsequent modification allowed the side sections of the shield to be folded so that they would be the same width as the carriage track on narrow roads. Its trails (as in the 1934 model) could be folded to reduce the overall length of the gun in the travel mode. The gun could be towed (for horse artillery, towed by a horse team) either with or without a limber by an artillery tractor such as the TL 37 (a FIAT-OCI 708 CM on mountain roads); it could not be broken down for pack transport. An ammunition limber was towed by another prime mover (at first the Pavesi mod. 30A, and later by the TL 37) in ordinary field artillery units.

As for the mod. 34, production never reached the level needed to meet requirements, thus when the war broke out, only an experimental battery of mod. 35 existed and only 68 had been delivered by September 1942, while 206 more were on order. In the following months, until June 1943, 54 more were produced.

The mod. 35 proved to be a reliable weapon. In 1942 it equipped the *Ravenna*, *Cosseria* and *Sforzesca* infantry divisions when they were sent to Russia to serve with the ARMIR, while the *Superga* Division was equipped with them during the campaign in Tunisia. In Sicily, in summer 1943, when the Allies landed, the *Napoli*, *Livorno* and *Aosta* infantry divisions were able to deploy a few batteries.

After the Armistice, a few pieces went to the armed forces of the RSI, namely to the 2nd Artillery Regiment assigned to the *Littorio* Division and to the 4th Artillery Regiment assigned to the *Italia* Division. The pieces taken over by the Germans were designated as the *7.5cm leFh 255(i)*.

In the south of Italy, where the government raised a small army operating alongside the Allied forces against the Germans, the howitzer equipped the first unit formed, the *11° Reggimento di artiglieria* assigned to the *I Raggruppamento Motorizzato* and later to the *Corpo Italiano di Liberazione*, until replaced by British weapons in summer 1944.

Prototype of the mechanically towed 75/18 mod. 1935. (Museo Storico della Guerra di Rovereto)

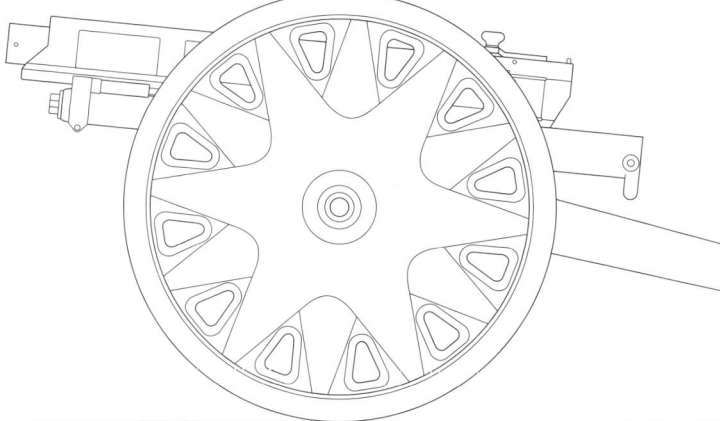

A 75/18 mod. 35 howitzer with its limber used for towing by horse teams. (Claudio Pergher Archive)

75/18 Mod. 35 howitzer.

Specifications:

Designation:	obice da 75/18 mod. 35
Adopted:	1935
Inventory 10/06/1940:	one experimental battery
Subsequent production:	118*
Originator:	Ansaldo- DSSTAM
Producer:	Ansaldo, OTO
Unit cost:	144,300 Italian lire (1939)
User countries:	Italy
Caliber:	75mm (2.95 inches)
Overall length:	1.557m (61.3 inches)
Weight in action:	1,100 kg (2425 lb)
Carriage:	Split trail
Wheel track:	1.15-1.45m (45.3-57.1 inches)
Wheel type/diameter:	semi-pneumatic tires on metal, elektron, or pressed steel wheels/1300mm (51.2 inches)
Breech type:	horizontal wedge
Recuperator type:	telescoping springs
Recoil length:	1,000mm maximum; 500mm minimum
Elevation:	-10° to +45°
Traverse:	50°
Muzzle velocity:	425 m/s (1395 fps)
Maximum range:	9,400 metres (10,280 yards); maximum effective 5,000 metres (5,468 yards)
Rate of fire:	8 rounds per minute
Ammunition types:	HE, AP and hollow charge
Shell weight (HE)	HE 6.4 kg (14.1 lb)

*   See previous footnote.

75/32 mod. 37 gun

The idea of a long-barrelled version of the 75/18 howitzer surfaced as early as 1929, and in fact the *cannone da 75/32 mod. 37* was based on the earlier *obice da 75/18 mod. 35* and shared many of its components and features to rationalize the use of raw materials and production lines. The need for a longer barrel was prompted by two basic considerations; the first was that the range of the 75/18 guns was woefully inadequate compared to that of other contemporary field guns such as the British 25-pdr and the German 10.5 cm Model 18, and the second was that a longer barreled gun could be used in the anti-tank role as well as in the field artillery role.

A static view of the 75/32 gun with its distinctive pepper-box muzzle brake. Note the stakes hammered into the ground to anchor the trails. (Claudio Pergher Archive)

Positive aspects of the project were that it was designed from the outset for towing by mechanical means (mainly by the TL 37 light artillery tractor) rather than by horse (although it could be towed by draft animals), and it had high enough muzzle velocity to be employed in the anti-tank role; somewhat offsetting these advantages was the fact that the design continued to use large trail spades hammered into the ground through the trail legs, making rapid changes in off-carriage traverse somewhat difficult to achieve. The prototype of the gun, initially with a 75/34 barrel with the same muzzle brake as on the 75/18 mod. 35, made its debut in 1937. Tests were carried out with a battery of five pre-series guns, and in 1938 an order was placed with Ansaldo Pozzuoli for 192 of the guns. The first series production guns, whose barrel length had been reduced to 75/32 and whose muzzle brake had been replaced with a new pepperbox-type, were not available until late 1941. Despite the fact that by 1943 additional orders had been placed amounting to a total of 542 guns and that in the summer of that year OTO La Spezia had been brought in as an additional producer (without, however, being able to deliver a single piece before the Armistice), by July 1943 only 172 had been completed.

75/32 guns of the 201st Motorized Artillery Regiment at Maniago del Friuli in June 1942 prior to leaving for the Russian front. (From the book by Paolo Zanlucchi E qui, quando fiorirà la terra? Lettere del Cappellano militare don Onorio Spada, marzo 1942 – settembre 1943, Egon Editions 2011)

The gun was a solid, reliable piece and was well liked by Italian gunners, but as related above, Italian industry was unable to keep up with the demand for the weapon. These circumstances were truly unfortunate for Italian gunners, because the 75/32 gun represented the most modern artillery piece assigned to divisional artillery and the only gun that was effective against enemy armour. The gun's initial operational employment was on the Russian front in 1941, where it equipped three groups (a total of 36 guns) of the *201° Reggimento di artiglieria motorizzato*. It performed quite well, especially in comparison with other anti-tank material assigned to Italian troops, but in such a small number could do little to stop the Soviet offensive that wiped away the ARMIR in winter

Catholic military chaplain Don Onorio Spada celebrating a Mass at Maniago del Friuli in June 1942 prior to departure of the 201st Motorized Artillery Regiment for the Russian front. (From the book by Paolo Zanlucchi)

Artillerymen of the 201st Motorized Artillery Regiment firing in the Ukraine in July 1942. (From the book by Paolo Zanlucchi)

A firing exercise in Italy with the 75/32 gun. (Claudio Pergher Archive)

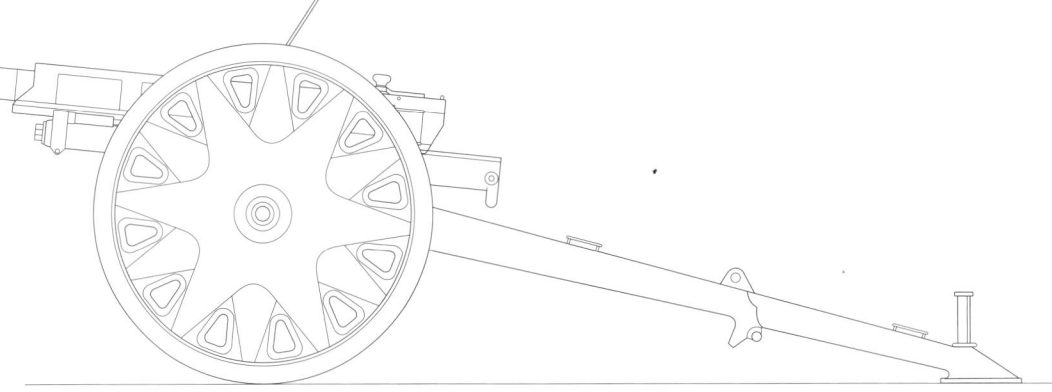

75/32 Mod. 37 gun.

1942/1943. By 1943 all of the 75/32 guns in Russia had been lost; five additional groups armed with the gun remained operational, of which two were in the *Brennero* Infantry Division's 9th Artillery Regiment, two with the *Ariete II* Armoured Cavalry Division's 235th Artillery Regiment, and one with the 3rd *Articelere* of the *Principe Amadeo Duca d'Aosta* Division. After September 1943, 48 of the 75/32 guns were pressed into service by the Germans with the designation of *FK 248 (i)*.

Specifications:

Designation:	cannone da 75/32 mod. 37
Adopted:	1941
Inventory	10/06/1940: 0
Subsequent production:	172
Originator:	Arsenale Regio Esercito di Napoli
Producer:	Ansaldo (Pozzuoli); OTO La Spezia
Unit cost:	156,300 Italian lire (1939)
User countries:	Italy
Caliber:	75mm (2.95 inches)
Length of barrel:	2.574m (101.3 inches)
Overall length:	3.345m (131.7 inches)
Weight in action:	1,200 kg (2,645.5 lb)
Carriage:	split trail
Wheel track:	1.18-1.48m (46.5 – 58.3 inches) (variable)
Wheel type/diameter:	initial production had semi-pneumatic tires on 1.20m (47.2 inch) elektron wheels; later production had pressed steel wheels with semi-pneumatic tires-
Breech type:	sliding wedge
Recuperator type:	telescoping springs
Recoil length:	1,000mm (39.37 inches) maximum; 600mm (23.62 inches) minimum
Elevation:	-10° to +45°
Traverse:	50°
Muzzle velocity:	624m/s (2047 fps)
Maximum range:	12,500 metres (13,670 yards)
Rate of fire:	10 rounds per minute
Ammunition types:	HE, AP, hollow charge
Shell weight (HE)	HE 6.3 kg (13.9 lb)

75/46 gun mod. 34, mod. 34M and mod. 40 anti-aircraft gun

At the end of the 1920s, as the *Regio Esercito* was taking stock of its overall artillery inventory and assessing requirements for new weapons, it became apparent that a replacement was needed for the ageing 75/27 C.K. and other assorted WWI vintage anti-aircraft guns of Italian and Austro-Hungarian manufacture. The results of early attempts by Ansaldo and OTO, who respectively developed 75/50 and 75/45 gun prototypes, were disappointing, leading the army to test a number of foreign weapons for possible adoption. One of the weapons, the Bofors 75/mm M29, caught the attention of Ansaldo engineers who used it as the basis for their design of the *cannone da 75/46*. It is interesting to note that a clandestine design team from Krupp was working in Sweden at the time of development of the Bofors Model 29, and that many elements of the Bofors design were later incorporated into the German 88mm *FlaK* 18. Thus, the Italian 75/46, which borrowed features from the Bofors Model 29, could be considered either a half-brother or a cousin to the iconic 88. The *cannone da 75/46 mod. 34*, adopted by the *Regio Esercito* in 1934, also proved to be an effective anti-tank gun.

The 75/46 was produced in three versions, the mod. 34 field model, the 34M, which was a version fitted with different wheels that allowed mechanical towing without the use of a limber, and the mod. 40, which had a static pedestal mount and was intended for homeland defence in fixed positions. The mobile field version of the gun was mounted on a central pivot that rested on a cruciform platform, which permitted a 360° traverse. For towing, the legs were folded together to form a carriage, and two wheels were mounted on one end while the other end was laid on a limber, attached to the tractor. The breech mechanism was a transversal wedge, which could be operated both automatically or manually.

The 75/46 incorporated virtually all of the desirable features that the *Regio Esercito* had requested: high muzzle velocity, high rate of fire, satisfactory elevation, and a stable firing platform. On the negative side, the barrel wore down rapidly and although, as with other contemporary Italian pieces, the barrel was made of tubes which could be separated cold so that when the inner liner wore down it could be replaced easily without withdrawing the gun from its position, it was necessary to reduce the powder charge in the ammunition, leading to a reduction in muzzle velocity to 750 m/s (2461 fps). This circumstance and the rapid improvement of aircraft capabilities resulted in a situation in which this gun became ineffective against the heavier bombers used by the Allies later in the war.

A 75/46 anti-aircraft gun in position in Russia during the winter of 1943. (USSME)

Fire control originally was provided by a *Gala mod. 37*, produced in Italy, replaced in part during the course of the war by the more capable *Gamma mod. 40* system produced in Hungary that could transmit the firing coordinates directly to the guns without the need to type them in and could track an aircraft flying at 540 km/h (335 mph) at 7,500 meters (24,600 feet); unfortunately, the fire control systems were always in short supply, in July 1943 only 11 of the 31 operational 75/46 batteries were equipped with these systems.

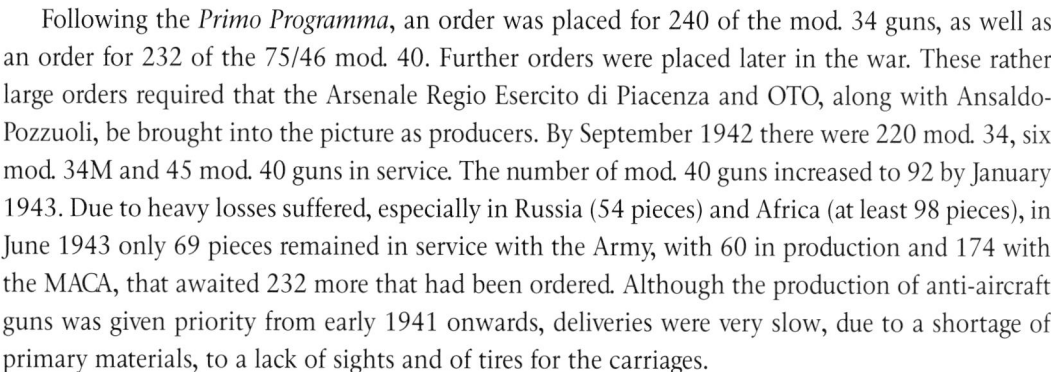

An initial order for 100 guns was placed in late 1933 or early 1934 and by October 1939 84 pieces had been delivered; in June 1940 the number of guns on hand had decreased to 76, probably explained by the fact that eight guns sent to Spain remained there. All of the available 75/46 guns were assigned to the *Regio Esercito*; the MACA had none.

Following the *Primo Programma*, an order was placed for 240 of the mod. 34 guns, as well as an order for 232 of the 75/46 mod. 40. Further orders were placed later in the war. These rather large orders required that the Arsenale Regio Esercito di Piacenza and OTO, along with Ansaldo-Pozzuoli, be brought into the picture as producers. By September 1942 there were 220 mod. 34, six mod. 34M and 45 mod. 40 guns in service. The number of mod. 40 guns increased to 92 by January 1943. Due to heavy losses suffered, especially in Russia (54 pieces) and Africa (at least 98 pieces), in June 1943 only 69 pieces remained in service with the Army, with 60 in production and 174 with the MACA, that awaited 232 more that had been ordered. Although the production of anti-aircraft guns was given priority from early 1941 onwards, deliveries were very slow, due to a shortage of primary materials, to a lack of sights and of tires for the carriages.

A 75/46 gun assigned to the 90ᵗʰ Gruppo *in Tunisia. (USSME)*

A 75/46 gun assigned to the MACA, with its associated fire control center. The MACA personnel are wearing the old-style Adrian helmet. (Claudio Pergher Archive)

A battery of 75/46 anti-aircraft guns. (Claudio Pergher Archive)

The fire direction center for a 75/46 battery. (USSME)

A battery of 75/46 anti-aircraft guns ready to fire. (USSME)

A 75/46 gun in travel order. (Fondazione Ansaldo)

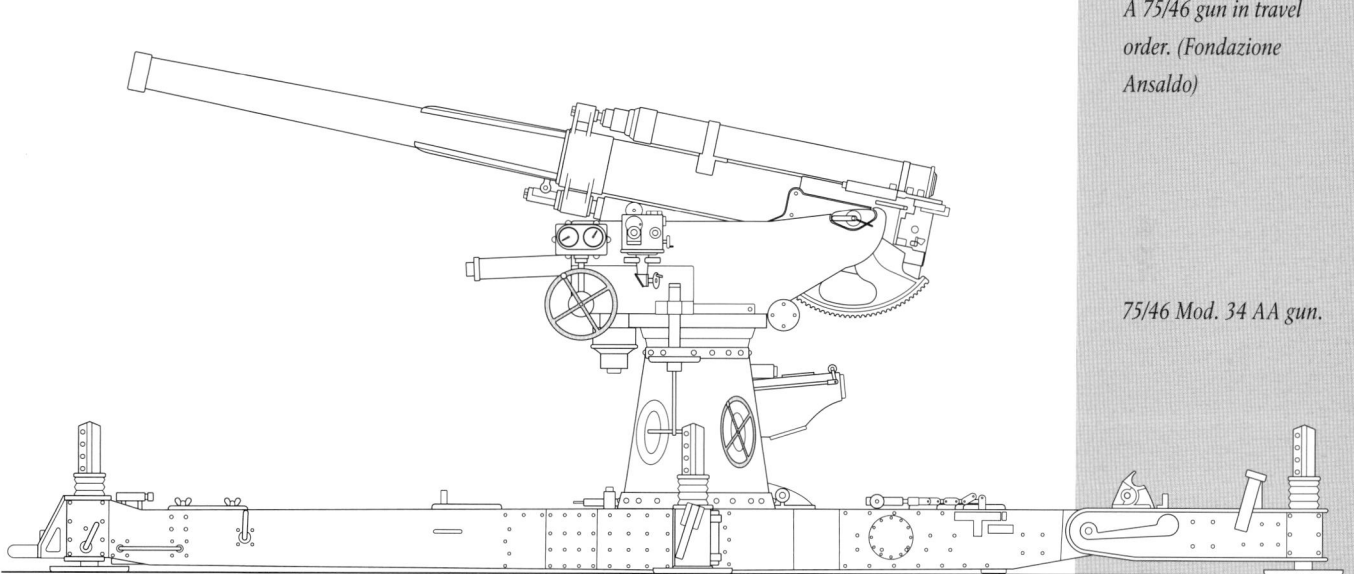

75/46 Mod. 34 AA gun.

The 75/46 saw its first action in Spain where two test batteries (eight guns) were sent during the civil war there. After that, either in the static or in the field version, it took part in every campaign fought by the Italian army in WWII. In Italian East Africa four static batteries were deployed, 16 guns in total, all of which were lost when the colony surrendered in May 1941. Two more static battalions served on the Greek-Albanian border during the campaign against Greece. The first field batteries were formed in 1941, grouped in two battalions, the IV and the XIX, and assigned to the CSIR. Three more battalions, the XXXVI, XXXVII and XXXVIII, joined the following year, with the two additional Italian army corps sent to Russia. Other field battalions, the XIV, XXXV, XL, XC and XCI, were sent to Tunisia in 1943, taking part in the final battles against the Allies on North African soil; it goes without saying that they could do little to stop the mounting tide of Allied aircraft and armoured vehicles. Another battalion was later sent to Greece, assigned to the *Brennero* Infantry Division. Eight batteries of the 75/46 were also deployed to Sicily, for defence of the ports.

After the surrender of Italy, production of 75/46 went on under German control, with the new designation of *7,5 cm FlaK – 264/3 (or 264/4) (i)*, for the static and field versions, respectively. The RSI armed forces obtained a few pieces that equipped some batteries of the anti-aircraft defences (*Artiglieria Contraerea – Ar.CO.*), while, in the south, the Allies deployed some batteries for defence of the ports.

Specifications:

Designation:	cannone da 75/46 C.A. mod. 34, mod. 34M and mod. 40
Adopted:	1934
Inventory 10/06/1940:	76
Subsequent production:	366 (by 30 June 1943)
Originator:	Ansaldo
Producer:	Ansaldo-Pozzuoli, Arsenale Regio Esercito di Piacenza, OTO
User countries:	Italy, Germany (after September 1943)
Caliber:	75mm (2.95 inches)
Length of barrel:	3.45m (135.8 inches)
Overall length:	7.40m (291.34 inches)
Overall width:	1.85m (72.83 inches)
Overall height:	2.15m (84.65 inches)
Weight in action:	3,300 kg (7275 lb)
Carriage:	folding cruciform pedestal mount on two-wheeled carriage
Wheel track:	1.30m (51.2 inches)
Breech type:	horizontal wedge
Recuperator type:	hydropneumatic
Recoil length:	1,100mm (43.3 inches) maximum; 610mm (24 inches) minimum
Elevation:	0° to +90°
Traverse:	360°
Muzzle velocity:	800 m/s (2625 fps)
Maximum effective ceiling:	8,500 metres (27,887 feet)
Rate of fire:	15 rounds per minute
Ammunition types:	AA; AT
Shell weight:	AA 10.64 kg (23.5 lb)

90/53 gun mod. 39, mod. 41P, mod. 41C anti-aircraft gun

The *cannone da 90/53* was very similar in appearance and performance characteristics to the iconic 88mm German *FlaK* 18 and *FlaK* 36 anti-aircraft guns. Although the 90/53 never was accorded the same coverage or respect as was the German 88 in press accounts and popular lore, if the objective truth were to be recognized and acknowledged, the 90/53 was in several respects a better gun than the 88. It was simpler to produce, it fired a heavier shell at a higher muzzle velocity, and had a higher effective ceiling than did the German guns; like the 88, it was also highly effective as

Towing test of a prototype 90/53 gun in travel order. (Claudio Pergher Archive)

a tank killer. Compared to contemporary Allied guns of the same general type, namely the British 3.7 inch (94mm) Mk 3 anti-aircraft gun and the US 90mm M1, the 90/53 had a higher muzzle velocity and a higher effective ceiling than either of the Allied guns. Succinctly and simply stated, the 90/53 was fully competitive with all of its contemporaries, German and Allied alike.

The 90/53 was based on a 90/50 naval gun that had been developed by Ansaldo; in 1938 the *Regio Esercito* put forth a requirement for an anti-aircraft gun to replace the 75/46 gun, and in 1939 the DSSTAM asked Ansaldo to develop a ground version of the naval gun. An order was placed for eight test guns, four of which were static versions designated the mod. 41P (the P standing for *posizione*, or static) and four of which were field versions, designated the mod. 41C (the C standing for *campale*, or field/mobile). The first static gun was delivered on 30 January 1940; tests carried out in April were very satisfactory.

The barrel was one piece, cast in steel and chrome, nickel and molybdenum, and shared with other modern Italian guns the feature of tubes that could be separated cold, directly on the battlefield, once the inner liner wore down due to use. The breech mechanism was a horizontal wedge which could be operated both manually or automatically. The platform while in battery assumed a cruciform configuration, with two lateral arms extending from the main frame. For towing, two two-wheeled dollies and a drawbar were added to the platform to convert the system to a trailer. Two different fire control systems were used with the 90/53: the first was the Hungarian designed *Gamma-Juhasz mod. 40*, and the second was the Italian BGS (Borletti-Galileo-San Giorgio) system. There were two versions of the BGS system, the first being a static version associated with the mod. 41P, and the second

A 90/53 anti-aircraft gun in firing position; note the leveling jacks on the cruciform platform. (Claudio Pergher Archive)

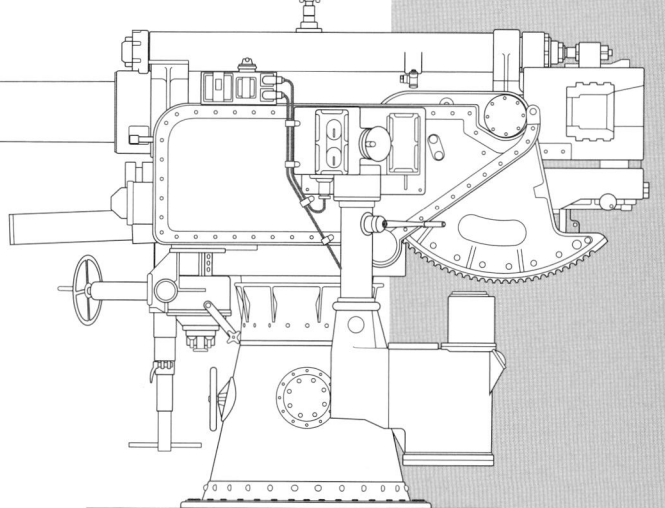

90/53 gun on pedestal mount.

A 90/53 gun mounted on a Lancia 3Ro truck. (Fondazione Ansaldo)

A 90/53 truck-mounted gun on a Breda 51 truck with reinforced chassis. (Fondazione Ansaldo)

mounted on a two-axle Viberti trailer for use with the mod. 41C mobile system. The BGS system could track aircraft flying between 1,200 meters and 12,000 meters at speeds up to 720 km/h (447 mph), which exceeded the capabilities of most aircraft of the era. A Calzoni-Galileo system also enabled the gun to track the target automatically. In late 1942 the BGS could be used in conjunction with German-supplied *Würzburg* radar, called *Volpe* (fox) in Italian. Unfortunately, all of this advanced technology was available only in limited quantities; in July 1943 only 23 of the 121 batteries assigned to the MACA could be equipped with the BGS system, obliging most batteries to rely on relatively ineffective barrage fire.

The first order placed was for 102 four-piece batteries, increased a few weeks later by a further 228 (*Primo Programma*). Later in 1940 order for an additional 1,600 more were placed, reduced in February 1941 to 480 (*Secondo Programma*). These included 300 pieces to be produced by OTO. A number of other subcontractors were involved, mainly in the production of mounts and fire control equipment; among these were Reggiane and CRDA (Cantieri Riuniti dell'Adriatico) for mounts. On the other hand, while delivery of the static version of the cannon was able to begin relatively quickly, although in not great numbers, the production of the field version was seriously delayed because the platform had to be redesigned several times before the army accepted it. The first 12 mobile platform mounts for the mod. 41 C were not delivered by Motomeccanica of Milan until December 1942. In February 1943 the Naples Arsenal ordered a new type of mobile platform to be produced by Ansaldo, consisting of a stamped rather than riveted frame, designated the mod. 43 mount. The definitive mount had wheels of the same diameter as the TM 40 trac-

Gun platform for a truck-mounted 90/53 gun. (Claudio Pergher Archive)

tor used to tow the gun. As a consequence, when WWII broke out there were no 90/53 guns in active service, and the first field batteries were not delivered until December 1942.

Due to delays in delivering the mod. 41C towed version, as a stop-gap measure in January 1941 the General Staff of the *Regio Esercito* directed Ansaldo to mount the 90/53 gun on both the 4 x 2 Lancia 3 Ro chassis and the 6 x 4 Breda *Dovunque* chassis, as well as for the successive development of a 90/53 tracked self-propelled gun, ultimately realized as the M 41M self-propelled gun mounted on an M.41 tank chassis (see separate entry). The prototype of the *autocannone* on the Lancia 3 Ro chassis was ready in February 1941. Due to the demonstrated capabilities and effectiveness of the gun, production was ordered using the Lancia 3 Ro as well as the Breda 51 specifically reinforced, designated the Breda 52. Ultimately, a number of other *autocannoni* utilizing the 90/53 gun on a variety of different chassis were also under consideration. A special Breda chassis was developed (in prototype only), the Breda *Tipo 102*, which was partially armoured and which mounted the 90/53 gun on a specially designed low-profile chassis. Plans were also under way to mount the 90/53 on a Breda Model 61 half-track chassis, but neither the *Tipo 102* nor the half-track mount progressed past the prototype or design stage, respectively.

During the war, due to increasing Allied air raids against Italy, production of the 90/53 was increased, being surpassed only by production of the 47mm Breda/ Böhler gun. Although by December 1940 Ansaldo had produced only 41 mod. 41P static position guns in addition to the

A 90/53 gun mounted on a Lancia 3Ro chassis.

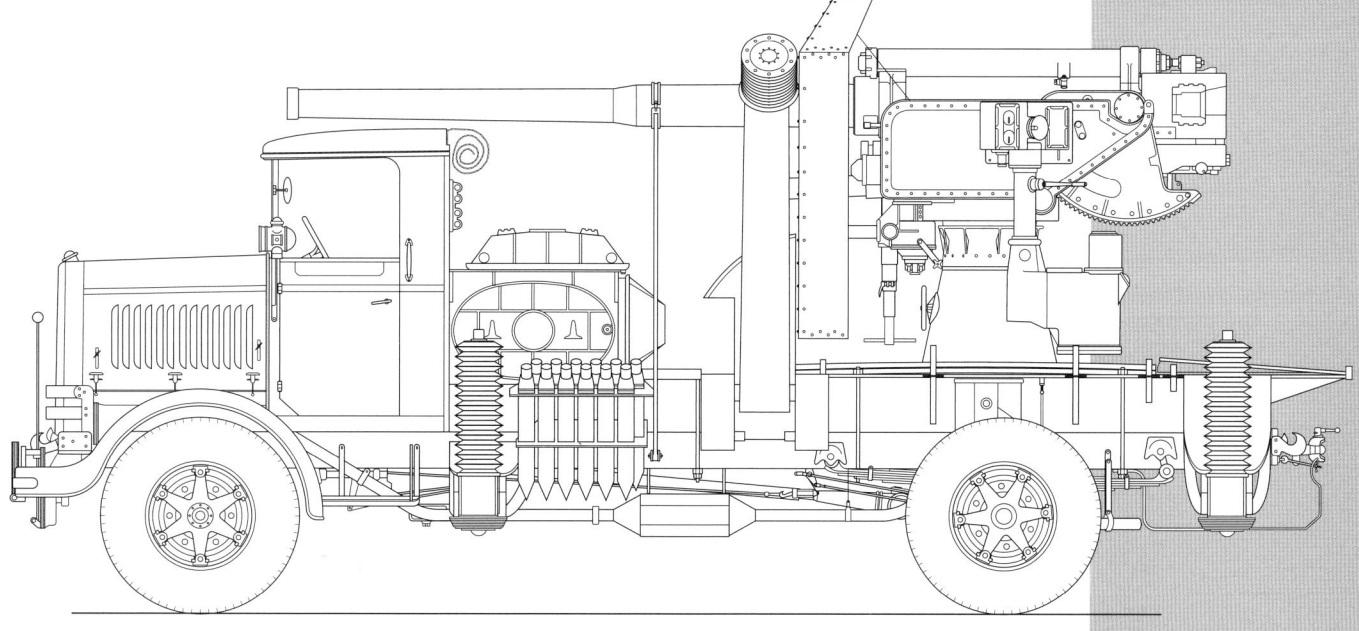

two test batteries, by the end of 1942 combined production of Ansaldo's Genoa and Pozzuoli plants amounted to 517 mod. 41P, 104 mod. 41C, and 96 mod. 39 guns fitted as *autocannoni*. During the first half of 1943 an additional 216 90/53 guns were produced. To those numbers must be added the OTO production, amounting to 30 by December 1942. However, as with so much other Italian equipment, production never managed to keep up with requirements and demand, and, taking into account losses suffered, in September 1942, the number of 90/53 in service amounted to 304 pieces for MACA, with orders for no fewer than 1,087, 52 for the Army, that awaited a further 660, and 96 *autocannoni*, with 26 more on order and by July 1943, only 593 static and mobile guns, as well as 29 mounted on trucks. Production shortfalls also affected the prime movers needed to tow the mobile 41 C guns; the tractor originally envisioned for the 90/53 was the Breda 32 heavy tractor, but that tractor proved to be too slow for the purpose. The more powerful Breda 41 was paired with the 90/53 as a towing vehicle, and plans called for the SPA *Dovunque* 41 ultimately to replace the Breda 41, but that vehicle did not enter service in time to be assigned to units. Other problems affected the production of Borletti mod. 41 fuses that allowed ammunition to reach the optimal muzzle velocity of 850 m/s; the majority of the ammunition used with mod. 36 and mod. 36R delay fuses had a muzzle velocity of only 710 m/s.

The first field batteries of 90/53 were deployed in the *autocannone* version at the beginning of 1942 in North Africa, assigned to the *Ariete (DI Gruppo)* and *Littorio (DIII Gruppo)* armoured divisions. They fought the 1942 campaign until the Battle of El Alamein. Later, another battalion, the DII, was sent to Tunisia, along with the *Centauro* Armoured Division. Another battalion of *autocannoni*, the DV, was deployed in Sicily, when the Allies landed in July 1943. In August 1943 the last significant operational use of the 90/53 by the *Regio Esercito*, along with German 88mm batteries, occurred during the evacuation of Sicily; eight fixed and

three mobile batteries on Sicily, and two mobile and one static battery on the opposite shore in Calabria provided anti-aircraft support.

Following the September 1943 Italian surrender to the Allies, some of the 90/53 guns assigned to the *Ariete II* Division's 135th Artillery Regiment saw action in the Italian attempt to defend Rome against German forces. The Germans seized 65 of the guns, as well as taking delivery of all ongoing and new production; Ansaldo produced 145 mod. 41P and 68 mod. 41C for the Germans, who in December 1944 had a total of 315 of the various types of the 90/53 in their inventory, 37 of which may have been produced by OTO. The German designation for the 90/53 was the *9.0 cm FlaK 41 (i)*. The 90/53 also served with RSI air and coast defence forces, as well as to a limited extent with Allied forces which deployed them in the newly established Italy Air Defence Area.

At the end of the war, an assortment of 90/53 guns and gun assemblies remained in Italy, including 620 barrels, 360 fixed mounts, and 158 mobile mounts. In early 1948, the new Italian Army possessed eight 90/53 guns in active units, with another 24 operating guns as well as a further 168 in need of repair or completion in depots; plans called for eventual refurbishment of a total of 200 guns, and ultimately seven air defence regiments were equipped with the 90/53. In 1951 a derivative of the 90/53 was also developed by the Naples Arsenal; the gun was a 90/74 on a mobile mount. An experimental battery of three guns was produced, but with the advent of surface-to-air air defence missiles, further development was abandoned. In the mid-1950s the British *Contraves F90BT* was adopted as the fire control system for the remaining 90/53 guns. The 90/53 continued to serve with both the Italian Army and the Italian Navy until 1970 when it was finally retired from service. The last actual operational use of the 90/53 appears to have been by Croatian coast defence units against the Serbian Navy during the fighting as Yugoslavia was breaking apart in 1990.

Specifications:

Designation:	cannone da 90/53 mod. 39, mod. 41P and mod. 41C
Adopted:	1939
Inventory 10/06/1940:	0
Subsequent production:	982
Originator:	Ansaldo
Producer:	Ansaldo, OTO

User countries:	Italy, Germany (after September 1943), Yugoslavia (post-WWII), Croatia (recently)
Caliber:	90mm (3.54 inches)
Crew:	9
Length of barrel:	5.039m (198.4 inches)
Overall length:	7.95m (313 inches) on trailer; 6.52m (256.7 inches) in battery
Overall width:	2.00m (78.7 inches) on trailer; 5.00m (196.9 inches) in battery
Overall height:	2.93mm (115.4 inches) on trailer; 2.00m (78.7 inches) in battery
Weight in action:	6,240 kg (13,757 lb); 8,950 kg (19,731 lb) travel weight
Carriage:	pedestal on cruciform platform
Wheel track:	1.994m (78.5 inches)
Wheel type/diameter:	8 spoke steel wheels with pneumatic tires/12.75"x32"
Breech type:	horizontal sliding wedge
Recuperator type:	hydropneumatic (dual)
Recoil length:	905mm at 0° elevation; 780mm at 85° elevation; the recoil regulator compensated for the elevation angle, preventing the breech mechanism from hitting the firing platform
Elevation:	-2° to + 85°
Traverse:	360°
Muzzle velocity:	830 m/s (2723 fps)
Maximum range:	17,470 metres horizontal; 12,000 metres ceiling
Rate of fire:	20 rounds per minute
Ammunition types:	AA, AP
Shell weight:	10.1 kg (22.3 lb) AA; 11.25 kg(24.8 lb) AP

149/19 mod. 37, mod. 41, and mod. 42 howitzer

The end of WWI saw a number of heavy field artillery types in service in the Italian Army, among these being several different types and models of 149mm pieces, including the Krupp 149/12, the Ansaldo 149/12 mod. 16, and several Škoda guns. The 1927 study by the Supreme Defence Commission had concluded that there was a need for 1,200 guns in 149mm and 152mm, and that all of the existing 149mm guns in the inventory should be retired due to their age and obsolete character. Two years later, in 1929 the DSSTAM requested both Ansaldo and OTO to produce prototypes of 105mm guns and 149mm howitzers of modern design. The requirements set forth by the Technical Service for the latter type were for a split trail gun with a range of no

Gun limber for a 149/19 howitzer. (Claudio Pergher Archive)

Prototype of the OTO 149/19 howitzer with the carriage limber and gun limber. (Fondazione Ansaldo)

less than 14 kilometers, a minimum range not greater than 2 kilometers at an angle of elevation of 15°, and a weight in battery not greater than 5.5 tons that could be placed in battery in fifteen minutes or less. Other requirements were that the guns should have 60° traverse and 70° elevation and should be capable of being broken down into two towed loads neither of which could exceed 3.5 tons. Both howitzers were submitted to the army in 1933, but both were rejected as not meeting the requirements. Both Ansaldo and OTO went back to the drawing board, eliminating details that were considered unnecessary. In 1934 Ansaldo presented its 149/21, with a carriage and wheels similar to that of the Ansaldo *cannone da 149/40*, and in 1935 OTO submitted a new prototype which, among other modifications, had eliminated the shield of the original prototype and had been redesigned so that when firing the wheels were raised so that the carriage rested on the ground. Both versions could be mechanically towed at 30 km/h, and could be put in battery in 12 minutes. Further modifications requested by the army led to acceptance of the OTO 1936 version, designated the *149/19 OTO mod. 37*. The howitzer as adopted had a replaceable barrel liner (that could be separated cold, directly on the battlefield), hydropneumatic equilibrators and recuperator, an interrupted screw breech mechanism, a split trail carriage with rubber-tired steel wheels, and could be towed either as a single unit or as two components and could be emplaced in battery, from its travel mode, in 30 minutes. Almost all of the components of the 149/19 were forged or stamped.

Ultimately, three versions of the 149/19 were built: the 16 pre-series *modello 37*, the *modello 41*, and the *modello 42*. The mod. 37 version of the 149/19 was separated into two loads for towing (4,000 kg for the gun tube itself, and 4,170 kg for the carriage), towed by a Pavesi tractor. Entry into service of the more capable SPA TM 40 medium artillery tractor enabled the howitzer to be towed as a single load. The 149/19 OTO mod. 42 consisted of the gun and a limber, and the 149/19 OTO mod. 42, which had an increased chamber capacity resulting in a greater range capability, consisted of the gun only, without a limber.

Sixteen pre-series pieces were ordered in 1938, but the first delivery was not made until the second half of 1940; these pieces were immediately placed in service due to the critical state of the army's heavy artillery inventory. In 1938, the requirement was fixed for a total of 632 149/19 howitzers to be built by 1943; of these, 312 were to be built by Ansaldo at its Pozzuoli works, and 320 by OTO *(Primo Programma)*. However, modifications continued to be made from 1938 on, and by 1940 the number of howitzers ordered rose to 792 from Ansaldo and 600 from OTO. Due to shortages of critical material, in spring 1941 the orders were reduced to only 521 pieces, to be added to the pre-series 16, but it was not until the end of 1941 that series production was very slowly under way. Actual production, however, fell far short of requirements: in 1941 only 16 guns were produced, by September 1942 147 howitzers of this type were in service, while, overall, by 1943, enough guns had been produced to equip 24 artillery groups. Total production during the

three year period 1941-1943 is quite uncertain, but it did not exceed much more than 400 pieces[1]. Furthermore, due to a chronic shortage of artillery tractors, the Pavesi and the TM40, the number of 149/19 howitzers that were able to reach the front line was even smaller.

The gun was regarded at the time by the Italians as one of the best guns available in its class; it was in fact at least equal to, or better with respect to range and weight, than any comparable contemporary weapons in the German, British, US, Soviet, French or other European inventories. However, due to the small number of guns produced compared to requirements, the howitzer was not able to replace all of the various types of WWI era 149mm artillery that the *Regio Esercito* had in its active inventory when WWII began.

The howitzer saw its first use only in Sicily, in July 1943, after the Allied landings, where it performed very well. The number of batteries deployed there is disputed by different sources[2], but what it is undisputed is the very good quality of the piece, reliable, accurate and quick to put in firing position. Despite the overall satisfactory performance of the gun, it could do little to stop the Allied forces on the island. On the other hand, the pieces assigned to the *135° Reggimento artiglieria corazzata* of the *Ariete II* Armoured Division were used to fire against the former German allies of the 3rd *Panzergranadieren* Division at the Monterosi strongpoint during the confused days of the defence of Rome that followed the surrender of Italy.

1 According to L. Ceva, *Storia delle Forze Armate in Italia*, page 345, the total production should be 436 pieces. According to *Storia dell'Artiglieria italiana*, Ansaldo produced 42 pieces in 1942 and 74 more until June 1943, i.e. a total of 116, which would leave 320 pieces to OTO. F. Minniti, *Il problema degli armamenti*, pag. 27, confirms the 320 pieces produced by OTO, and the 116 by Ansaldo. On the other hand, N. Pignato, *L'obice da 149/19 OTO 1937* slightly reduces this latter figure, quoting OTO sources that reported first 312 and later 304 pieces ordered (the difference might be due to the 16 pre-series pieces, already assigned), and not all of them delivered.

2 A. Santoni, *Le operazioni in Sicilia e Calabria*, page 499 onwards, reports the *CLVII Gruppo* assigned to the XII Army Corps, a battery within the *XXX Gruppo Pluricalibro*, assigned to the XVI Army Corp and the *CLVIII Gruppo* assigned to the *Piazza Marittima* (Port Defense Authority) of Messina-Reggio Calabria. *Storia dell'artiglieria italiana*, page 855 onwards, considers the *CLI* and the *CLVII Gruppo* on the island at the moment of the invasion, and one more battalion arriving afterwards. N. Pignato, *L'obice da 149/19 OTO 1937*, page 25, reports the same two battalions, assigned to the XVI Army Corps, and an additional battalion to the XII Army Corps. F. Cappellano, *Le artiglierie del Regio Esercito nella seconda guerra mondiale*, page 124, increases the number of battalions to five.

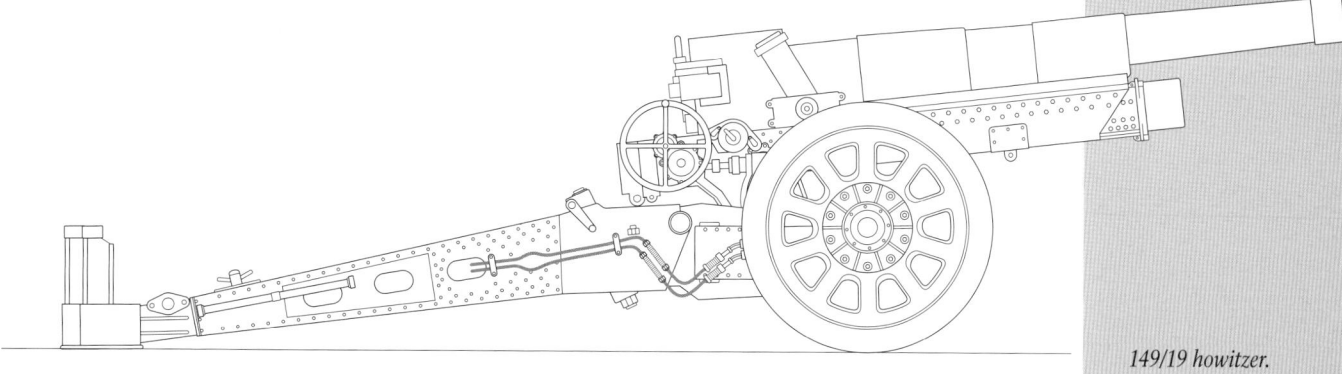

After 8 September 1943, the guns located on Italian territory controlled by the Italian Royal Government were organized as the *CLXXVI Gruppo artiglieria* assigned to the *11° Reggimento artiglieria motorizzato* that equipped the *Corpo Italiano di Liberazione* and employed operationally from 8 July to 24 September 1944. In northern Italy 121 of the howitzers were seized by the Germans who designated them *15 cm sFH 404 (i)*; an additional 13 howitzers were produced by Italian industry for German use subsequent to September 1943. Other howitzers of this type remained in the hands of the RSI, in the north, and equipped the artillery regiments of three divisions of the ENR, the *2° Reggimento artiglieria*, assigned to the *Littorio* Division, the *3° Reggimento artiglieria*, assigned to the *San Marco* Divison, and the *4° Reggimento artiglieria* of the *Italia* Division, with a battalion of 12 pieces for each regiment, as well as equipping two coastal batteries in Liguria and two fixed batteries in Fiume (now Rijeka).

Following the war, 96 of the 149/19 howitzers were recovered, of which 26 needed repairs. The heavy artillery regiments of the reconstituted Italian Army were organized with two groups each, one group equipped with the British 5.5 inch howitzer and the other with the 149/19. The regiments equipped with the 149/19 were the 3rd, 4th, 6th, 8th, 27th, and 41st. The post-war guns were

A group of 149/19 howitzers taken during the post-war period, towed by TM48 artillery tractors. (Gianna Olivero Archive)

149/19 howitzer.

refitted with pneumatic tires in place of the semi-pneumatic tires, leading to redesignation of the models as the 149/19 OTO mod. 42/50 and the 149/19 OTO mod. 41/51. Initially the TM 40 medium artillery tractor was used as the towing vehicle, but this was later replaced by the TM 48 medium and finally by TM 50 heavy tractors. Beginning in 1950 the 149/19 and British 5.5 inch howitzer in Italian heavy field artillery regiments began to be replaced by the 155mm US M114 howitzer. Following an experimental conversion to 155mm, the 149/19 continued to serve in a limited capacity until 1974 when it was finally removed from service, replaced by the 155mm FH-70.

Specifications:

Designation:	obice da 149/19 mod. 37, mod. 41 and mod. 42
Adopted:	1937
Inventory 10/06/1940:	1
Subsequent production:	436
Originator:	OTO
Producers:	OTO and Ansaldo
Unit cost:	837,000 Italian lire (1939)
User countries:	Italy
Caliber:	149.1mm (5.87 inches)
Length of barrel:	3.034m (119.5 inches)
Length of rifling:	2.831m (111.5 inches)
Overall length:	5.90m (232.3 inches)
Overall width:	2.30m (90.6 inches)
Weight::	5,650 kg (12,456 lb) in action; 5,780 kg (12,743 lb) travel weight
Carriage:	split trail
Wheel type/diameter:	8-spoke steel wheels/1.30m (51.2 inches)
Breech type:	interrupted screw
Recuperator type:	hydropneumatic
Elevation:	-5° to +60°
Traverse:	50°
Muzzle velocity:	597 m/s (1,959 fps)
Maximum range:	15,320 metres (16,754 yards)
Rate of fire:	1-3 rounds per minute
Ammunition types:	HE, AP
Shell weight:	HE 42.55 kg (93.8 lb)

149/40 mod. 35 gun

In the context of Italy's artillery modernization, in 1930 the Artillery Inspectorate of the *Regio Esercito* requested both the Arsenale Regio Esercito di Napoli and Ansaldo to submit proposals for a new 149mm cannon to replace the old WWI era 149/35 (initially designated as 149A) and the 152/37 and 152/45 guns. The requirements laid down called for a gun weighing no more than 11 tons in battery that could be broken down into two or three loads for towing, that had a range of at least 20,000 metres, and that could be placed in battery in no more than one hour. Both prototypes were presented in 1933; the Naples Arsenal based its prototype on the old 149/35 gun, lengthening the barrel slightly to 37 calibers (149/37), while Ansaldo presented a completely new 149/40 gun. Although tests of both entries proved satisfactory, the Ansaldo version was chosen over that of the Naples Arsenal, mainly because the Ansaldo version rested on a platform while firing, whereas the Naples Arsenal version rested on its wheels. Between December 1933 and December 1934 the Ansaldo gun was subjected to extensive trials at the Nettuno firing range; in early 1935 the gun was sent back to Ansaldo's Genova plant for modifications to improve stability while firing and to reduce the number of pieces necessary during transport. In June 1935 the new gun was officially adopted as the *cannone da 149/40, mod. 35*, and an initial order for 48 was placed on 15 July 1935. The main visual difference between the Ansaldo prototype and the production model was the configuration of the wheels, which in the prototype had eight steel spokes, while the production model switched to wheels with eight large diameter holes. In December 1938 an order was

placed for an additional 132 guns, and in May 1940 yet another 590 were ordered, bringing the total to 722 pieces. However, shortages of raw materials, coupled with priority accorded to anti-tank, anti-aircraft, and divisional artillery pieces, led to scaling back the order to 108 guns in early 1941. Ultimately, only 51 149/40 guns were produced for the Italian Army.

The slow rate of production of the 149/40 was exacerbated by the fact that there was also a lack of heavy artillery tractors needed to tow the guns, limiting their ability to be employed with motorised elements as well as at the army level. Even when enough Breda heavy tractors became available, towing the gun as a single load was not feasible; it had to be broken down into two loads consisting of a gun load weighing 7,800 kg (17,196 lb) and a carriage load weighing 6,540 kg, (14,418 lb) towed at a speed of about 19 km/h (12 mph). This, of course, meant that twice as many of the scarce tractors were needed for each gun and battery.

The Ansaldo engineers deserve credit for designing what was unquestionably a first-rate gun. The 149/40 mod. 35 was a state of the art gun for its time. It had an inner barrel liner that could be removed from the tube and replaced in about an hour, even under field conditions. Its split trail

Prototype of the 149/40 photographed at the Ansaldo works at Cornigliano in 1935. The spoked wheels were later replaced by different style steel wheels. (Fondazione Ansaldo)

The 149/40 on its gun limber. (Fondazione Ansaldo)

The 149/40 carriage limber during rough terrain tests carried out at Ansaldo's Cornigliano works in 1935. (Fondazione Ansaldo)

An advertising brochure published by Ansaldo in 1938. (Fondazione Ansaldo)

allowed a wide traverse arc; stability was assured both by the fact that the entire carriage was lowered to the ground, the wheels being slightly raised off the ground while firing, and the trail legs were further anchored by driving trail stakes into the ground at the end of each leg. The added stability provided by the trail stakes was offset by the fact that, although hammering the stakes into the ground may have been easy under certain conditions, removing the stakes when the gun had to be reoriented was a labour intensive and time-consuming process. With respect to performance, the 149/40 was as good as or better than any of its contemporaries, including the US155mm M1A1 *Long Tom* cannon; the German *15cm Kanone 18* and *15cm Kanone 39*, whose barrels were considerably longer than that of the 149/40, had higher muzzle velocities and greater range, but fired a lighter shell. Unfortunately for the *Regio Esercito*, only a fraction of the guns required were ever produced.

Although delivery of the initial order of these modern and powerful pieces of artillery had been completed by 1940 and a first battalion had been formed, the XXXIII *Gruppo*, they could not be assigned to front line units until the following year due to lack of heavy tractors, and were used as coastal artillery instead.

In 1941 three mobile groups were formed, the XXXI, XXXII and XXXIV, while the XXXIII, formed earlier, also received its tractors. The first battalion to see use was the XXXIII, which in April 1941 was sent to Yugoslavia, assigned to the *2ª Armata*. After the campaign in the Balkans it was deployed to North Africa, within the *8° Raggruppamento artiglieria d'armata*, and took part in the Axis offensive of spring-summer 1942 towards Egypt. In autumn of that year it was deployed at El Alamein. Afterwards, it accompanied the retreat of the Italian troops and fought again in Tunisia, with the remaining six pieces. The other three groups were sent to Russia in 1942 within the

9° *Raggruppamento artiglieria d'armata* of the ARMIR. There they had the opportunity to engage in action before being wiped out by the Soviet offensive of winter 1942, which caused the loss of the entire 8th Army.

After the surrender of Italy in September 1943, and until the end of the war, the Germans obtained 13 more pieces produced by Ansaldo that were used as static artillery with the designation *15 cm K 408 (i)*.

The Italian Army also had plans to mechanize the 149/40 by mounting it on a modified heavy tank chassis (see specific entry).

A 149/40 gun in North Africa, February 1942. (USSME)

A 149/40 battery in North Africa. (USSME)

49

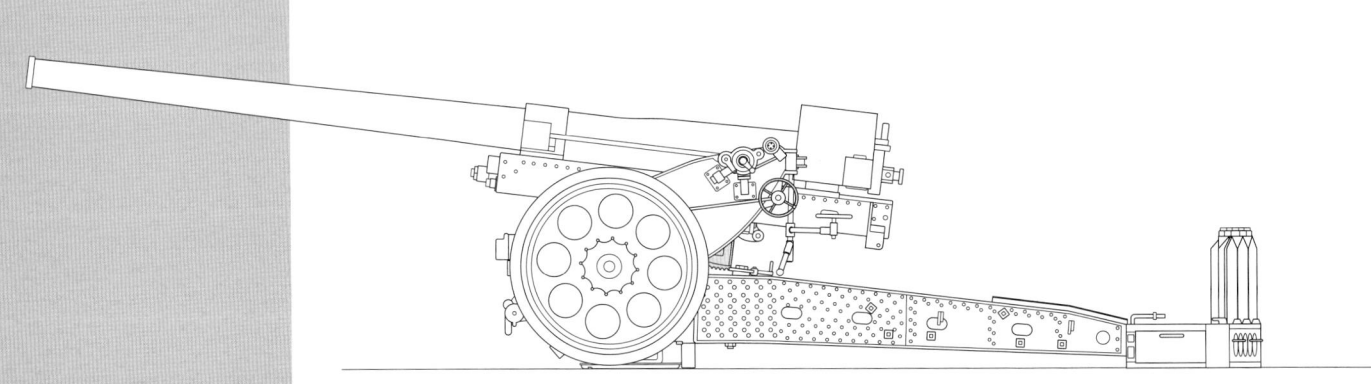

149/40 Mod. 35 gun.

Specifications:

Designation:	cannone da 149/40 mod. 35
Adopted:	1935
Inventory 10/06/1940:	48
Subsequent production:	3 for the *Regio Esercito*; 13 after the Armistice for the German army
Originator:	Ansaldo
Producer:	Ansaldo (Genoa)
User countries:	Italy, Germany (after September 1943)
Caliber:	149.1mm (5.87 inches)
Crew:	9
Length of barrel:	6.36m (250.4 inches)
Overall length:	6.70m (263.8 inches) in travel position
Overall width:	2.10m (86.7 inches) traveling; 6.40m (252 inches) with split trails extended
Weight:	14,340 kg (31,614 lb) traveling; 11,430 kg (25,199 lb) in action
Carriage:	split trail
Wheel type/diameter:	8-hole steel wheels with semi-pneumatic tires/1400mm (55.1 inches)
Breech type:	horizontal wedge
Recuperator type:	hydropneumatic
Recoil length:	1,400mm maximum; 800mm minimum
Elevation:	0° to + 45°
Traverse:	57°
Muzzle velocity:	800 m/s (2625 fps)
Maximum range:	23,700 metres (25,928 yards)
Rate of fire:	1 round per minute normal; 2-3 rounds per minute possible
Ammunition types:	HE
Shell weight:	46.2 kg (101.4 lb)

210/22 mod. 35 howitzer

As well as inviting submissions for a new heavy gun, in 1929 the *Regio Esercito* also requested bids for a large howitzer to replace the panoply of siege howitzers and bombards extensively used during WWI. Despite the impression given by the unique wheel arrangement that this was an outmoded design, the 210/22 howitzer, an Army-level system, was one of the Italian Army's most modern artillery pieces in WWII; it was designed by the DSSTAM. Development was begun by Ansaldo in autumn of 1932, and a prototype produced at its Pozzuoli works was presented in 1935. It was not accepted for service until 1938, when a production order was placed for 24 units (12 each from Ansaldo and OTO). Even though OTO had been brought on board to produce the 210/22, the production rate remained very slow, and when Italy entered the war, although 24 howitzers had been delivered, eight of those had been sold to Hungary where it was known as the 21cm 39.M[1], leaving only 16 available for the Italian army. The 1939 artillery modernization program

1   With modifications, it was also produced in Hungary by MAVAG (the Hungarian State Railway workshops) as the 21cm 40.M and 40a.M. In 1941 a license was also granted to the Japanese Imperial Army to produce the howitzer.

called for OTO and Terni to produce a total of 66 210/22 howitzers by June 1941, followed in 1940 by 280 more, but the shortage of raw materials that plagued Italian industry as a whole resulted in an inability to produce the required numbers. Consequently, in February 1941 the original order was reduced from 66 to 46 and the second order was dropped altogether. Production of this excellent weapon, however, remained agonizingly slow[2]. It appears that only about 52 were delivered to the *Regio Esercito* by the end of 1943.

The gun tube consisted of an outer tube and an inner sleeve that could be removed when the gun was cold; the inner sleeve could be replaced in about 30 minutes. The split-trail carriage had two road wheels with semi-pneumatic tires per side, very much resembling a tank bogey. When in

2   As for other pieces, different sources are not consistent about the total number of pieces produced during the war. According to F. Minniti, *Il problema degli armamenti...* page 26, OTO produced 36 howitzers by end of 1942, but has no figures for the year 1943, while according to F. Cappellano e N. Pignato, *L'obice da 210/22 mod. 35*, page 8, the total production should be 46, but only 30 in 1942 and 16 more in 1943.

A wooden mockup of the 210/22 howitzer at Ansaldo's Cornigliano works. (Fondazione Ansaldo)

The 210/22 howitzer in the Ansaldo factory yard. (Fondazione Ansaldo)

battery, the wheels were raised off the ground and the gun rested on a firing platform under the main axle, providing exceptional stability for the gun. The howitzer could rotate through a full 360° arc while in battery. If necessary, the system could be broken down into as many as four loads for transport, although under ideal conditions it could be towed as one load. The howitzer components were towed by Breda heavy artillery tractors, and the system could be put into or taken out of action in about 30 minutes. Although new ammunition was developed for the 210/22, it could also fire the same ammunition as did the WWI 210/8 howitzer.

The limited production run meant that the gun saw relatively little operational use; the first and only unit to be equipped with this powerful howitzer was the *LXXIII Gruppo*, consisting of three batteries of four pieces each, 176th, 177th and 178th, assigned to the *9° Raggruppamento artiglieria d'armata*, deployed to the Ukraine in August 1942 as part of the ARMIR. In September, the entire artillery regiment was completely reorganized, to have three battalions (XXXI, XXXIV and LXXIII) armed with a battery of 210/22 howitzers and two batteries of 149/40 guns each. The 176th Battery remained with the *LXXIII Gruppo*, while the 177th and 178th were assigned to the XXXI and *XXXIV Gruppo*, respectively. In this configuration, the *Raggruppamento* was deployed on 14 December 1942 near the Don River, but only four days later, in the face of the Red Army winter offensive aimed at isolating the 6th German Army in Stalingrad, the Italian retreat began and the guns of the *9° Raggruppamento* had to be abandoned.

In 1943 a new battalion was formed, the *LXXIV Gruppo*, that never saw action. Other howitzers produced in 1943 could not be assigned due to lack of heavy tractors and remained in Italian Army depots where they were found by the Germans after the surrender of Italy. The *Wehrmacht* thought highly of the piece, and had Ansaldo continue production, obtaining 22 more howitzers, used as static artillery, with the new designation of *21cm H 520 (i)*.

Following the war, from April 1952 to June 1955 one group of the reconstituted Italian Army was equipped with eight of the howitzers, which were then replaced by 8-inch howitzers provided by the US. In 1969 the remaining 210/22s were retired from service, but all eight survive in various museums and military installations in Italy.

Specifications:

Designation:	obice da 210/22 mod. 35
Adopted:	1935
Inventory 10/06/1940:	16
Subsequent production:	36 for the *Regio Esercito*; 22 after the armistice for the German army
Originator:	Ansaldo
Producer:	Ansaldo (Pozzuoli); OTO
User countries:	Italy, Hungary, Germany (after September 1943)
Caliber:	210mm (8.27 inches)
Length of barrel:	5.01m (197.25 inches)
Length of rifling:	4.62m (181.89 inches)
Overall length (towed):	7.10m (279.5 inches)
Overall length (in battery):	6.20m (244 inches)
Overall width (in battery):	7.66m (301.6 inches)
Weight:	24,030kg (52,977 lb) travelling; 15,885kg (35,020 lb) in action
Carriage:	split trail, with under-carriage firing table
Wheel type/diameter:	bogey type steel wheels with 6 holes and semi-pneumatic tires
Breech type:	interrupted screw
Recuperator type:	hydropneumatic
Elevation:	0° to +70°
Traverse:	75°
Muzzle velocity:	560m/s (1837 fps)
Maximum range:	15,400 metres (16,842 yards)
Ammunition types:	HE, AP
Rate of fire:	One round every 2 to 4 minutes, depending on angle of fire
Shell weight:	101.5 kg (223.77 lb) mod. 35 HE

210/22 Mod. 35 howitzer

WWI GUNS

65/17 gun

The *cannone da 65/17*, first conceived in 1902, was designed by the Torino Arsenal. Originally designated as the *cannone 65A* (i.e. *acciaio*, steel) to distinguish it from other pieces made of *bronzo* (bronze, B) or *ghisa* (cast iron, G), it was adopted by the *Regio Esercito* in 1910 to equip the mountain artillery regiments. The 65/17 was the first gun to be entirely conceived, developed and built in Italy that incorporated a recoil mechanism, and for its time it was a modern piece, even though so much time had elapsed between its original concept and its adoption that it could no longer be considered the latest word in mountain artillery, especially with respect to its elevation and traverse capabilities. The first order for the guns was placed in 1911 for enough guns to equip 12 batteries, and units began receiving the gun in 1913. By May 1915 the gun equipped 14 mountain artillery groups, and on the eve of WWI 212 pieces were in the inventory; 685 more were introduced during the war but by the end of the war only 523 had survived.

As a pack weapon conceived for mountain warfare it could be broken down into five components for transport by mules; in addition, mules were used to carry two boxes containing ten rounds in each box. The gun could also be towed in one piece either by horses or by tractors, like the small FIAT OCI 708 CM. Its simple design allowed it to be put into battery in a matter of minutes. The gun had a fixed single trail, was mounted on metal rimmed wooden-spoke wheels, and could be fitted with a shield. It was fitted with a steel barrel, with an interrupted screw breech mechanism, and had a constant recoil system. It was an accurate, reliable weapon whose production continued through the end of the war until 1918 at both the Turin Arsenal and the Naples Army Arsenal. Ammunition types were HE, shrapnel, and canister. Muzzle velocity was 320 to 355 m/s (1,050 to 1,165 fps), depending on ammunition type.

Although in WWI the 65/17 was issued to Italian mountain artillery units, it was not a true mountain howitzer and consequently was not an ideal weapon for the role, as it lacked sufficient elevation to be used effectively in the mountains. This shortcoming was compensated to some extent by placing the wheels of the gun on an earthen berm or ramp, thus significantly elevating the muzzle end of the piece. This makeshift arrangement also enabled the gun to be used in an anti-aircraft role[1].

A battery of 65/17 guns in Tunisia being towed by light tricycle motor tractors. (USSME)

---

1 The gun was also experimentally mounted on a dirigible, but the experiment was not further pursued.

A battery of 65/17 guns deployed in the anti-tank role in Tunisia, spring 1943. (USSME)

A 65/17 battery of the Spezia Air Transportable Division in Tunisia (USSME)

In 1920 the 65/17 was replaced in mountain artillery units by the Škoda 75/13 mountain howitzer (see separate entry), large numbers of which had been captured or acquired as war booty by the Italians, as the Škoda was a more capable weapon and was well suited as a pack weapon. In 1926 the gun was assigned to infantry regiments on the scale of one 3-gun section per regiment, increased to four guns per regiment in 1934. In 1925, on an experimental basis, a 65/17, with a smaller shield, was fitted with rubber tires and a limber to increase mobility, but was still drawn by horses.

In the 1920s, several batteries of the 65/17 took part in operations to reconquer Libya. On occasion, the gun was carried aboard FIAT 15*ter* trucks to provide mobility. In 1936 the gun was widely used in the war in Ethiopia where it equipped divisional level artillery units as well as infantry support detachments. Also in 1936, a total of 343 guns of this type took part in the Spanish Civil War, issued to Spanish Nationalist as well as Italian artillery units, where it proved to be an effective anti-tank weapon.

Beginning in 1935 the 65/17 began to be replaced by the 47/32 (see separate entry above) in the infantry support role. The 65/17 guns were then redistributed either to GaF and MVSN units, or were placed in fixed fortifications. However, when Italy entered the war many infantry regiments were still equipped with the 65/17. Manufacture of the gun was resumed in 1937 in order to fill an order for 249 new guns to replace those worn out or lost during the campaigns in Spain and Ethiopia. In order to adapt the gun to being towed by truck, in 1939 the wood artillery wheels

A 65/17 gun fitted with a shield, being used in an urban environment by partisans in April 1945. (Istituto Piemontese per la Storia della Resistenza Torino)

on a certain number of pieces were replaced by elektron wheels with solid rubber tires. In April 1940 there were 700 65/17 guns in the inventory, and although ammunition stocks overall were plentiful, there was a shortage of anti-tank ammunition for the guns. By December 1942, the number of 65/17 guns in the inventory had dropped to 444.

In WWII, the 65/17 was widely used and saw action on all fronts in which the Italians were engaged. In North Africa the 65/17 initially was mounted on FIAT 634 trucks, but beginning in spring of 1941 these guns were mounted on captured British Morris CS8 light trucks, and formed part of the so-called *batterie volanti*, or "flying batteries", that were quite effective as mobile artillery attached to Italian reconnaissance units and, later, with the *Giovani Fascisti* Division. Essentially, the shield and wheels were removed from the guns, which were then mounted on specially fabricated mounts that could rotate 360°, fixed to the truck beds. These improvised truck/gun combinations proved to be fairly successful systems; a total of seven batteries (28 guns) were equipped with these guns, which functioned effectively in the anti-tank role as well as in the conventional artillery role. In Italian East Africa, where the gun was assigned to the 60th Artillery Regiment of the *Granatieri di Savoia* Division, some batteries used camels as pack animals for the 65/17. Later, the 80th Artillery Regiment of the *Spezia* Air Transportable Division sent to fight in Tunisia[2], had these light pieces

2   This unit had been created and equipped for the invasion of Malta, scheduled for spring 1942 and then called off in favor of the Axis offensive to the Delta that ended at El Alamein. It was finally deployed in Tunisia.

Unique image of a self--propelled gun towing a 65/17 gun during a parade staged by the partisans in Torino in May 1945. (Istituto Piemontese per la Storia della Resistenza Torino)

The 65/17 was mounted on a Morris-Commercial CS8 with a body lengthened by the Italians. The vehicle carried spare jerrycans for fuel and water. (Ralph Riccio files)

A Morris CS8 with its 65/17 gun belonging to the 1ᵃ Batteria Volante, 1° Gruppo, 136° Reggimento Artiglieria Corazzato (*1ˢᵗ Flying Battery, 1ˢᵗ Group, 136ᵗʰ Mobile Artillery Regiment*) in Tunisia in 1943. (LT Silvio Monte)

The side and rear panels of the CS8 could be lowered to allow the gun to easily traverse. (Ralph Riccio files)

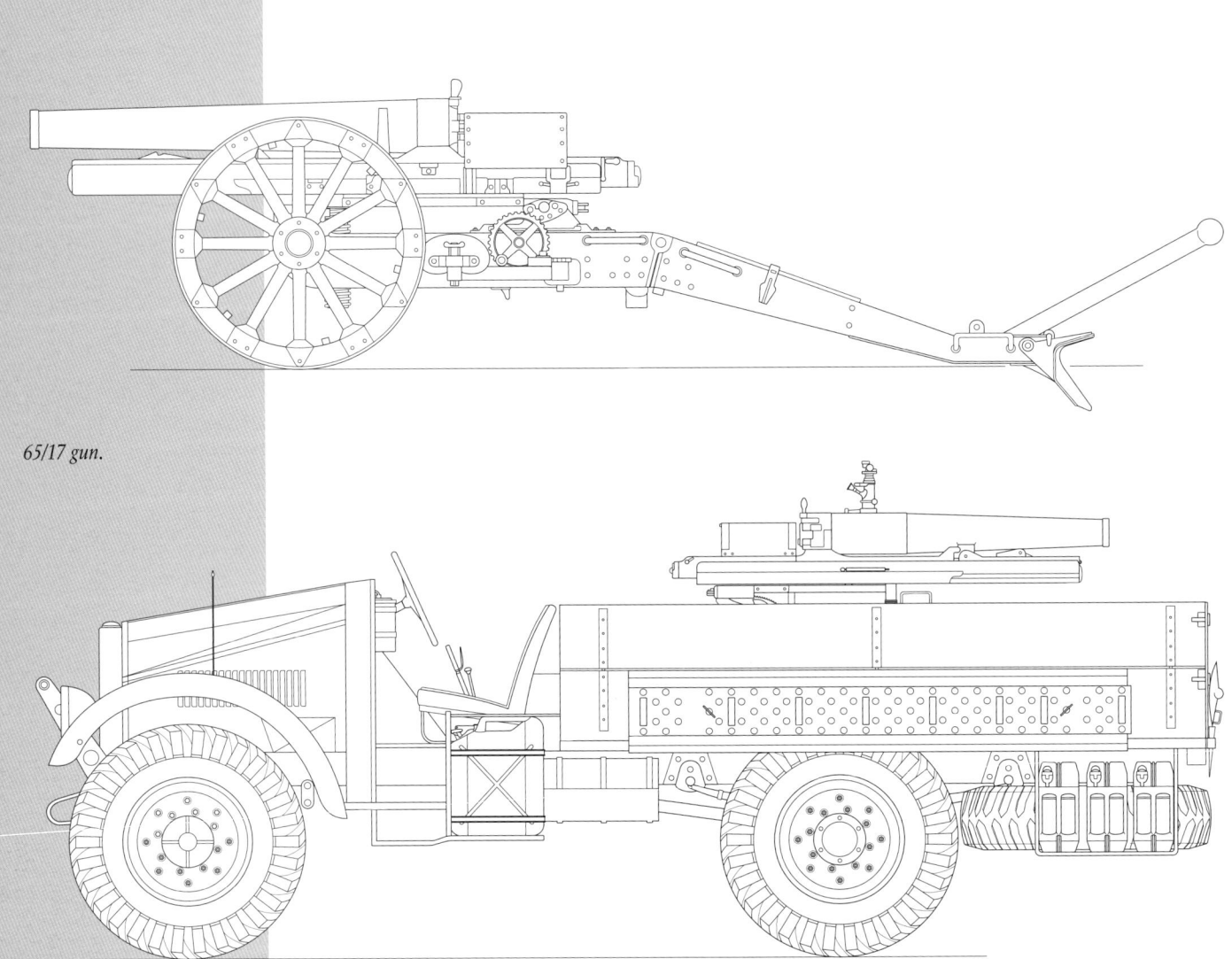

65/17 gun.

65/17 gun on Morris CS8 light truck.

adapted for towing with specially modified Guzzi *Trialce* motor-tricycles. Its regiment was formed of two battalions of two batteries, on 4 guns and 4 motor-tricycles each. Numerous coastal batteries in Italy and in the Balkans were equipped with 65/17 guns to defend against possible landings.

Despite its age, during WWII the 65/17 showed itself to still be an effective weapon. Its larger caliber and EP ammunition provided anti-tank performance superior to the newer 47/32 gun. When using the EP ammunition, the 65/17 more than held its own when compared to the much newer British 6-pdr anti-tank gun; the 6-pdr shell could penetrate about 76mm of armour plate, while the 65mm EP round could penetrate up to 120mm at roughly the same range.

After September 1943, the 65/17 continued to be used by Italian units belonging to Mussolini's RSI. The *Barbarigo* Battalion of the *Xª MAS Division* employed the 65/17 against the Allied landings at Anzio, and the *3º Reggimento Bersaglieri Volontari* was also equipped with a few 65/17 guns. Guns in German service were designated the *6.5 cm GebK 246(i)*. Following the liberation of Corsica, the Italians ceded eight 65/17 guns to the Free French Forces.

Specifications:

Designation:	Initially (January 1918) designated as 65-A (the A signifying acciaio, or steel); subsequently the designation was changed to 65 da montagna, and from 1926 the gun was known as the cannone d'accompagnamento da 65/17
Adopted:	1913
Inventory 10/06/1940:	700
Originator:	Arsenale Regio Esercito Torino
Producer:	Westinghouse (Vado Ligure) for slide and cradle; Terni, Naples Arsenal and Turin Arsenal for the guns and carriages; the firm of Franchi-Gregorini was also involved in some aspects of manufacture

User countries:	Italy, Spain, Ecuador, Germany (after September 1943)
Caliber:	65mm
Length of barrel:	1.15m (45.275 inches)
Overall length:	3.57m (140.5 inches)
Overall width:	1.00m (39.4 inches)
Overall height:	1.25m (49.2 inches)
Weight in action:	556 kg (1226 lb)
Carriage:	single trail
Wheel track:	960mm (37.7 inches)
Wheel type/diameter:	wood spoke artillery wheels with 12 spokes/700mm (27.5 inches)
Breech type:	eccentric screw
Recuperator type:	spring
Recoil length:	950mm
Elevation:	-7°30" to +20°
Traverse:	8°
Muzzle velocity	320-355 m/s (1050-1165 fps)
Maximum range:	6,500 metres (7,108 yards); effective anti-tank range 500 metres (547 yards)
Rate of fire:	6-12 rounds per minute
Ammunition types:	HE, shrapnel, canister, AP (1936), EP (1942)
Shell weight	HE 4.23 kg (9.33 lb); AP 4,23 kg (9.33 lb)
Armour penetration:	76mm-120mm (3-4.7 inches) depending on ammunition type.

75/13 howitzer

The *obice 75/13* was the Italian designation for the *7.5cm Škoda Gebirgskanone M. 15* howitzer used by the Austro-Hungarian Army as well as by Bulgaria and Turkey during WWI. The M.15 was based on an earlier export model, the M.13, which had been sold to Costa Rica, Ecuador and Uruguay, as well as being ordered by China. In 1914 52 of the guns ordered by China were requisitioned and introduced into the Austro-Hungarian Army as the M.14 "China Type."

The howitzer could be broken down into seven components, not including a separate ammunition load, that could be carried in four loads by pack animals, or alternately could be towed with the assistance of a drawbar by animals. It was also tested for towing by artillery tractors, particularly the FIAT OCI 708 CM mountain tractor. The heaviest of the components was the breechblock weighing 110 kg (243 lb). The gun tube was of monobloc construction fitted into a heavy reinforcing jacket. The recoil mechanism, which was variable with the inclination of the barrel, was fitted into the cradle, and the cradle, recoil mechanism, tube, and jacket were mounted on the carriage trunnions. The carriage was riveted steel with a modified box trail and was fitted with wooden artillery wheels. The gun was fitted with a shield weighing some 86 kg (190 lb), and thus was problematic if the shield was routinely carried when used as a pack howitzer in the mountain environment. A separate shield was also provided to protect the ammunition, but was not always used. The 75/13 normally used explosive ammunition, but occasionally it was used as an anti-tank gun, using armour piercing or hollow charge EP rounds.

The M.15 itself first entered service with the Austro-Hungarian Army in April 1915, and between 1915 and 1918 a total of 2,174 were produced. Ultimately it became one of the most widely used mountain guns in Europe, as

Preparing to fire with a 75/13 howitzer in Dalmatia, May 1943. (USSME)

A 75/13 howitzer being towed by a mule team in Croatia, April 1943. (USSME)

A 75/13 howitzer in a commanding position overlooking the Bay of Ploca in Croatia, spring 1943. (USSME)

after the war it served with the Austrian, Czech, Hungarian, Romanian, Bulgarian and Turkish armies, as well as with the Italian Army, which obtained 393 complete guns, plus an additional 323 gun tubes and 268 mounts as war reparations. It was immediately pressed into service to replace the less capable 65/17 mod. 13 mountain gun used during WWI

In 1933, due to dwindling stocks of the Škoda originals, the Italians decided to reproduce the gun in Italy, and by 15 August 1937 a total of 840 were on hand, and in 1938 a further 96 were ordered. In 1934 the idea was proposed to mount this weapon on a self-propelled mount to provide artillery support to Italian armoured formations; the idea, however, was never implemented. At the outset of the war in 1940 the total available had risen to 1,187; in February 1941 the Italian Army Staff authorized an order for the manufacture of a further 500 75/13 howitzers, although how much of the order was actually completed is unknown, and by 30 September 1942 the number had risen to 1,213. Supplementing the 75/13 howitzers, the inventory also included 67 Škoda 75/15 howitzers (ex-Yugoslav mod. 28s)[1]. In addition to equipping alpine artillery units, the 75/13 also was used in the pack artillery elements of field artillery units.

Between the wars, the gun served in the war against Ethiopia, both on the northern and southern fronts. During WWII, the howitzer served on all fronts[2]. An increasing number of pieces were deployed to Albania, with a maximum of 608 in April 1941, and, including some batteries manned by Albanian crews, fought against the Greeks. The howitzer also saw action in Italian East Africa (32 pieces) and in Russia where 72 of them equipped the artillery regiments of the three alpine divisions (*Julia*, *Tridentina*, and *Cuneense*) on that front. Some batteries reached the Tunisian front with the *Superga* Division while, in Sicily, the howitzer was deployed by the *Aosta* and *Assietta* Divisions.

Following 8 September 1943, Italian artillerymen on the islands of Corsica and Cefalonia and in the Balkans and Albania used their 75/13 howitzers effectively against the Germans; during the Italian Campaign, the *Corpo Italiano di Liberazione*, which operated with the Allied forces until summer 1944, included the pack artillery *IV Gruppo* (a battalion of 3 batteries) equipped with this material. On the opposing side, several RSI units were equipped with the howitzer, notably the *Monterosa* alpine division and the *Littorio*

1   They were identical to the *obice da 75/13* except for the length of their slightly longer barrel (about 1500mm/59 inches) which enabled the gun to achieve a greater maximum range (9,200 meters/10,061 yards), compared to that of the 75/13, firing the same ammunition.

2   Its use in North Africa is controversial: while F. Cappellano, *Le Artiglierie del Regio Esercito...*, and N. Pignato *L'obice da 75/13 ...*do not mention it, *Storia dell'artiglieria Italiana*, pages 600 and 601 reports some pieces operating with the 8th Army Corps Artillery Regiment and with the *Trento* Division during the battle of El Alamein

A pack-mounted 75/13 howitzer. (Gianna Olivero Archive)

75/13 pack howitzers of the Gruppo San Giorgio of the Xª MAS ready to fire during the fighting in Italy, winter 1944/45. (Istituto Panzarasa Trieste)

A section of 75/13 howitzers belonging to the Gruppo S. Giorgio of the Xª MAS in action on the Friuli front during the winter of 1944/45. (Istituto Panzarasa Trieste)

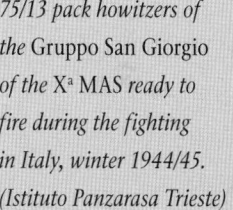

61

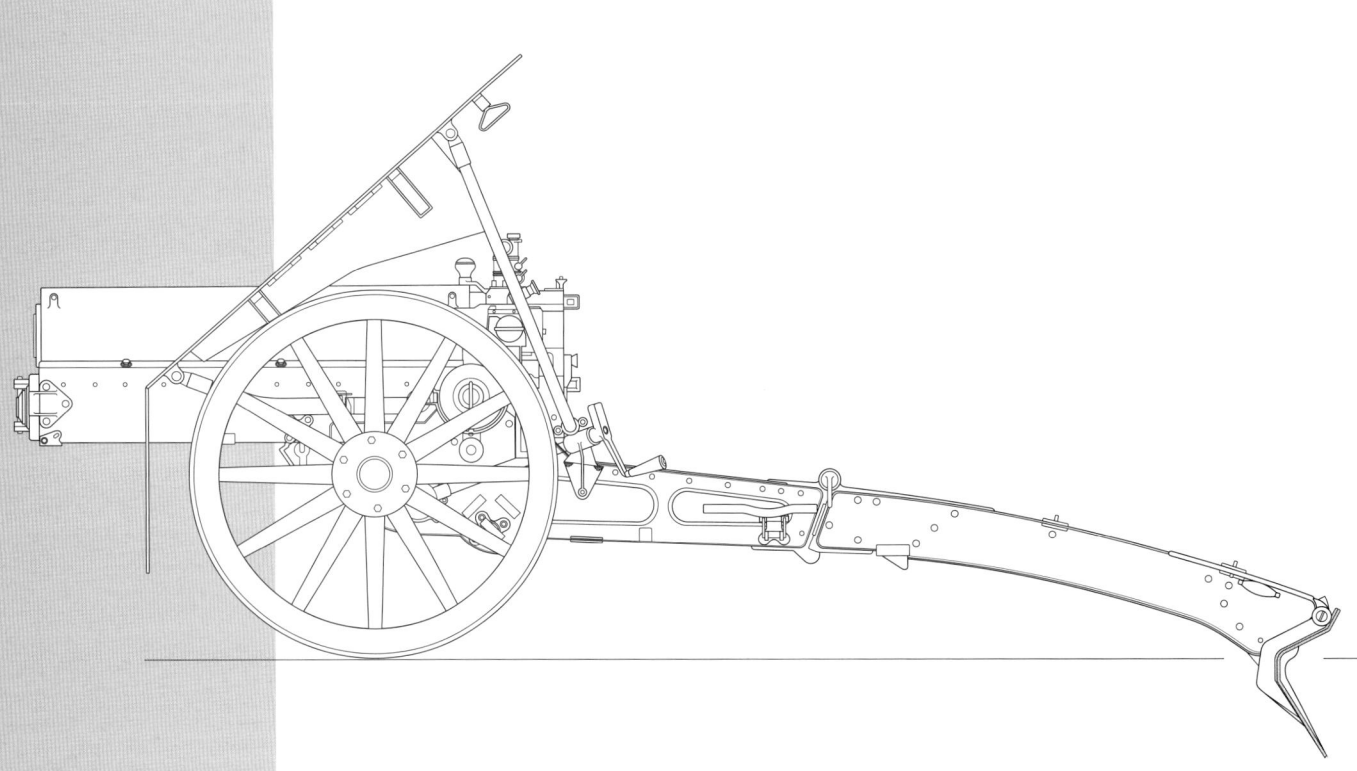

75/13 howitzer.

Division of the ENR, as well as the *San Giorgio* artillery battalion of the *X^a MAS*. The Germans also pressed some of them into service designated as the *7.5 cm GebK 259(i)*. Among other units, the Italian *Waffen SS* Division had some pieces assigned.

The 75/13 howitzer had an extremely long service life. More than 200 of these artillery pieces survived the war and were refurbished by the Turin Arsenal. When in the post-war era Italian Army mountain artillery units were re-formed each of the mountain artillery regiments of the five alpine brigades had one battalion equipped with the 75/13. *Belluno*, the first of the battalions, was ready by 27 August 1947. These battalions continued to use this weapon until 1962, when it started being replaced by the OTO-Melara 105/14 mod. 56 howitzer.

Specifications:

Designation:	obice da 75/13 - ex Austro-Hungarian 7.5 cm *Gebirgskanone* M. 15
Adopted by Italy:	after WWI (captured, war booty)
Inventory 10/06/1940:	1,187
Subsequent production:	none
Originator:	Škoda, Plzeň (Bohemia, now part of the Czech Republic)
Producer:	Škoda
User countries:	Austria-Hungary, Italy, Austria, Bulgaria, Czechoslovakia, Hungary, Yugoslavia, Poland, Romania, Turkey, Germany (after September 1943)
Caliber:	75mm (2.95 inches)
Crew:	9 (gun commander plus 8 crew)
Length of tube:	1.155m (45.5 inches)
Length of rifling:	975mm (38.4 inches)
Overall length:	3.57m (140.6 inches)
Overall height:	1.28m (50.4 inches)
Weight in action:	613 kg (1351 lb)
Carriage:	modified box trail
Wheel track:	900mm (35.4 inches)
Wheel type/diameter:	wood spoke artillery wheels, 12 spokes/800mm (31.5 inches)
Breech type:	horizontal semi-automatic sliding wedge
Recuperator type:	hydrospring
Recoil length:	900mm maximum; 440mm minimum
Elevation:	-10° to +50°

Traverse:	7°
Muzzle velocity:	354 m/s (1161 fps)
Maximum range:	8,250 metres (9,022 yards)
Rate of fire:	4-5 rounds per minute normal; 8 rounds per minute maximum
Ammunition types:	HE, shrapnel, AP
Shell weight:	HE 6.35 kg (14 lb)

75/27 mod. 06 gun

In 1902 the *Regio Esercito* realized that the time had come to replace its old model 75A 75mm field guns, mounted on rigid carriages, with a more modern gun of similar caliber that incorporated a recoil system. A number of guns were tested, including a modernized version of the 75A, a 73mm Krupp gun, and a 75mm Krupp gun; the 75mm Krupp gun was chosen as a result. In 1906 the gun was accepted for service designated simply as the 75/27, but subsequently was redesignated as the mod. 1906 to distinguish it from the 75/27 French Déport adopted by Italy in 1911 (and designated the 75/27 mod. 11; see separate entry following). Krupp was asked to supply both complete pieces and spare parts to be assembled directly in Italy. In 1907 an order was placed for enough guns to equip 48 batteries (39 field batteries and nine horse-drawn batteries). Guns for a further 68 batteries were to be built in Italy at the arsenals at Naples and Turin, but in 1912 production was suspended due to the Italian Army's decision to adopt the French Déport gun; 1,005 had been built. Production was resumed at Ansaldo and Armstrong in Pozzuoli in 1916 in order to meet wartime requirements, and between 1916 and 1919 a total of 2,400 were produced, and used extensively in WWI.

The gun was sturdily constructed and was reliable; its pole trail, however, restricted its elevation. It had a constant recoil mechanism, a steel outer barrel with a liner, and was fitted with a 4mm (0.16 inch) shield to protect the gunners. Its original configuration featured wooden spoke artillery wheels that were standard on virtually all similar field pieces during WWI. Towing was

A 75/27 mod. 06 gun fitted with metal wheels from the Museo Storico della Guerra di Rovereto collection. (Enrico Finazzer)

Field test in North Africa of the "carrello elastico" carrying a 75/27 mod. 06 gun. The arrangement does not seem to be very satisfactory, as the carrello's wheels have sunk deeply into the sand. (Claudio Pergher Archive)

originally by horse traction, three two-horse pairs, which could achieve a speed of 8-10 km/h (about 5-6 mph), but between the wars some dozens of pieces were adapted to mechanical traction, either with the adoption of the *carrello elastico* and, later, with the replacement of the original wheels with new metal wheels of elek-tron or stamped steel with semi-pneumatic rub-ber tires for direct towing by light artillery trac-tors, principally the TL37. An experiment that took place between 1938 and 1940 to form two motorised artillery battalions, with the mod. 06 guns carried on Lancia Ro cargo bodies and low-ered by hand winches to put them into firing po-sition, was not successful.

The gun could use an optical panoramic sight for direct fire or an elevating arc for indirect fire; open sights consisting of a blade front sight and notched rear sight were fixed to the gun itself. It fired mainly explosive ammunition, but for special purposes, as in the anti-tank role, it could use armour piercing or hollow charge (*EP* and *EPS*) rounds. However, its effectiveness as an anti-tank gun was rather low even with the special ammunition, and effective range was limited to about 700 meters

The first time the 75/27 model 1906 saw service dates back to 1911, during the war declared by Italy against Turkey (1911/1912), fought mainly in Libya, which became an Italian colony. Later, it

A 75/27 mod. 06 piece with metal wheels in action at El Mechili in February 1942. (USSME)

was extensively used during WWI, and in 1918, despite losses due to destruction, attrition, and capture, 1,451 were still in Italian service. To a limited extent, the 75/27 mod. 06 were used as anti-aircraft guns, mounted on specially constructed concrete and wood gun mounts that allowed elevating the barrel to approximately 90°; time-fused ammunition was used in the anti-aircraft role. Towards the end of the Great War a shortage of horses compelled the conversion of two regiments into portee batteries.

The 75/27 mod. 06 continued to soldier on following WWI, not only with the army but also with GaF and colonial units, as well as being assigned to static positions. The GaF itself had 59 batteries equipped with the 75/27 mod. 06 in

A battery of 75/27 mod. 06 guns firing against tanks at El Mechili in February 1942. (USSME)

Italy, 8 in Libya, and 21 in Albania. It saw action during Italy's several inter-war conflicts, including the Italian reconquest of Libya and the Ethiopian campaign; about a hundred pieces saw action during the Spanish Civil War serving with both the Italian "volunteer" troops and Spanish Nationalist forces. Fully 330 were supplied to the Spanish government after the civil war. Some were ceded to Albania, and 36 batteries were furnished to Poland who used them in its successful 1920 war against the Soviet Union.

On the eve of Italy's entry into WWII, about 1,700 guns of this type remained in service, some 101 used as static artillery in fortified bunkers on different mounts, and, along with their contemporary, the French-origin 75/27 mod. 11, they formed the backbone of the divisional artillery regiments, with as many as two battalions out of three and, even though unable to match the capabilities of most of the Allied artillery they faced, bore the brunt of the Italian artillery's work-

Battery fire by 75/27 mod. 06 guns against tanks at El Mechili, February 1942. (USSME)

load. The gun served on almost all of the fronts where Italian troops fought, except for Italian East Africa, where the 77/28 gun (see separate entry later) was deployed with colonial troops, and Russia, where the 75/27 model 1911 was sent instead. The 75/27 mod. 06 was used mainly in the North African campaign, where it was at a serious disadvantage compared to the excellent, much more modern British 25-pdr. Taking a leaf from the British, in 1943 a circular platform similar to that used with the 25-pdr was developed that enabled a full 360° traverse for the mod. 06, but this entered service too late to be of any use in North Africa. By May 1941 there were only 75 of these guns left in Africa, of which six still retained the old wood spoke artillery wheels. By October of 1941 the number of mod. 06 guns in North Africa had risen to 263, then being reduced to only 93 guns following the British *Operation Crusader*. During the campaign in North Africa, some German field batteries had been issued the mod. 06 as a stop-gap measure until sufficient German equipment could be furnished.

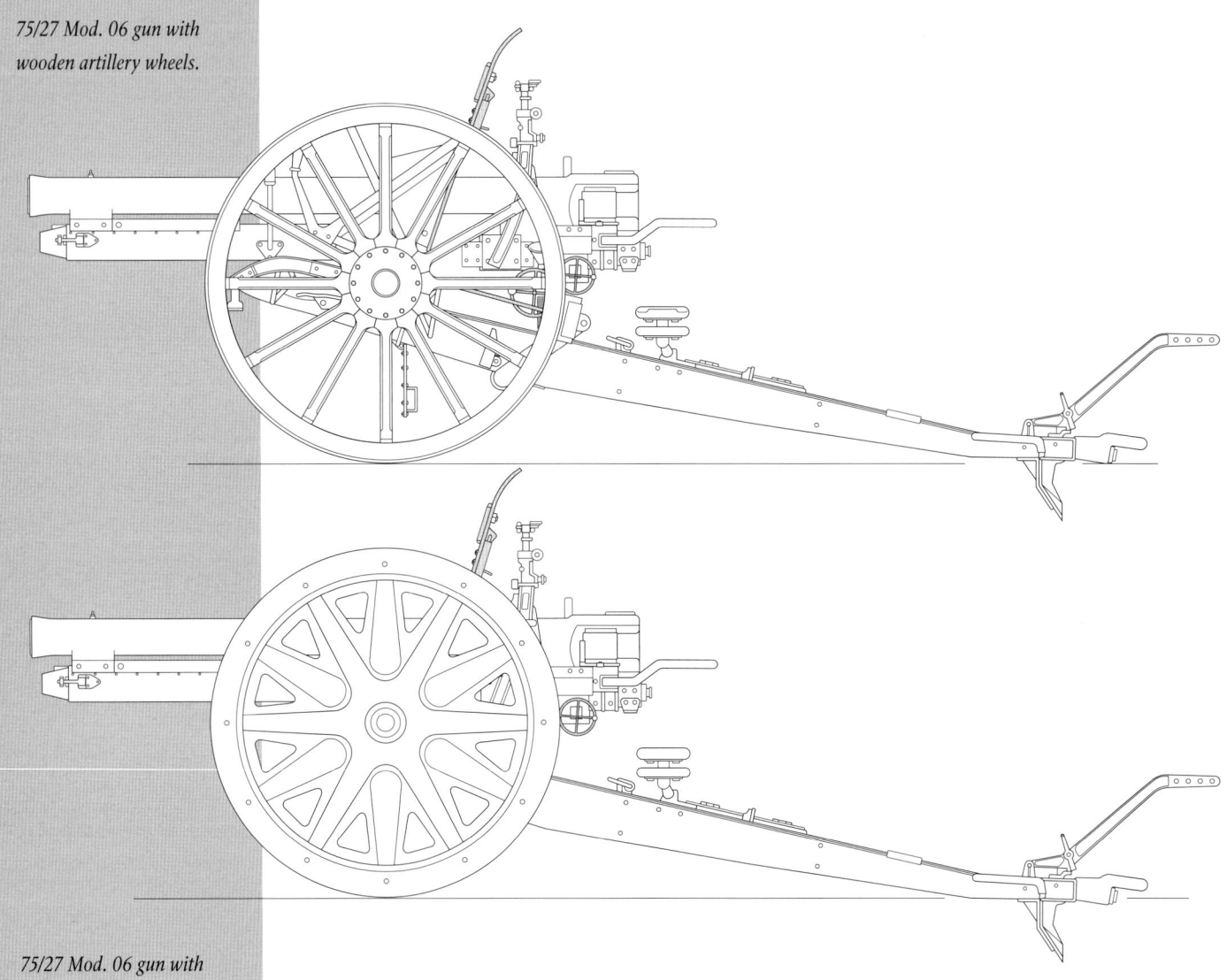

75/27 Mod. 06 gun with wooden artillery wheels.

75/27 Mod. 06 gun with pressed steel wheels.

April 1943 still saw a significant number of the mod. 06 and mod. 11 guns in the inventory, numbering 2,106 combined on all fronts, including many that had been relegated to static duties along the Italian coastline.

The 75/27 mod. 06 guns produced in Italy were supplemented to a very limited extent by similar guns captured by the Germans and ceded to Italy; these included 38 captured in Belgium, which were assigned to Sardinia, an undetermined number captured in Holland built by Siderius, and some ex-Yugoslav and Greek guns. After September 1943, many dozens of these guns, taken over by the Germans were designated the *7.5cm FK 237 (i)*. A number of the mod. 06 also equipped some RSI units, primarily in fixed positions.

Specifications:

Designation:	cannone da 75/27 mod. 06
Adopted by Italy:	1906
Inventory 10/06/1940:	1,699
Subsequent production:	none
Originator:	Krupp A.G. , Essen
Producer:	Krupp (initial production); Italian Army arsenals (Naples and Torino) series production
Unit cost:	80,000 Italian lire (1918)
User countries:	Italy, Poland, Spain, Germany (after September 1943)
Caliber:	75mm (2.95 inches)
Length of tube:	2.25m (88.6 inches)
Weight in action:	1,015 kg (2238 lb) with shield

Carriage:	single pole trail
Wheel track:	1.52m (59.8 inches)
Wheel type/diameter:	originally 12-spoke wood artillery wheels with steel rims; later (about 18/100 of the guns in service) received new axles whose wheels were elektron alloy and later metal spoke wheels with solid or semi-pneumatic tires/1.30m (51.2 inches)
Breech type:	horizontal sliding wedge
Recuperator type:	four springs
Elevation:	-10^0 to $+16^o$
Traverse:	7°
Muzzle velocity:	502 m/s (1,647 fps)
Maximum range:	10,240 metres (11,199 yards)
Rate of fire:	6-8 rounds per minute
Ammunition types:	HE, chemical (gas), inert training
Shell weight:	HE 6.35 kg (14 lb)

75/27 mod. 11 gun

The *Regio Esercito* was less than completely happy with the performance of the Krupp 75/27 gun that had been adopted in 1906. The difficulty encountered in moving the Krupp gun over rough terrain coupled with its very limited traverse and elevation capability led the Italians to reconsider their choice and to seek a possible alternative. Accordingly, in 1910 they ran a series of tests with a Déport, initially in France and then in Italy, firing some 2,800 rounds, including rapid fire tests, of both French and Italian ammunition at varying ranges and under varied weather conditions. Following the tests the Italian Army bought two batteries of Déports for operational testing, followed by a competition that included a Krupp model, as well as a Schneider in addition to the Déport, ultimately selecting the rapid fire Déport which, like the earlier Krupp, was a 75/27 gun.

In order to clearly distinguish between the two guns, the Krupp was designated as the *cannone 75/27 mod. 06*, and the Deport as the *cannone 75/27 mod. 11*, reflecting the respective years of adoption (1906 and 1911). The most significant difference between the two guns was the split trail of the Déport which allowed a much greater elevation than the Krupp was capable of. The variable recoil system of the Déport was radically different than that of the Krupp, actually consisting of two recoil systems that worked in concert with each other, limiting recoil to about a quarter that of the mod. 06. The Déport, which was fitted with a 4mm (0.16 inch) thick gunner's shield

Russia, autumn 1941; a battery of 75/27 mod. 11 guns. (USSME)

67

similar to that of the mod. 06, was easily recognizable by the prominent box housing above the barrel that contained the recoil mechanism. As for the 75/27 mod. 06, towing was originally by animal, mainly by the use of horses; the gun, along with its ammunition limber, was towed by three two-horse teams.

The initial order was for enough Déports to equip 100 batteries; in order to cope with the size of the order Vickers Terni headed a consortium of 27 Italian companies engaged in producing the gun itself and its ammunition. In its typical role it used mainly explosive ammunition, but during WWII this gun was also used, as well as more or less every other Italian piece, as an anti-tank gun, firing armour piercing and hollow charge ammunition.

In May 1915 the *Regio Esercito* had 532 Déports equipping 125 field artillery batteries assigned to divisional and corps artillery regiments. In September 1918, due to continued production during the war and despite combat losses there were 820 pieces in the Italian inventory. The mod. 11 gave a very good account of itself during the war, with capabilities superior to those of its principal Austrian counterpart, the *8cm Škoda Mod 1905*. Its overall capabilities were impressive enough for the Italians to assign 43 batteries equipped with Déports to anti-aircraft duties. The Déports in the anti-aircraft role were mounted on specially designed mounts consisting of a wooden framework that in turn was mounted on a concrete pedestal that enabled the barrel to be elevated to about 80° and that allowed the entire assembly to rotate a full 360°; the shields were removed from the guns and special sights were fitted. During WWI, one battery of mod. 11 was exported to Romania; Russia also received some mod. 11s, and curiously, some Italian-built Déports were also provided to France.

During the inter-war period, the 75/27 mod. 11 remained as a first-line weapon in the artillery regiments of the infantry divisions, while a number of improvements to increase range and mobility were made. Variable charge ammunition was introduced that increased range by

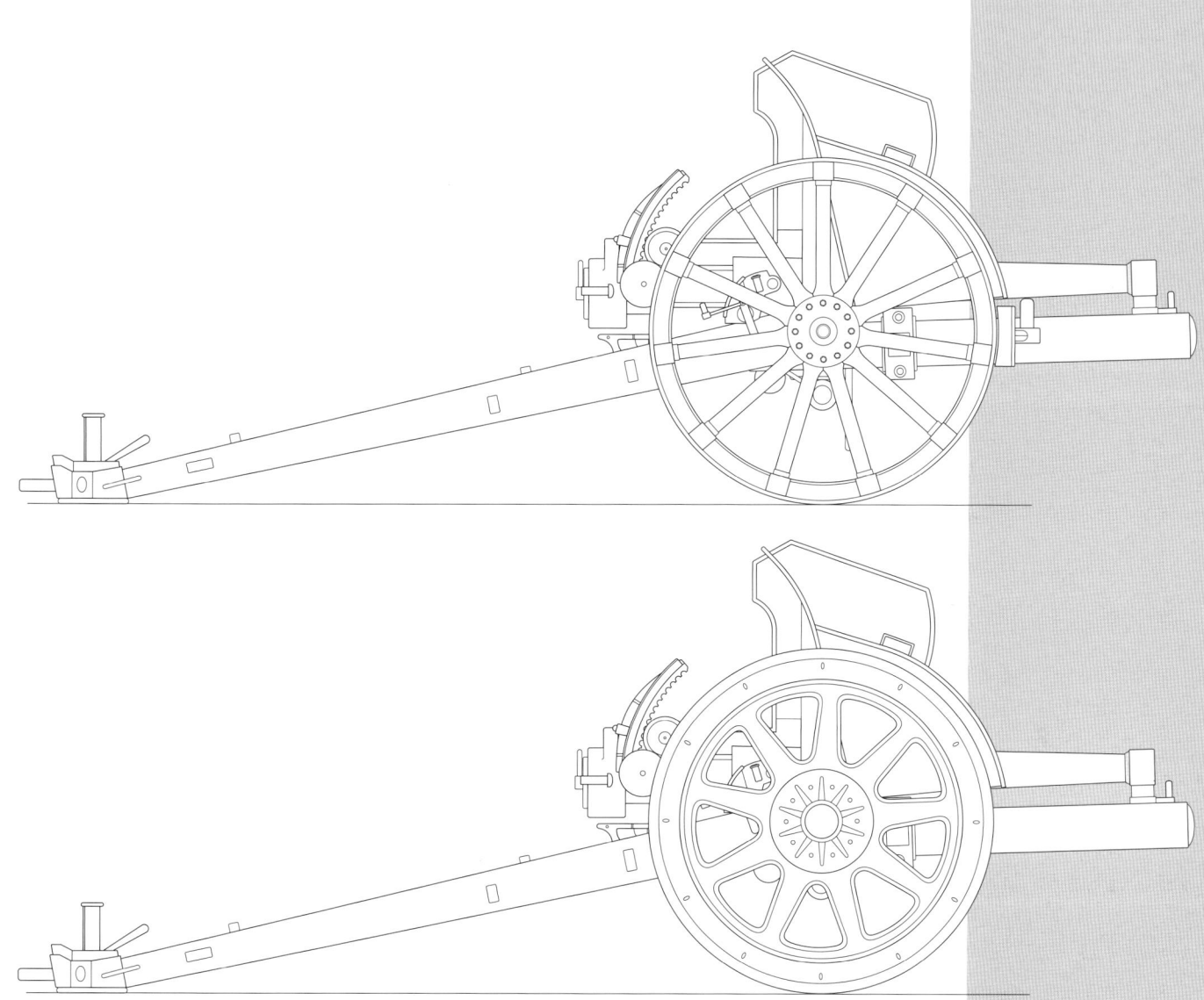

2,000 meters; ultimately, over a dozen different types of ammunition were provided for the mod. 11, covering a spectrum from the original basic HE round through chemical, smoke, and EPS hollow-charge ammunition. Various attempts, not unique to the mod. 11, were made to improve mobility; in the twenties these included mounting the guns portee-style on truck beds, that proved unsatisfactory. Later the *carrello elastico* was adopted and finally metal wheels with semi-pneumatic rubber tires were mounted replacing the original wooden wheels on some three hundred pieces. The Déports commonly were towed by either the FIAT OCI 708 CM light tracked tractor or the TL 31 and subsequently the SPA TL 37 wheeled light artillery tractor. On 1 June 1940, Italian artillery had 1,073 of the horse-drawn type, while 268 had already been modified for mechanical towing

The mod. 11 saw action during the Spanish Civil War, with 50 being sent to support the Italian force fighting alongside the Spanish Nationalist forces; the surviving batch of those guns were ceded to Spain following the civil war. Two batteries of the mod. 11 were also sold to Poland.

During WWII, the 75/27 mod. 11 was employed operationally on all fronts in which the Italians fought, except for Italian East Africa. It was the gun of choice in Russia, to the exclusion of the 75/27 mod. 06, although it served alongside the mod. 06 in North Africa. At the beginning of the war, the armoured divisions in that theater – which were to receive the 75/32 instead - replaced their 75/27 mod. 11 with the mod. 06 for unknown reasons. Of the 108 mod. 11 guns in North Africa in 1942, by February 1943 only ten remained. The circular firing platform developed for the 75/27 mod. 06, copied from the British, was also suitable for use by the mod. 11. Three batteries of the mod. 11 were mounted on SPA TL 37 light tractors in North Africa in 1942 to form a battalion of *batterie volanti* (flying batteries) to provide better mobility; the gun/tractor combination

75/27 Mod. 11 gun with wooden artillery wheels and with pressed steel wheels and rubber tires.

was a local conversion and proved fairly effective. These *batterie volanti* were initially assigned to reconnaissance units and later to the *Giovani Fascisti* Division.

A good number (262 by 1 March 1944) of Déport 75/27 mod. 11 guns, pressed into service by the Germans after September 1943, were designated as the *7.5 cm FK 244 (i)*. Some 75/27 mod. 11s were also used by RSI units.

Following the war, a number of the 75/27 mod. 11 were retained in service; in 1949 they were fitted with an improved suspension system and pneumatic tires.

Specifications:

Designation:	cannone 75/27 mod. 11
Adopted by Italy:	1911
Inventory 10/06/1940:	1,341
Subsequent production:	none
Originator:	Déport (France)
Producer:	Italian consortium led by Vickers Terni
Unit cost:	86,000 Italian lire (1918)
User countries:	Italy, France, Romania, Russia, Spain, Poland, Germany (after September 1943)
Caliber:	75mm (2.95 inches)
Crew:	4
Length of tube:	2.132m (83.9 inches)
Overall length:	4.16m (163.8 inches) in battery; 8.50m (334.65 inches) traveling
Overall width:	1.90m (74.8 inches) traveling
Overall height:	1.70m (66.9 inches)
Weight in action:	1,076 kg (2372 lb)
Carriage:	split trail
Wheel track:	1.595m (62.8 inches)
Wheel type/diameter:	originally 12 spoke wood artillery wheels with steel rims; later more than 300 received new axles whose wheels were of the 9 pressed metal spoke type with semi-pneumatic tires/1.30m (51.2 inches)
Breech type:	automatic breech with eccentric screw
Recoil length:	1.36m
Elevation:	-15° to + 65°
Traverse:	52° 9'
Muzzle velocity:	500 m/s (1640 fps)
Maximum range:	10,200 metres (11,555 yds)
Rate of fire:	6-8 rounds per minute
Ammunition types:	HE, AP, WP, smoke (semi-fixed)
Shell weight:	6.3 kg (14 lb) HE

75/27 mod. 12 gun

The *cannone da 75/27 mod. 12* was a slightly modified version of the earlier Krupp *cannone da 75/27 mod. 06*. The gun itself was unaltered, with changes limited primarily to the carriage and breechblock. A heavier breechblock shifted the centre of gravity further to the rear, the seats were mounted on the trail instead of on the shield, the upper part of the shield was no longer hinged, and the spade was modified. The mod. 06/12 guns retained their wood spoke artillery wheels throughout their operational life.

The earliest 75/27 mod. 12 guns delivered by Krupp were assigned to the light artillery's horse-drawn batteries called *Voloire*. At the outset of WWII, 51 of the mod. 12 were available and equipped a group in each artillery regiment of Italy's three *celere* (essentially cavalry) divisions – the *Principe Amadeo Duca d'Aosta* (PADA), *Emanuele Filiberto Testa di Ferro*, and *Eugenio di Savoia*, the so called *Reggimenti Artiglieria a Cavallo* or *Articelere*. In early 1941 the three *Articelere* were detached from their divisions and sent to North Africa, leaving the mod. 12 guns behind and re-equipped with towed 100/17 guns. In June 1941 24 of the mod. 12 guns were brought together

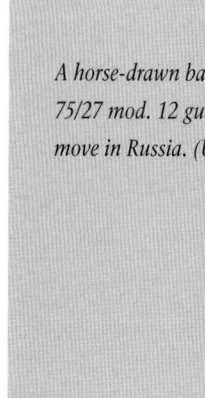

A horse-drawn battery of 75/27 mod. 12 guns on the move in Russia. (USSME)

A 75/27 mod. 12 gun in Russia; its wheels are on a berm and its trail in a dug-out position to allow a high degree of elevation. (USSME)

again in three groups of two batteries each and formed a full horse-drawn regiment which was then assigned to the PADA Division, part of the CSIR. In spring 1942 the division lost its cavalry component and had the mod. 12 guns replaced by two groups of mechanically towed 75/27 mod. 11 guns and one of 100/17 howitzers, and the horse drawn batteries remained in Russia with the cavalry squadrons as the *Raggruppamento Truppe a Cavallo*. Although most of the guns were retired from service in the post-war period, in 1966 one horse-drawn battery was organized outside of normal establishment authorization; this battery is a ceremonial battery that carries on the tradition of the *Voloire*, that dates back to 1831.

Specifications: Except as noted below, specifications are as for the 75/27 mod. 06

Designation:	cannone da 75/27 mod. 12
Adopted by Italy:	1912
Inventory 10/06/1940:	51
Subsequent production:	none
Producer:	Krupp A.G., Essen
Weight in action:	900 kg (1984 lb)
Wheel type:	12 spoke wood artillery wheels with steel rim/1300mm (58.18 inches)
Elevation:	-12° to +18.5°

75/27 C.K. anti-aircraft gun

Just before WWI the *Regio Esercito* acknowledged the new menace and the potential of aircraft used in warfare[1] and decided that it was necessary to adopt a specific weapon to counter it. The study was commissioned to the *Arsenale Regio Esercito di Napoli* (Artillery Arsenal of Naples), that designed an anti-aircraft gun based on the existing 75/27 model 1906 piece, in accordance with the recommendations of the so-called *Commissione Krupp* (Krupp Commission, which had been involved with acquisition of the original Krupp gun from Germany), hence the abbreviation C.K. Production started a few months before Italy entered WWI and deliveries of the new piece started in 1915. At the beginning, the priority was given to static artillery for the defence of critical locations, but later some dozens of pieces were mounted on a specially modified heavy truck, the Itala X, for mobile use.

The *cannone da 75/27 C.K.* has its roots in the German 75/27 Krupp gun that the Italians examined for purchase in 1913. The onset of WWI, which saw Italy and Germany on opposite sides, put an end to dealing with Germany for acquisition of the Krupp guns, but Italy had already begun domestic production and by September 1915 could field mobile air defence batteries. As mentioned, the piece was based on the 75/27 model 1906, from which it took the barrel and was chambered for the same ammunition as the Krupp 75/27 mod. 06 field gun. The field carriage was replaced by a pedestal mounted on the rear of the truck. During firing, the truck itself was stabilized using jacks and outriggers. These truck-mounted guns were the genesis of the *autocannone* in Italy. The total number of 75/27 C.K. produced during the war amounted to 165 systems, including reserve stocks. Of these, 72 were *autocannoni*, the rest being either mounted on trailers or in fixed installations. Throughout WWI the 75/27 C.K. gave a good account of itself.

After hostilities ceased in 1918, the surviving 75/27 C.K. systems were the only anti-aircraft guns retained in Italian service, even though by then they were obsolete. Additionally, in 1926

During the inter-war period these 75/27 CK guns were assigned to the 1st Gruppo of the 2nd Anti-Aircraft Regiment. The guns are mounted on the Ceirano CMA chassis. (FIAT)

1   The first bombing by airplane was carried out by the Italian army in Libya in 1911, during the war against Turkey. At the time it consisted simply of some bombs thrown by the pilot from the open cockpit, but the path was open for increasingly sophisticated and effective ordnance delivered by aircraft in the future.

the *Regio Esercito* ordered another 57 guns in order to form a further 14 batteries that were to be mounted on a more modern truck chassis, the Ceirano 50 C.M.A., developed specifically for the gun. At the same time, the Ceirano chassis began to replace the Itala X chassis of the older surviving pieces and a *GALA* fire control system was assigned to the mobile batteries.

In 1935-1936 two batteries (16 guns) of the 75/27 C.K. were deployed to Ethiopia, although the air threat there was minimal. Still later, five batteries were assigned to the *Comando Truppe Volontarie* (Volunteer Troop Command) in Spain, even though they were deemed to be of limited capability, but were retained in service due to the lack of more suitable equipment. Two battalions (I and II) were deployed in Italian East Africa.

By far the largest number of Italian truck-mounted artillery systems employed during WWII was comprised of the WWI vintage 75/27 C.K. systems, still mounted on the Ceirano 50 C.M.A. truck chassis. In October 1939, prior to Italy's entry into WWII, the *Regio Esercito* still had some 166 75/27 C.K. guns in active service. The system formed the mobile anti-aircraft battalions of each army corps and served in all theaters except Russia. As many as three battalions were deployed in North Africa as early as 1937, although it was widely accepted that the Ceirano was too heavy to move in a desert environment and therefore unable to move outside the few roads of the colony of Libya. The XX battalion was assigned, without great success, to the *Brigata Corazzata Speciale*, an armoured brigade formed in 1940, hastily gathering together all the armoured units deployed in that area. It is questionable whether the pieces could have been better adapted to anti-tank support, as had been demonstrated by the use of anti-aircraft guns in the anti-tank role by the Germans in France, but no one in the Italian Army hierarchy had the thought of using them in this new role at the time. Interestingly, a few of the *autocannone da 75/27 C.K.* that had been captured by the British in North Africa subsequently were recaptured by the Germans who used them in the anti-tank as well as air defence role.

A 75/27 C.K. that had been captured by the British in North Africa, and subsequently captured by the Germans from them and emblazoned with German insignia. The gun is in the travel position. (Ralph Riccio files)

In mid-1941 there were 11 operational battalions equipped with the 75/27 C.K., two of which were in Albania and Greece. Several infantry divisions received one group each of this system for mobile air defence, although in 1942 some of these battalions were stripped of their drivers and transformed into fixed air defence sites. The batteries of the *VIII Gruppo* were still in service in Sicily in July 1943 when the Allies landed on the island, although by that time the gun was totally inadequate to counter the absolute air superiority of the Allied air forces.

Specifications:

Designation:	cannone da 75/27 C.K.
Adopted by Italy:	1915
Inventory 10/06/1940:	166
Subsequent production:	none
Originator:	Krupp AG
Producer:	Arsenale Regio Esercito di Napoli
User countries:	Italy
Caliber:	75mm (2.95 inches)
Length of tube:	2.25m (88.6 inches)
Overall length:	2.195m (86.4 inches)
Weight in action:	1,030 kg (2,270 lb)
Carriage:	pedestal mount
Wheel track:	none (pedestal mount)
Wheel type/diameter:	none
Breech type:	horizontal wedge
Elevation:	0° to + 70°
Traverse:	360°
Muzzle velocity:	510 m/s (1673 fps)
Maximum range:	6,100 metres (6,671 yards)
Rate of fire:	15 rounds per minute
Ammunition types:	AA
Shell weight:	6.1 kg (13.5 lb)

77/28 mod. 5 and mod. 5/8 gun

The 77/28 gun was the designation given by the Italians to the WWI *Škoda 8 cm M 5 and M5/8* field gun. Although referred to by the Austro-Hungarians as an 8 cm gun, its actual caliber was 7.65 cm (76.5mm), rounded to 77mm in Italian parlance. Development by Škoda began in 1902, and a number of prototypes were tested with differing breech, carriage and recoil designs, culminating in a definitive model adopted in 1905 and designated the *8 cm Feldkanone M 5*. The gun had a cast bronze or iron barrel, had a wedge-type breech, fired fixed ammunition, and was fitted with a shield. A modified version of the gun, designated the M 5/8, was designed for mountain transport and warfare; it was much simpler to break down than the M5 and could be broken down into three loads. The M5 could be towed by animals, but was eventually adapted to mechanical towing by means of the *carrello elastico*. In some cases, it was also transported directly on trucks.

The mod. 5 and 5/8 guns captured by the Italians or acquired by Italy after WWI as war reparations were used in the Italian colonies to a limited extent during WWII. The *Regio Esercito* decided to deploy the 77/28 in the colonies and equip the local colonial troops with this piece in Italian East Africa and Libya. In this role it fought during the initial phases of WWII. Later, in 1942, dozens of these pieces were assigned to some infantry divisions in North Africa, such as the *Brescia*, *Bologna*, and *Pavia* divisions, which used this veteran piece as an anti-tank gun, in the absence of

A 77/28 gun on display at the Museo Storico della Guerra di Rovereto. *Note the unusual stamped metal wheels. (Enrico Finazzer)*

77/28 gun.

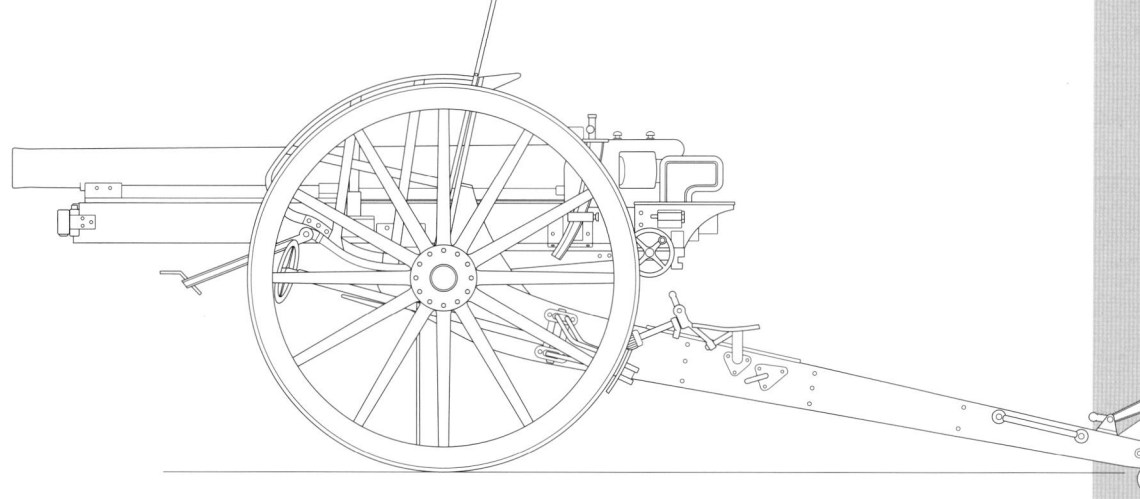

anything better at hand; these divisions took part in the battle of El Alamein using this equipment. Other 77/28 guns were assigned in 1943, in Tunisia, to the *Centauro* Armoured Division, to the *Spezia* Air Transportable and to the *Trieste* motorised divisions as well as to the special desert unit called *Raggruppamento Sahariano* (Sahara Battlegroup).

The 77/28 guns captured by Germany after September 1943 were redesignated as the *7.65 cm FK (i)*.

Specifications:

Designation:	cannone da 77/28 mod. 5 and mod. 5/8 - ex Austro-Hungarian 8 cm *Feldkanone* M 5 and 8 cm *Feldkanone* M 5/8
Adopted by Italy:	after WWI (captured, war booty)
Inventory 10/06/1940:	245
Subsequent production:	none
Originator	Škoda, Plzeň (Bohemia, now part of the Czech Republic)
Producer:	Škoda; Böhler
User countries:	Austria-Hungary, Italy, Hungary, Yugoslavia, Czechoslovakia, Austria, Germany (after September 1943)
Caliber:	76.5mm
Length of tube:	2.285m (89.96 inches)
Weight in action:	1,050 kg (2315 lb)
Carriage:	box trail
Wheel track:	1.61m (63.39 inches)
Wheel type/diameter:	12 spoke wood wheels with steel rims/1.30m (51.18 inches)
Breech type:	horizontal sliding wedge
Recuperator type:	hydro-spring
Elevation:	-7° to +18°
Traverse:	8°
Muzzle velocity:	536 m/s (1,759 fps)
Maximum range:	8,500 metres (9,296 yards) HE; 6,100 metres (6,671 yards) shrapnel
Rate of fire:	8 to 10 rounds per minute
Ammunition types:	HE, shrapnel
Shell weight:	6.34 kg (13.76 lb) HE; 6.68 kg (14.73 lb)

100/17 mod. 14 and mod. 16 howitzer

Prior to WWI, Škoda had developed and produced two modern 10 cm mountain howitzers, the *M8 and M10*, which were the first howitzers of the Austro-Hungarian army to be provided with a hydraulic barrel recoil mechanism using the adjustable recoil principle. They were, however, considered unsatisfactory because the ammunition they fired was that of the earlier Škoda M99 field howitzer. Accordingly, Škoda developed a new 10 cm field howitzer, the M14, that with modifications became the M16 mountain howitzer, developed specifically for the mountainous terrain of the Italian theater. In comparison to the M14, the M16 had a much narrower wheel track of 950 mm that was largely compatible with the width of mountain tracks, and the wheels themselves were smaller in diameter than those on the M14. The carriage, whose ground clearance was increased, was also modified to allow elevations up to 70°, and the barrel counter-recoil spring was strengthened while the brake cylinder was made smaller. Overall, the M16 was also almost 200 kg (440 lb) lighter than the M14. Both the M14 and M16 were also designed for

North Africa, summer 1942. A 100/17 howitzer engaged in barrage fire. (USSME)

easy disassembly into three loads that could be drawn by teams of two heavy draft horses in tandem harness, that is, one behind the other rather than side by side. The three loads of the M 14 weighed 600 kg (1,323 lb) each for the carriage and the shields, and 980 kg (2,161 lb) for the gun assembly load; for the M16 the loads were 750 kg (1,654 lb) for the gun assembly, 570 kg (1,257 lb) for the cradle and shield, and 670 kg (1,477 lb) for the carriage. The M14 could be disassembled for transport in about 15-20 minutes by a squad of 15 men, whereas the M16 could be disassembled in somewhat less time by the crew. The M16 could also be transported by sledge, rather than on its wheeled trailers, in the snow. The combined output of the Škoda plant in Plzeň and the Böhler plant in Kapfenberg, which built the howitzers under license, was 6,458 barrels and 4,077 carriages for the M 14 and 346 barrels and 541 carriages for the M 16.

The end of WWI saw Italy furnished with a virtual glut of the two versions of the 100/17: there were 1,339 mod. 14 and 95 mod. 16 howitzers as complete guns. Of these 212 were scrapped because they were beyond repair. Subsequently, another 915 gun tubes and 735 carriages for the mod. 14 and 557 gun tubes and 56 carriages for the mod. 16 were received as war reparations. The guns were refurbished at the Naples Army Arsenal, with some work subcontracted to private firms.

Initial issue of the 100/17 was to a truck-borne mixed field artillery regiment in 1919 that tested the feasibility of transporting various types of artillery pieces aboard trucks. In the 1930s, as with most other WWI artillery pieces in the Italian inventory, in order to adapt the 100/17 to

A 100/17 Model 16 on a Lancia 3Ro heavy truck. (Ralph Riccio files)

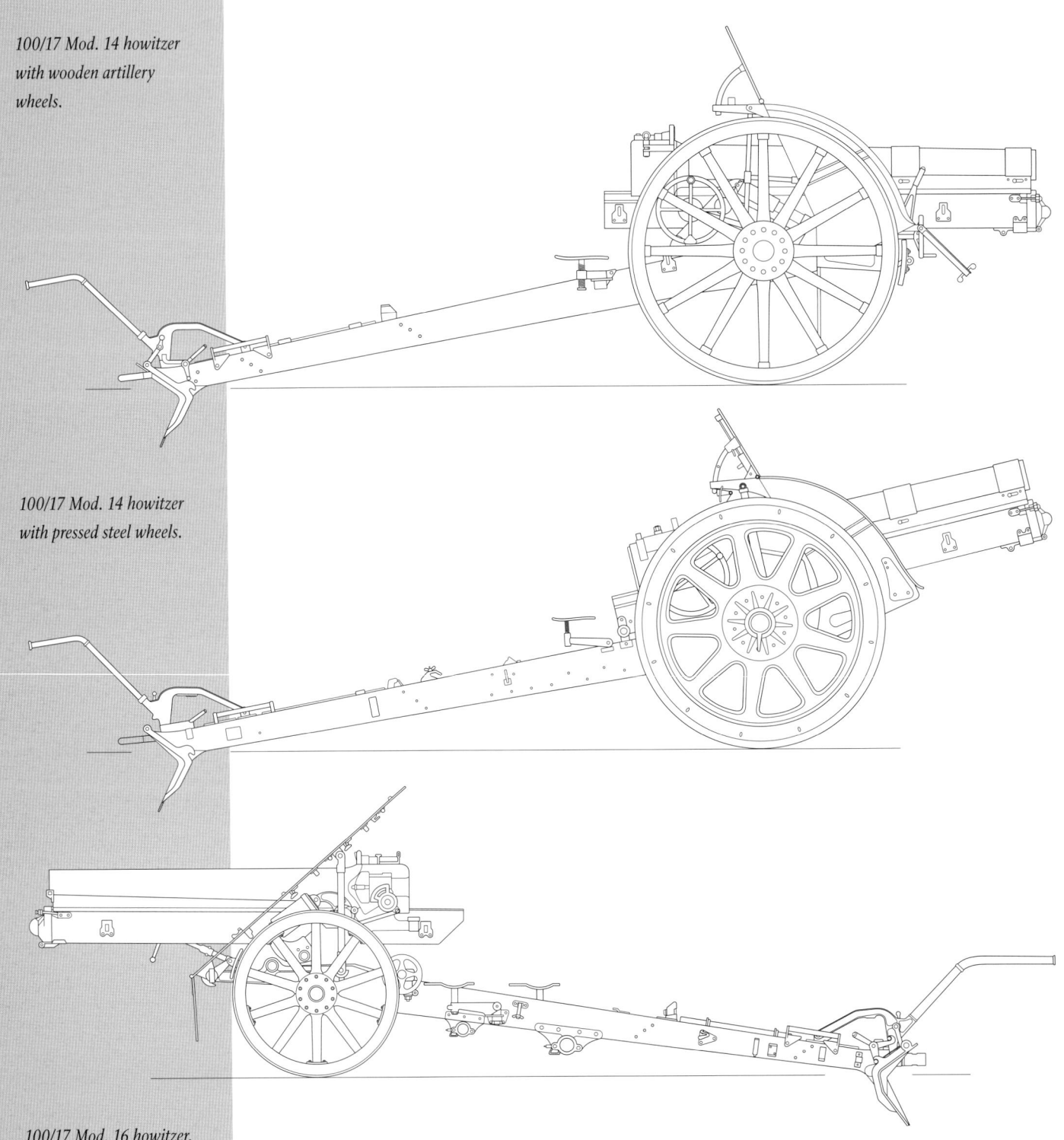

100/17 Mod. 14 howitzer with wooden artillery wheels.

100/17 Mod. 14 howitzer with pressed steel wheels.

100/17 Mod. 16 howitzer.

mechanical towing, at first they were mounted on the *carrello elastico* while others - starting in late thirties – had their wood wheels replaced by steel or alloy wheels fitted with semi-pneumatic tires and without the two seats in front of the shield (designated the 100/17 T.M.). Unfortunately, the process was very slow, and by June 1940 only about 200 howitzers had the new wheels, while the majority of the others continued to travel at animal pace.

Although the Italians had obtained a large number of 100/17 howitzers, the corresponding stock of ammunition was low. The Italians undertook to remedy this by producing their own ammunition, the mod. 32 shell, which increased the range of the gun by 500 metres. In 1942 the Italians also developed the EP anti-tank ammunition followed by the EPS in 1943 for use with the 100/17.

In 1935 and 1936 the 100/17 motorised batteries took part in the Ethiopian campaign (30 howitzers in Eritrea and 35 in Somalia) and later in the Spanish Civil War 1936-39 (at least 208 pieces, some of which were supplied to the Spanish troops). The beginning of the war in 1940 saw

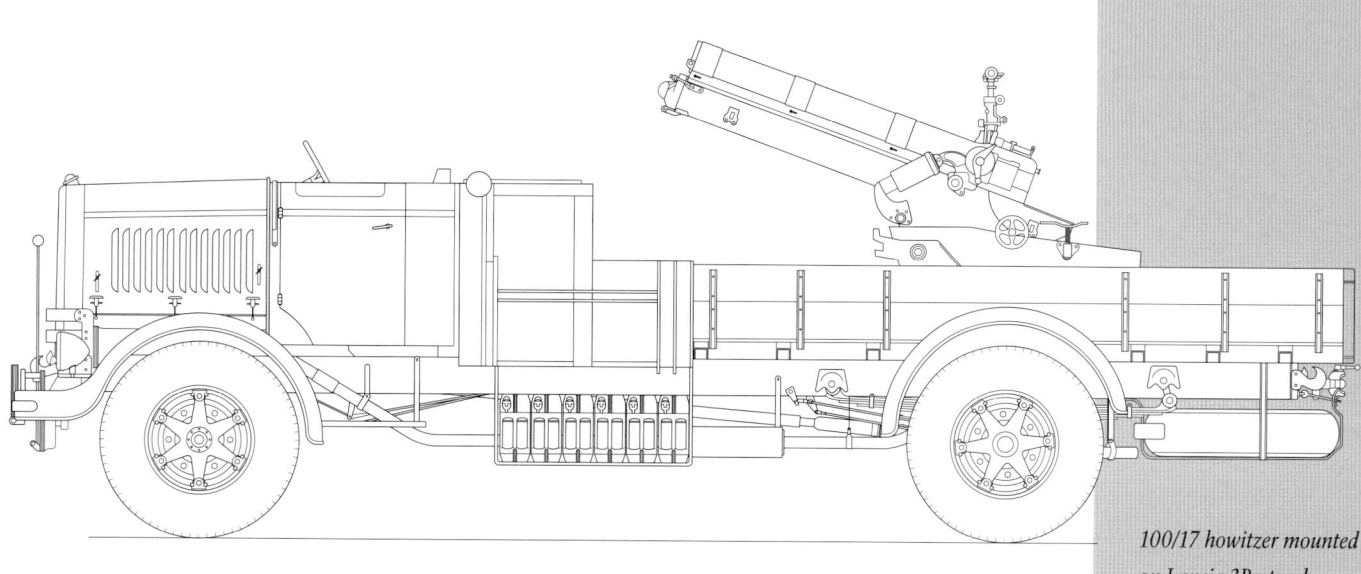

100/17 howitzer mounted on Lancia 3Ro truck.

the Italian artillery park with 1,524 of the mod. 14 howitzer still either horse-drawn, in fixed positions, or modified for mechanical towing by the Spa TL 37 light artillery tractor. There were also 181 mod. 16 mountain howitzers available, bringing the total of the two versions of the 100/17 to 1,705 pieces. Along with the 75/27 gun, during WWII the 100/17 howitzer was the backbone of the Italian army divisional artillery, that included a battalion of 100/17 in most of the artillery regiments. As a consequence, the 100/17 appeared on every front where the Italians fought, although in both North Africa and Russia the range of the 100/17 was found to be inadequate compared to the artillery it faced. In addition, by 1940 some 40 batteries of the 100/17 were assigned to GaF fixed defensive positions.

In North Africa four batteries of 100/17 guns were mounted on Lancia 3Ro trucks with modified platforms and the cabs cut to allow 360° traverse, to form a battalion. These local conversions, along with various other types of guns mounted on either Italian or captured Commonwealth trucks, fought alongside the other truck-mounted artillery batteries[1] within reconnaissance units, in 1941, later to be assigned to the *Giovani Fascisti* Division and fight until the very end of the African campaign in Tunisia. They were a very effective means of providing mobile artillery to support Italian forces in the desert.

By June 1943 there were 37 artillery groups still equipped with the mod. 14 (11 of which were motorised), and ten groups equipped with the mod. 16. Following the September 1943 Italian surrender, the Germans confiscated 133 of this howitzer which they redesignated as the *10cm leFH 315 (i)*, together with 64 mod. 16, renamed *10cm FH 316 (i)*. The Germans used these pieces mainly as static artillery. The RSI armed forces fielded a number of horse-drawn 100/17 groups and batteries, like the 1st Artillery Regiment of the *Monterosa* Division, the 3rd Artillery Regiment of the *San Marco* Division and the *San Giusto* artillery battalion of the *Xa MAS* Division, as well as several fixed defensive batteries.

During the post-war period, as part of the Somalia Security Corps authorized by the UN, in 1950 a battery of 100/17 T.M. was sent to Somalia. The guns were either towed by the TL 37 light tractor or were mounted portee-style on Lancia 6 Rom trucks, marking the final use of portee artillery by the Italian Army.

In Italy itself five battalions of two batteries each remained equipped with the 100/17 converted with new wheels, axles and 360° platform into the 14/50 model. In the mid-1950s the 100/17 mod. 14/50 was replaced as mountain howitzer by the Oto Melara 105/14 mod. 56. It was then recalibrated as 105 NATO and had the barrel lengthened to 22 calibers and provided with a muzzle brake. With these modifications the piece, now designated the 105/22 mod 14/61, remained in service within the motorised brigades until the late 1980s.

---

1   See above for the mounted 65/17 and 75/27 guns

Specifications:

Designation:	obice da 100/17 mod. 14 e mod. 16 - ex Austro-Hungarian 10 cm *Feldkanone* M.14 and 10 cm *Gebirgshaubitze* M.16
Entry in Italian service:	after WWI (captured, war booty)
Inventory 10/06/1940:	1,705
Subsequent production:	none
Originator:	Škoda, Plzeň (Bohemia, now part of the Czech Republic)
Producers:	Škoda; Böhler
User countries:	Austria-Hungary, Italy, Hungary, Austria, Poland, Yugoslavia, Czechoslovakia, Rumania, Turkey, Spain, Germany (after September 1943)
Caliber:	100mm (3.94 inches)
Length of tube:	1.93m (76 inches)
Overall length:	5.30m (208.7 inches)
Overall width:	1.78m (70 inches) mod.14; 900mm (35.4 inches) mod.16
Weight in action:	1,417 kg (3,124 lb) mod 14; 1,235 kg (2,723 lb) mod. 16
Carriage:	box trail
Wheel track:	1.55m (61 inches) mod. 14; 950mm (37.4 inches) mod. 16
Wheel type/diameter:	10 spoke wood wheels with steel rims; upgraded with elektron wheels and semi-pneumatic tires/1.30m (51.2 inches) mod. 14; 900mm (35.4 inches) mod. 16
Breech type:	horizontal wedge
Recuperator type:	spring
Recoil length:	1.37m (53.9 inches) maximum; 500mm (19.7 inches) minimum
Elevation:	-8° to +48° mod. 14; +70° maximum for mod. 16
Traverse:	5°
Muzzle velocity:	407 m/s (1335 fps)
Maximum range:	9,200 metres (10,061 yards)
Rate of fire:	4-6 rounds per minute
Ammunition types:	HE, shrapnel, AT
Shell weight:	13.8 kg (30.4 lb) HE

105/28 gun

The *cannone da 105/28* was an Italian field gun based on the French *canon de 105mm de campagne système Schneider*, which in turn was based on the Russian Putilov 106.7mm M1910-12 gun. In 1913 France had adopted the *canon de 105mm Modèle 1913*; the Italians, who at the time had a 105mm gun designed by Déport under development by Vickers Terni, were very impressed by the Schneider design and chose to abandon further development of the Déport design in favour of the Schneider. Because at the time Italy was still part of an alliance with Germany, a license to produce the Schneider was obtained in secret, and production of the gun was begun by Ansaldo-Genoa in 1914. The Italian model differed from the French model only in its traverse mechanism, which was improved over the French version and allowed the gun to traverse without moving the direction of the wheels. The gun, with the wood spoke, steel-rimmed wheels and box trail characteristic of the era, was designed to be towed with a limber by six horses. When being towed the gun and cradle were retracted to the rear on the carriage, while during firing they were returned to the forward position.

Production of the 105-A, as it was originally designated (the A suffix stood for *acciaio*, or

A lineup of 105/28 guns at a barracks in Italy. (Claudio Pergher Archive)

steel) began in September 1914, and was first issued to units in June 1916. Sources differ as to how many 150/28s were produced, some claiming a total of 2,050 and others claiming 1,730, plus 1,131 guns in 106.7mm that originally had been destined for export to Czarist Russia. At the end of the war, 426 of the guns were in active units, while an undetermined number were held in reserve. Production continued until 1919.

The 105/28 gun had a steel barrel reinforced at the rear by an external sleeve, and an interrupted screw breech mechanism, mounted on a box trail carriage fitted with a spade. It was originally fitted with 133 cm diameter (52.36 inches) steel-rimmed twelve-spoke wooden wheels, and had a 4.5 mm (0.18 inch) thick shield to protect the gunners. Ammunition included high explosive as well as armour-piercing and hollow charge (EP and EPS) ammunition for use in anti-tank role.

Originally it was designed for animal traction, by retracting the barrel on the carriage and resting it on a limber that was pulled by the animals, but during the course of WWI tests were conducted to adapt it to mechanical towing by simply towing it by heavy trucks. During the inter-war years, in common with many other Italian artillery pieces, the 105/28 was initially adapted for mechanical towing on paved roads by placing the entire gun on a *carrello elastico*. The earliest prime mover was the FIAT 18 BLR truck, later replaced by the Pavesi heavy field artillery tractor which managed to tow the gun at a maximum speed of 18 km/h (about 12 mph). Later, but as early as 1938, a number of 105/28 guns began to be modified for towing at a higher speed, particularly on desert terrain; the gun was fitted with elektron wheels with semi-pneumatic *Celerflex* tires, the brake system was modified, and a new type of tow hook was fitted. This arrangement allowed the gun to be towed without a limber by a TM 40 tractor at speeds up to 40 km/h. During the war the elektron wheels were replaced by pressed steel wheels.

Operationally, during WWI the 105/28 served alongside the Ansaldo 149/12 howitzers in the corps level heavy field artillery groups. As a gesture of Allied solidarity and cooperation the *14° Gruppo*, equipped with these guns, was sent to France to operate with the *9ª Gruppo Artiglieria Pesante Campale*. The 105/28 was a very reliable gun; throughout the war there were only six reported accidental explosions with this type of gun. On the debit side, the gun barrel tended to wear quickly, ammunition was somewhat weak, and compared to the 10.4cm Austro-Hungarian guns, the 105/28 was outranged by some 2,000 meters. After being widely used in WWI, the piece remained in active service with the Italian army. Prior to the outbreak of WWII, the 105/28 saw action in the 1935-36 Ethiopian war (8 in Somalia), and the civil war in Spain, where 403 of the guns were sent.

At the outbreak of WWII, the 105/28, with a total of 956 pieces in service, still formed, along with the 149/13 howitzer (see later) the backbone of the *raggruppamenti d'artiglieria di corpo d'armata*, and thus it appeared on every front of the war where Italian units were deployed.

In Italian East Africa, a total of 59 were present in 15 batteries at the beginning of the war, but they could do little to stop the British offensive once it started. They were all lost during the campaign that led to the surrender of the colony in May 1941. Three battalions participated in the invasion of Greece, in October 1940, attached to the *26° Raggruppamento di artiglieria di Corpo d'Armata*.

In North Africa, where the guns were constantly at a disadvantage against the British 25 pdr, during the same period, there were eight battalions assigned to the four *Raggruppamenti di artiglieria di corpo d'armata*, plus four independent batteries equipped with the 105/28, assigned to static artillery duties around the major Libyan cities. All of them were lost during the British counteroffensive of December 1940-January 1941 which almost put an end to the Italian presence in North Africa. Subsequently, an undetermined number of the 105/28 guns were shipped to North Africa along with the new divisions assigned there, and took part in all the following phases of the war, from the siege of

A 105/28 gun in a dug-in firing position in North Africa, October 1941. (USSME)

Tobruk to El Alamein to, finally, the defence of the bridgehead of Tunisia, where only 33 of the guns were still available, reduced to 14 at the battle of Enfidaville, in April 1943.

Many battalions were sent to Russia in spring 1942, assigned to the *2° Raggruppamento d'artiglieria*, of the *II Corpo d'Armata*, as well as to the divisional artillery regiments of the infantry divisions forming that army corps, *Cosseria, Ravenna* and *Sforzesca*, with a battalion for each regiment, in an attempt to enhance their firepower. In fact, the experience of the previous year had demonstrated that the Italian divisions were severely undergunned on that front.

Also in Sicily, at the time of *Operation Husky*, several dozen of 105/28 guns were deployed, either as field or as static artillery. The *XXI Gruppo* and the *XLVIII Gruppo* were assigned to the *12° Raggruppamento di artiglieria* attached to the *XII Corpo d'Armata*[1], while the *X, XVI* and the *XXIX Gruppo* were assigned to the *40° Raggruppamento* assigned to the *XVI Corpo d'Armata*.

After the surrender of Italy, many pieces remained in the hands of the Germans, who used them mainly as static artillery on the Gustav and the Gothic Line, renamed *10,5 cm Kan 338 (i)*. A few pieces were used by the armed forces of the RSI, in particular a battery of the *San Giorgio* artillery group was used against the Anzio bridgehead in spring 1944 to support the *Barbarigo* Battalion of the *Xª MAS*.

---

1   According to A. Santoni, *Le operazioni in Sicilia e in Calabria*, page 502, attached to this army corps there was a third battalion, the *XXII Gruppo*.

Camouflage nets used to mask 105/28 guns from aerial observation. (Claudio Pergher Archive)

In the south of Italy, a battalion of 105/28 equipped the *11° Reggimento d'artiglieria*, attached to the *I Raggruppamento Motorizzato* and later to the *Corpo Italiano di Liberazione*.

During the post-war period a number of 105/28s were retained in reserve stocks until 1951, when they were removed from the inventory.

Specifications:

Designation:	cannone da 105/28
Originator:	Schneider (France)
Adopted by Italy:	1914
Inventory at 10/06/1940:	956
Subsequent production:	none
Producer:	Ansaldo-Genoa
Unit cost:	121,000 Italian lire (1914)
User countries:	Italy (original French model as *canon de 105mm Modèle 1913* in France), Germany (after September 1943)
Caliber	105mm (4.13 inches)
Length of tube:	2.987m (117.6 inches)
Overall length:	6.925m (272.6 inches) in battery; 7.079m (278.7 inches) travel
Overall width:	1.95m (76.8 inches)
Overall height:	1.828m (72 inches)
Weight in action:	2,170 kg in battery (4,784 lb)
Carriage:	box trail
Wheel track:	1.65m (65 inches)
Wheel type/diameter:	12 spoke wood wheels with steel rims/1.33m (52.4 inches), elektron or pressed steel wheels with semi-pneumatic *Celerflex* tires/1.30m (51.22 inches)
Breech type:	eccentric screw, Schneider pattern
Recuperator type:	hydropneumatic
Recoil length:	1.20m (47.28 inches)
Elevation:	-5° to +37°
Traverse:	14°
Muzzle velocity:	565 m/s (1854 fps)
Maximum range:	11,425 metres (12,495 yards) with the original ammunition
	12,780 metres (13,976 yards) with mod. 32 ammunition
Rate of fire:	from 1 round per minute to a maximum of 4 rounds per minute
Ammunition types:	HE, AP, smoke
Shell weight:	HE ammunition: 16.24 kg (35.8 lb); Mod. 32 ammunition: 16.3 kg (35.95 lb); hollow charge ammunition (EP): 14 kg (30.87 lb)

105/28 gun.

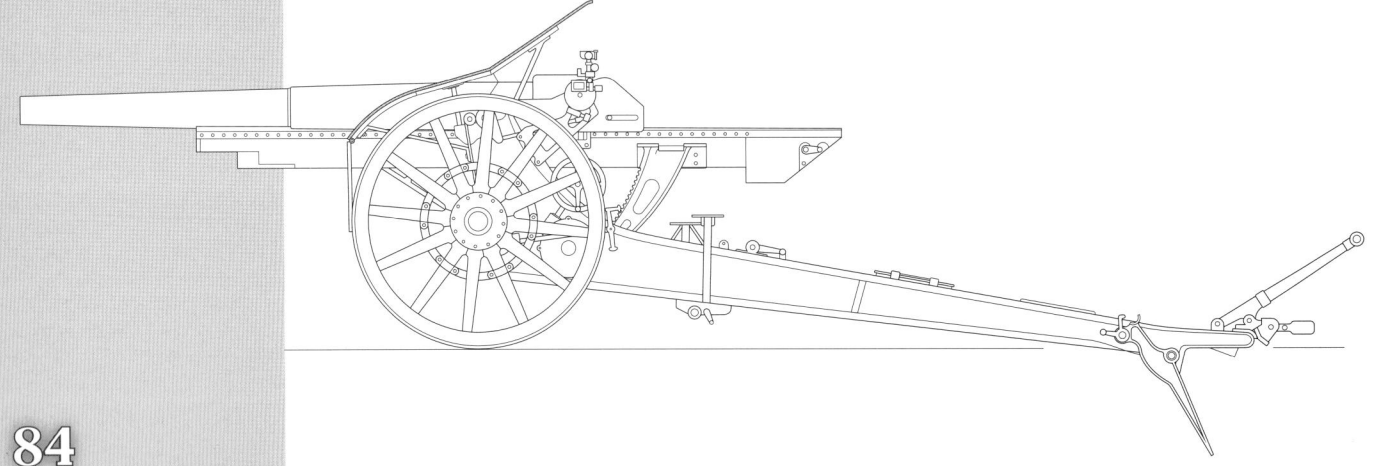

104/32 – 105/32 gun

The *cannone da 105/32* gun was the Škoda *10.4 cm Feldhaubitze*[1] *M.15* re-bored from 104mm to 105mm. The gun originally was conceived as a heavy flat trajectory siege gun, with requirements being laid down in 1902. The first cast bronze prototype, built by the Austro-Hungarian Artillery Ordnance Factory (*Artilleriezeugsfabrik,* or AZF) in Vienna, was ready in early 1909 but did not prove satisfactory; accordingly, Škoda was requested to provide an experimental gun which was tested in the summer of 1910. The gun was initially designated as the *10.4 cm Belagerungkanone* (siege gun), which with modifications became the M 12, and with further modifications the M 13. After further testing, orders for mass produc-

A 105/32 gun in position along a tree line. (USSME)

tion were placed with both Škoda and Magyar Àgyùgyàr (the Hungarian Gun Factory in Győr) in November 1914. The definitive gun was designated the *M 15 10.4 cm Feldkanone* and was used in the heavy artillery role rather than as a siege gun as originally intended. Škoda and the Hungarian Gun Factory produced a total of 577 105/32 guns during WWI; of these, some 260 were obtained by the Italians either as captured weapons or as war reparations

All factors considered, the gun did not have any innovative features, but was for its time an effective and reliable piece of artillery. The carriage was a standard box trail, with two wooden wheels; the steel barrel was reinforced with two external rings, one in the rear and another in the mid-section. The breech mechanism was a horizontal sliding wedge and recoil was constant. As was normal for its era, it was designed for animal towing, although it was adapted by the Italian army to mechanical towing by way of the *carrello elastic*o towed by a Pavesi tractor. If necessary it could be split in four loads for towing on mountain roads. It maintained its original wooden wheels throughout the war. The *Regio Esercito* used first this gun during the Ethiopian campaign (1935-1936), still in its original caliber. It was not until 1938-39 that the barrel was re-bored to 105mm at the *Arsenale Regio Esercito di Napoli*; the change in caliber allowed the Italians to use existing stocks of Italian ammunition.

1   The designation *Feldhaubitze* instead of *Feldkanone* was confirmed by the *Heeresgeschichtliches* Museum, Vienna directly to Ralph Riccio, in an E-mail dated 15 July 2010.

An artillery crew preparing to fire a 105/32 gun in Tunisia in spring 1943. (USSME)

104/32 gun.

Upon Italy's entry into the war in June 1940 there were 12 corps artillery groups equipped with the 105/32. The 105/32 saw action on a number of fronts including Russia, Tunisia and Sicily. In Russia the 105/32 equipped army corps artillery such as the *30° Raggruppamento di artiglieria di corpo d'armata*, of the CSIR, that included the *LX, LXI* and *LXII Gruppo*. The following year, when two more army corps were sent to the Eastern Front, more battalions, LI, LII and LIII, reached Russia within the *11° Raggruppamento di artiglieria di Corpo d'Armata*, assigned to the *Corpo d'Armata Alpino* (Alpine Troops Army Corps). The 105/32 was favoured in Russia over the 105/28 because of its greater range capability (16,200 meters compared to 13,976 meters for the 105/28). However, the greater range was offset by the fact that the 105/32 was significantly heavier than the 105/28, causing mobility problems, and leading to requests, which went unanswered, to replace the 72 105/32 guns in Russia by the 105/28. Other battalions, the LVII, LVIII and LIX, were sent to Tunisia at the end of 1942, within the XXX Army Corps, when the Axis troops made their last stand against the Allied forces landed in Morocco and Algeria. In Sicily the gun was used in the coast defence role. By June 1943 the remaining 105/32 guns equipped only four artillery groups.

After the surrender of Italy in September 1943, a few guns were taken over by the Germans, who used them mainly as static artillery, renaming them *10,5 cm K320 (i)*, while some others were used by the armed forces of the RSI, among them the *San Giorgio* artillery battalion of the *Xᵃ MAS* that deployed them at Anzio in spring 1944. There was no post-war role for these guns.

Specifications:

Designation:	cannone da 105/32 - ex Austro-Hungarian 10.4 cm *Feldhaubitze* M.15
Entry in Italian service:	after WWI (captured, war booty)
Inventory 10/06/1940:	238

Subsequent production:	none
Originator:	Škoda, Plzeň (Bohemia, now part of the Czech Republic)
Producer:	Škoda; Magyar Àgyùgyàr (Győr)
User countries:	Austria-Hungary, Italy, Hungary, Yugoslavia, Romania, Germany (after September 1943)
Caliber:	104mm originally; re-bored by Italian arsenal to 105mm
Length of tube:	3.36m (132.3 inches)
Overall length:	3.64m (143.3 inches)
Weight in action:	3,299 kg with shield (7,273 lb)
Carriage:	box trail
Wheel track:	1.60m (63 inches)
Wheel type/diameter:	12-spoke wood wheels with steel rims/1.30m (51.18 inches)
Breech type:	horizontal wedge
Elevation:	-10° to +30°
Traverse:	6°
Muzzle velocity:	685 m/s (2247 fps)
Maximum range:	16,200 metres (17,717 yards)
Rate of fire:	up to10 rounds per minute
Ammunition types:	HE, shrapnel
Shell weight:	17.5 kg (38.6 lb) HE

149/12 mod. 14, mod. 16 and mod. 18 howitzer

On the eve of WWI, in 1913, Italy accepted the proposal of Krupp for a 12 caliber heavy field howitzer, then named the *obice da 149 A mod. 14*, to be produced in Italy by Ansaldo. The performance of the 149 A proved disappointing, resulting in a somewhat improved version, designated the 149/12 mod. 16, fitted with a new carriage to provide greater stability, and a new recoil system. The Model 16 was followed by yet another version with a different carriage, designated the 149/12 mod. 18. According to Ansaldo, 1,220 tubes and 990 carriages were built (including the mod. 16 and mod. 18 versions). The military were not satisfied with them even after their improvement and after the war they were gradually passed to the reserve. However, they were once again put into limited field service during the early days of WWII.

In June 1940 592 M14s, redesignated as the *149/12 mod. 14*, were on hand in the Italian inventory, as well as 116 mod. 16 and mod. 18 guns. For towing by motor vehicle, the entire gun, wood wheels included, was mounted on a *carrello elastico*; they do not appear to have been upgraded by replacing the wood wheels with steel wheels and semi-pneumatic tires as was done with many other WWI era guns. Two groups (24 howitzers) of the mod. 14 were sent to Spain during the Civil

An Ansaldo 149/12 howitzer. (Claudio Pergher Archive)

War, and some batteries equipped with the mod. 16 were deployed to Libya in 1941, mostly as static artillery with the GaF. During the course of the WWII all of these howitzers were phased out of the heavy field artillery regiments and were relegated to fixed positions. Both Krupp-origin howitzers were replaced in service by the much more capable and reliable Škoda 149/13 obtained as war booty and successively by the OTO 149/19 howitzer. After 1943, the 63 howitzers of this type confiscated by the Germans were designated as the *15cm sFH 400 (i)*.

A 149/12 howitzer, possibly with a GaF crew, in a camouflaged and revetted position in North Africa. The individual weapons carried by the crew include the Model 1891 cavalry carbine and either the Model 1891 TS or TSM carbine (USSME)

Specifications:

Designation:	obice da 149/12 mod. 14, mod. 16, and mod. 18
Adopted:	1913
Inventory 10/06/1940:	708
Originator:	Krupp, Essen
Producers:	Ansaldo (Genova); Breda; Arsenale di Torino; Vickers-Terni; Franchi-Gregorini
Unit cost:	105,000 Italian lire
User countries:	Italy, Germany (after September 1943)
Caliber:	149.1 mm (5.87 inches)
Length of tube:	2.09m (82.3 inches)
Overall length:	5.61m (220.9 inches)
Overall width:	1.63m (64.2 inches)
Overall height:	1.858m (73.1 inches)
Weight in action:	2,344 kg (5167 lb)
Carriage:	box trail
Wheel track:	1.48m (58.3 inches)
Wheel type/diameter:	12 spoke wood artillery wheels with steel rims/1.30m (51.2 inches)
Breech type:	horizontal sliding wedge
Recuperator type:	hydropneumatic variable recoil
Recoil length:	1.25m
Elevation:	-5° to +43°
Traverse:	5°
Muzzle velocity:	300 m/s (984 fps)
Maximum range:	8,760 metres (9,580 yards) maximum; 6,900 metres (7,546 yards) effective
Rate of fire:	1 round every two minutes
Ammunition types:	HE, shrapnel
Shell weight:	HE 41 kg (90.4 lb)

149/12 Mod. 14 howitzer.

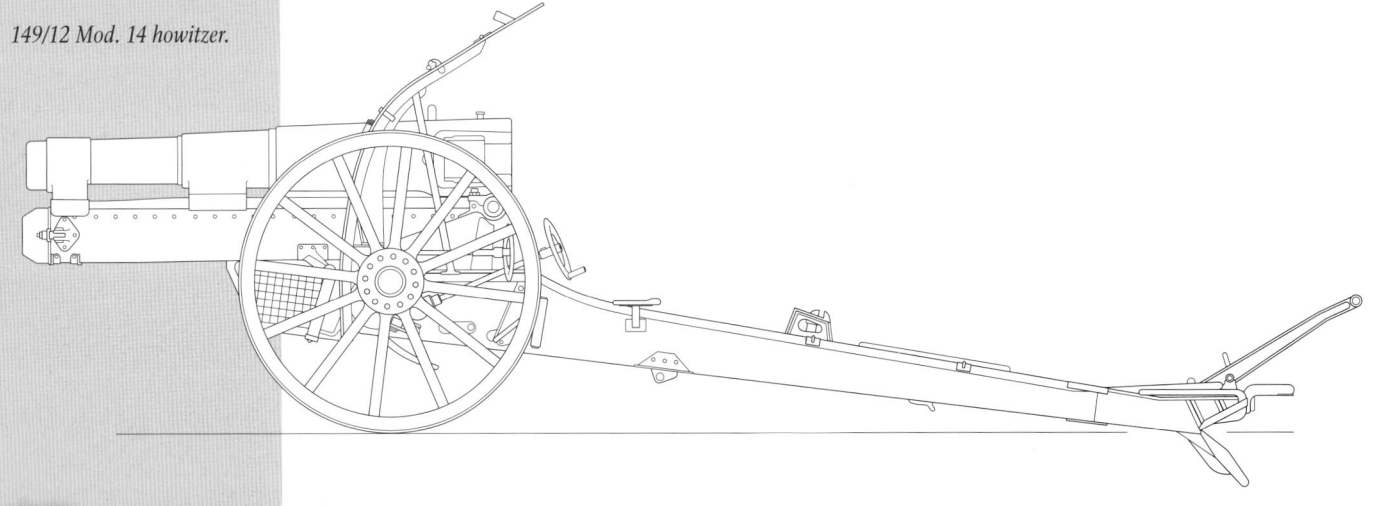

149/13 howitzer

The *obice 149/13* began life as the WWI vintage Austro-Hungarian *15cm schwere Feldhaubitze M.14*, introduced into Austro-Hungarian service in 1914, later followed by a modified version designated the Model 14/16. The gun was a Škoda product and reflected that firm's usual standards of robustness and technical innovation. The M14 was based on the earlier Škoda M12, of which only eight test guns were built, that had an adjustable barrel recoil system with a pneumatic recuperator. The carriage was a single trail type, fitted with the classic spoked wooden artillery wheels, ending with a spade that was hammered into the ground to stabilize the piece during fire. It could be fitted with a 5mm (0.2 inches) shield of either the straight or curved variety. Its steel barrel was strengthened in the rear, near the breech, and in the middle by two reinforcing rings. The breech mechanism was a horizontal sliding wedge. The M14 fired separate loading ammunition.

The 14/16 was the Model 14 that incorporated a number of significant improvements, including a redesigned cradle that allowed a maximum elevation of 70°, a strengthened carriage and trail, and a slightly longer barrel. In the Austro-Hungarian army, both models normally were horse drawn in two loads or broken down into four separate trailer loads for towing in mountainous terrain: the gun load weighed 1,290 kg (2,844 lb), the breech weighed 870 kg (1,918 lb), the carriage weighed 1,400 kg (3,087 lb), and the shield weighed 750 kg (1,654 lb). However,

Austro-Hungarian 149/13 (15 cm) howitzers abandoned at Ladaro, in the province of Trento, in November 1918. (Museo Storico della Guerra di Rovereto)

A 149/13 howitzer mounted on a carrello elastico, *towed by a Pavesi artillery tractor. (Museo Storico della Guerra di Rovereto)*

A 149/13 gun in a bunker position in Russia. (USSME)

although originally designed exclusively for animal towing, the model 14/16 was adapted to mechanical traction during the course of WWI, as its reinforced carriage was able to withstand the relatively higher speed. Between the wars the *Regio Esercito* also adopted this piece for towing in one load with the *carrello elastico*, towed by a Pavesi tractor and later, in a limited number of howitzers, it replaced the wooden wheels with metal wheels.

The victory of 1918 led to the capture of 281 Model 14 and 32 Model 14/16, but 142 were scrapped because of their poor condition. Additional numbers later were obtained as war reparations. Like other Austro-Hungarian pieces they were rushed into service with the *Regio Esercito*, which had been directly exposed to its effectiveness during the course of WWI.

During the 1920s and 1930s the 149/13 began to replace the Krupp designed 149/12 howitzers, license built by Ansaldo, in the *Regio Esercito*; the 149/12, which had proven to be inferior to the 149/13, were relegated to the static artillery role. Four of the 149/13 were sent to Italian East Africa in 1935-36. Late in the thirties, as previously mentioned, the Italian 149/13s were modernized by replacing the steel-rimmed wood wheels with steel wheels and semi-pneumatic tires. Ballistic performance was slightly improved by the introduction of new ammunition for the piece, which allowed a slightly longer range (400 meters additional); a Cortese-Falcone panoramic sight was provided. Despite its solid construction and its improved mobility, however, by 1940, when some 490 available guns equipped the corps-level heavy field artillery regiments, it was outclassed by both similar WWI era guns still in service in other armies as well as by newer guns that had come upon the scene and was constantly outranged by enemy artillery.

The 149/13 was, in June 1940, the standard howitzer for army corps artillery, along with the 105/28 or 105/32 guns, and until early 1942, when the new Italian produced 149/19 howitzer began to enter service (see separate entry above), the 149/13 served on virtually every front in which the Italians fought. It saw action in the Alps against France in June 1940, in Italian East Africa, and in North Africa where 48 took part in the defence of Tobruk in December. The 149/13 also took

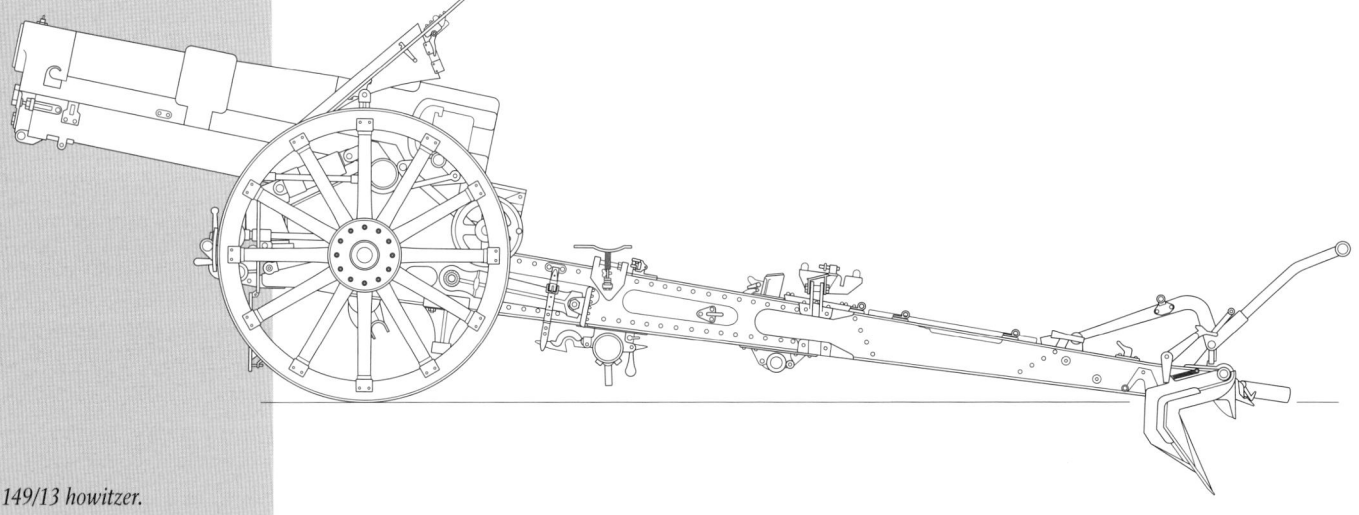

149/13 howitzer.

part in the campaigns against Yugoslavia and in Russia, where 48 guns served; three groups were assigned to the defence of Sicily. In June 1943 there were still 24 groups equipped with the 149/13, two of which were assigned to the defence of Naples.

A few 149/13s, probably three batteries, remained in service as static or coastal artillery with RSI forces after September 1943. One of the batteries was used along the Gothic Line against the Allies. As was common practice, after September 1943 the Germans seized 46 of these guns and used them, mostly in heavy field artillery batteries in Italy, as the *15cm sFH 401*.

Specifications:

Designation:	obice da 149/13 - ex Austro-Hungarian 15cm *schwere Feldhaubitze* M.14 and M14/16
Entry in Italian service:	after WWI (captured or war booty)
Inventory 10/06/1940:	490
Subsequent production:	none
Originator:	Škoda, Plzeň (Bohemia, now part of the Czech Republic)
Producer:	Škoda; Magyar Àgyùgyàr (Győr)
User countries:	Austria-Hungary, Italy, Austria, Czechoslovakia, Greece, Hungary, Romania, Yugoslavia, Germany (after September 1943)
Caliber:	149.1mm (5.87 inches)
Length of tube:	2.09m (82.28 inches) M.14; 2.12m (83.46 inches) M 14/16
Weight in action:	2,344 kg (5168 lb) M.14; 2,765 kg (6096 lb) M 14/16
Carriage:	box trail
Wheel track:	1.23m (48.43 inches)
Wheel type/diameter:	12-spoke wood wheels, replaced by 10-spoke steel wheels/1.0m (39.4 inches)
Breech type:	horizontal wedge
Recuperator type:	hydropneumatic
Elevation:	-5° to + 43° M.14; -5° to +70° M14/16
Traverse:	6°
Muzzle velocity:	336 m/s (1102 fps)
Maximum range:	6,900 metres (7,546 yards) M.14; 8,800 metres (9,624 yards) M 14/16
Rate of fire:	2-3 rounds per minute
Ammunition types:	HE, shrapnel (several versions)
Shell weight:	42.5 kg (93.7 lb) HE

149/35 gun

In 1940 the *cannone da 149/35* was an extremely antiquated artillery piece, but in the absence of sufficient quantities of more modern pieces of the same caliber, constituted the most available army-level artillery piece, with 923 available on 1 June 1940. Development of the gun began in 1896, and the gun was adopted with a rigid carriage by the *Regio Esercito* in 1901, on the cusp of the era in which recoil systems were being incorporated on gun carriages. This gun, originally designated the 149A (the A standing for *acciaio*, steel) had been designed to replace the previous 149G (G standing for *ghisa*, cast iron), with a more modern steel piece, and was produced by the Armstrong factory in Pozzuoli, near Naples. Overall, the gun's characteristics reflected the age of its adoption. The main features of this gun, that distinguished it from every other piece of artillery deployed by any army during WWII, was the fact that the barrel was rigidly mounted on the carriage; it had no recoil system, and no traverse capability.

The wheels were fitted with large grouser pads (referred to as *Bonagente* chains in Italian) strapped around the circumference, and when fired, the entire gun recoiled onto long inclined ramps; the tail of the frame rested in a sort of sled that slid along the ground during recoil. Once the gun had rolled back down the ramps to its approximate in-battery position, it often had to be relayed for the next round. It took about two hours to emplace the gun. Despite all of the drawbacks and problems associated with the gun that made the 149/35 more suitable as a museum piece than for use as a combat weapon, it did have the advantage of being able to hurl a projectile

An Ansaldo 149A cannon, later designated the 149/35. (USSME)

weighing more than 45 kg (88.2 lb) a distance of about 17,500 metres (19,138 yards) with a reasonable degree of precision. For towing, it was normally split in two loads, towed separately by two tractors, but for short distances it was also possible to move the gun as one load, laying the carriage on a limber and removing the grousers.

A 149A with Bonagente grouser pads and the inclined ramp that took up some of the recoil forces. (Andrea and Antonio Tallillo)

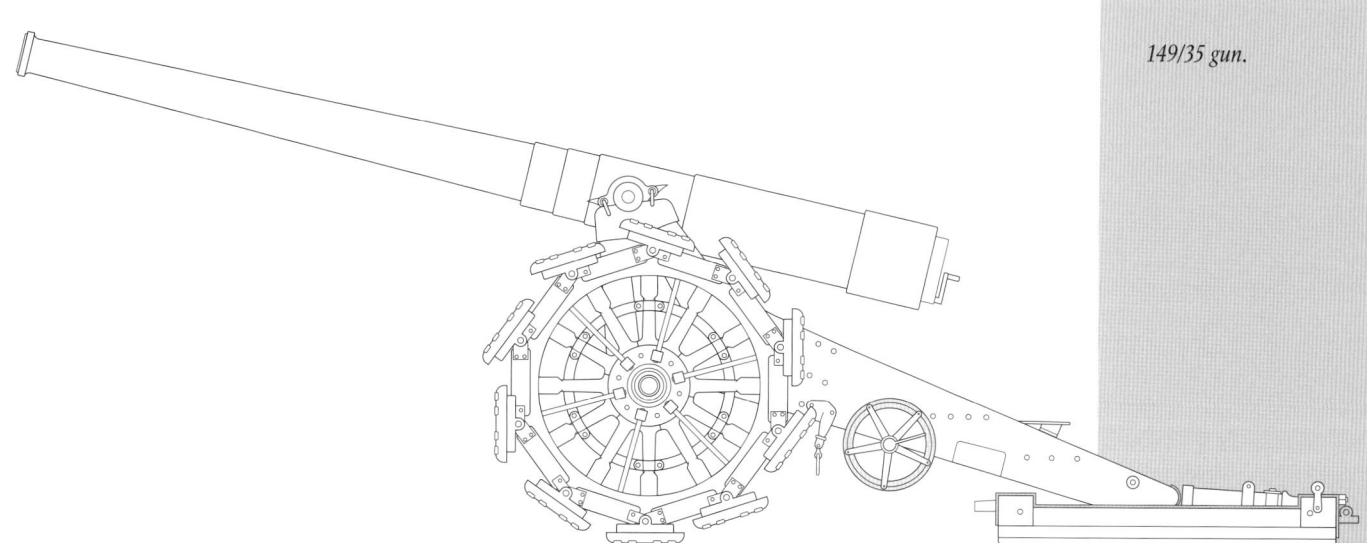

In 1911 the Italians, realizing that it was necessary to update the gun by adopting a more modern carriage with a recoil system, approached both Krupp in Germany and Schneider in France to submit proposals for a new carriage. It was not until 1915 that the Krupp design was selected, but shortly thereafter the project was cancelled in view of the deteriorating political and military situation between Germany and Italy. By September 1918 a total of 598 149/35 guns were in service and had served well throughout WWI.

Following the war, attempts were again made to modernize the gun's carriage and mobility. In 1921 the gun was mounted on a box trail recoil carriage developed by the Naples Arsenal, but was not further developed because a split trail carriage was found to be required; this ultimately led to development of the much more modern 149/40 gun (see separate entry). In 1933 some improvements were made to the suspension system that allowed for slow speed mechanical towing by a Breda 32 heavy tractor.

Between the wars, six, or possibly eight, of these guns were sent to Spain during the Spanish Civil War with the old Pavesi-Tolotti tractors, but do not appear to have particularly distinguished themselves in action there. Due to their age and operational limitations, a great number of the 149/35 were relegated to fixed positions along Italy's border; in 1940 the GaF had 60 batteries equipped with this gun.

Once Italy entered the war, the gun, despite its obvious limitations, saw service on a number of fronts, either in the army artillery regiments or as static artillery. It was not deployed in Italian East Africa, nor in Russia, where the *Regio Esercito* sent the little modern heavy artillery it had, such as the 149/40 and the 210/22 (see separate entries). In 1940 it participated in Italy's brief campaign against France, without registering any noteworthy success. Shortly thereafter, with 72 149/35 guns available in Albania, it saw action against both the Greeks and the Yugoslavs. In Libya in early 1940, 48 of the guns were assigned at army level, and a further 37 were subordinate to the GaF there; by January 1942 the number in North Africa had dropped to 46. In June 1943, 16 battalions continued to be equipped with the 149/35, in addition to numerous pieces that were assigned to coast defence duties in Italy, with Italian forces in France, Dalmatia, Greece, and the Aegean Islands. A number of the 149/35 were deployed in Sicily, assigned both to the 6th Army Artillery Regiment and to the coast defence role with the GaF.

Specifications:

Designation:	cannone da 149/35
Adopted:	1901
Inventory 10/06/1940:	923
Subsequent production:	None
Originator:	Arsenale del Regio Esercito di Torino
Producer:	Ansaldo
User countries:	Italy

Caliber:	149.1mm (5.87 inches)
Length of tube:	5.464m (215 inches)
Overall length:	6.825m (268.7 inches)
Overall width:	1.90m (74.8 inches)
Overall height:	2.31m (91 inches)
Weight in action:	8,600 kg (18,960 lb)
Carriage:	rigid
Wheel track:	1.48m (58.3 inches); 1.868m (73.5 inches) with *Bonagente* grousers
Wheel type/diameter:	wood spoke wheels/1.56m (61.4 inches)
Breech type:	cylindrical screw
Recuperator type:	none
Elevation:	-10° to +35°
Traverse:	0°
Muzzle velocity:	651 m/s (2136 fps)
Maximum range:	17,500 metres (19,138 yards)
Rate of fire:	One round every six minutes
Ammunition types:	HE, shrapnel
Shell weight:	45.96 kg (109.35 lb) HE

152/37 gun

The *cannone da 152/37* was another one of the many Škoda types turned over as reparations to Italy at the end of WWI and subsequently incorporated into its artillery inventory. The original designation of the gun in Austro-Hungarian service was the *15 cm Autokanone M. 15/16*, derived directly from the M 15 motorised gun, a 15 cm gun that made its debut in 1915. The M 15 had an elevation of only 30°, but in 1916 a modified design was developed with an arc type elevating mechanism and repositioned trunnions allowing a 45° elevation; the modified design was introduced in early 1917. The M 15/16 was a sturdy and reliable heavy field gun, without particularly remarkable characteristics that distinguished it from other artillery pieces of the period, with a variable recoil mechanism, a horizontal sliding breech, a box trail, iron wheels, and a curved gun shield. The steel barrel had two reinforcing rings, one in the rear position the other in the centre of the barrel itself. The Austrian designation of *Autokanone* was due to the fact that this was the first Austro-Hungarian gun designed for motor transport. The gun had to be broken down into two loads for towing by heavy tractors; one

A 152/37 gun in travel order being prepared for towing in Greece, March 1941. (USSME)

A 152/37 being readied to fire in North Africa. (Claudio Pergher Archive)

A 152/37 gun being transported on a trailer in North Africa, November 1941. (USSME)

152/37 gun.

load consisted of the gun carriage and weighed 8,440 kg (18,607 lb), and the second load, consisting of the gun itself weighed 9,000 kg (19,842 lb). Towing speed was about 10 km/h (6 mph) and the time required to place the gun in battery was about three hours. In Italian service during WWII towing in two loads was performed by a Breda 32 heavy tractor, although there is some evidence of transport on a truck trailer, at least in North Africa.

Of the 43 complete M. 15/16 guns built by Skoda and one extra carriage, fully 30 of the guns ended up in Italian hands. During the 1920s the guns in Italian service were refurbished by Vickers Terni, and range was increased from 20,000 metres to 22,000 metres (21,872 to 24,059 yards), while the weight of the two loads decreased to 7,900 kg (17,417 lb) for the carriage and 8,500 kg (18,739 lb) for the gun.

In June 1940 there were four battalions, with a total of 29 guns, equipped with 152/37, numbered from LI to LIV, assigned to army artillery regiments. Their initial employment in WWII was against France in June 1940; later, in March 1941 the LI battalion was deployed in Greece while the LII (134th and 135th batteries) went to North Africa in 1942, and took part in the Axis offensive that ended at El Alamein. By September 1942 only one four-gun battery remained operational in North Africa, while another seventeen 152/37 guns remained in service in Italy itself and on various Italian islands as coast defence guns. After September 1943, 152/37 guns taken over by the Germans were designated as the *15.2cm K 410 (i)*.

Specifications:

Designation:	cannone da 152/37 - ex Austro-Hungarian 15 cm *Autokanone* M. 15/16
Adopted by Italy:	After WWI (captured, war booty)
Inventory 10/06/1940:	29
Subsequent production:	None
Originator	Škoda, Plzeň (Bohemia, now part of the Czech Republic)
Producer:	Škoda
User countries:	Austria-Hungary, Italy, Czechoslovakia, Germany (after September 1943)
Caliber:	152.4mm (6 inches)
Length of tube:	6.00m (236.2 inches)
Overall length:	9.85m (387.8 inches)
Overall width:	2.30m (90.6 inches)
Weight in action:	11,900 kg (26,235 lb)
Carriage:	box trail
Wheel track:	1.75m (68.9 inches)
Wheel type/diameter:	steel wheels with two staggered rows with 12 spokes to each row/ 1.50m (59 inches)
Breech type:	horizontal wedge
Recuperator type:	hydropneumatic
Recoil length:	1800mm maximum; 800mm minimum
Elevation:	-6° to +45°
Traverse:	6°
Muzzle velocity:	692 m/s (2,270 fps)
Maximum range:	21,840 metres (23,885 yards); maximum effective 16,000 metres (17,498 yards)
Rate of fire:	1 to 2 rounds every two minutes
Ammunition types:	HE, shrapnel
Shell weight:	HE 54 kg (119 lb)

GERMAN OR WAR BOOTY GUNS

20/65 FlaK 30, 38 and *Flakvierling* (Rheinmetall)

The *FlaK* 30 was a Rheinmetall-Borsig development based on the Solothurn ST52, and was introduced into service in 1935. The gun was mounted on a trailer that had a horse-shoe frame with two wheels into which the gun mounting itself fitted; the wheels and frame could be easily disengaged and the mount then dropped to the ground and leveled with hand cranks, resulting in a triangular base that allowed 360° traverse. Ammunition was fed from 20-round magazines, but the rate of fire, at 120 rpm, was not particularly impressive. There was also a tendency to jam at times. These shortcomings led Rheinmetall, apparently working with Mauser, to develop an improved version. Mauser revised the breech mechanism to deliver a cyclic rate of 420-480 rpm, but the practical rate was 180-220 rpm. The improved version was designated the *FlaK* 38. Although the *FlaK* 38 supplemented the *FlaK* 30 it never completely replaced it in German service. In addition, a very lethal mount consisting of four *FlaK* 38 weapons was developed, designated *Flakvierling 38*.

Italy received the first batch of *Flakvierling* as early as in July 1940, when four of them were mounted on two *FlaK Schützwagen* (armed train wagons) offered by Hitler himself to Mussolini to enhance the aerial defence of mobile headquarters operating in the proximity of the frontline. This train, designated the C/20, did serve to provide anti-aircraft defence in many parts of Italy where aerial attacks were particularly heavy or where it was necessary to defend train lines and train traffic against low level attacks. In February 1943 the train was sent to Sicily, in that period suffering from heavy air attack, to protect the traffic between Messina and Palermo. In July one car was in Messina, and it operated there until it was destroyed by its crew when the island was evacuated; the other car was in Naples.

However, it was not until 1942 and the first half of 1943 that Italy received a number of the *Flakvierling* from Germany, as the utility of this weapon had been demonstrated and Italian tests for a quad mounting based on the 20/65 Breda mod. 35 or the 20/70 Scotti were proceeding very slowly. In 1942 30 *Flakvierling* arrived, followed by 75 more by summer 1943. Some of these weapons went to the *Regia Marina*, that used them on motor torpedo boats, as well as on the aircraft carrier *Aquila* that was under construction, while waiting for similar Italian weapons. With additional *Flakvierling* the *Regio Esercito* formed a few more armed trains to increase the defence of railroad traffic in the south of Italy.

Comparatively less important was the supply of *FlaK* 30 and 38 systems, due to the sufficient production of that caliber by Breda and Scotti, the Italian weapons having basically the same characteristics as the German weapons. The number of pieces is believed to be 264, attached to the *FlaK* 88 batteries or used for territorial defence. Furthermore, the *Regio Esercito* had acquired some other *FlaK* 30 and 38 from Greece as war booty, at the end of the campaign in spring 1941.

A 2 cm FlaK *mod. 38 on its wheeled carriage; this piece is part of the collection at the* Museo Storico della Guerra di Rovereto. *(Enrico Finazzer)*

After the surrender of Italy, as might well be expected, the *FlaK* guns were taken over by the previous owners. Thirteen of the guns were mounted by Viberti on *camionette* AS43 produced under German control and slightly modified to host the weapon.

Specifications:

Designation:	cannone-mitragliera 20/65 da 20mm mod. 30 carrellato, modello 38, complesso binato e quadruplo c.a. Mauser da 20/65 - original designation *Flugzeugabwehrkanone* 30, 38, and *Flakvierling*
Originator:	Rheinmetall-Borsig AG, Düsseldorf
Producer:	Rheinmetall-Borsig AG, Düsseldorf
User countries:	Germany, Italy, Holland, Finland, China
Caliber:	20mm (0.787 inches)
Crew:	5 for *FlaK* 30 and *FlaK* 38; 7 for *Flakvierling*
Length of tube:	2.30m (90.6 inches) *FlaK* 30; 2.2525m (88.7 inches) *FlaK* 38 and *Flakvierling*
Overall length:	4.08m (160.6 inches) *FlaK* 30; 3.988m (157 inches) *FlaK* 38; 4.33m (170.5 inches) *Flakvierling*
Overall width:	1.81m (71.3 inches) *FlaK* 30 and 38; 2.42m (95.3 inches) *Flakvierling*
Overall height:	1.60m (63 inches) *FlaK* 30; 2.166m (82.3 inches) *Flakvierling*
Weight in action:	470 kg (1,036 lb) *FlaK* 30; 412 kg (908 lb) *FlaK* 38; 1,514 kg (3,338 lb) *Flakvierling*
Elevation:	-10° to +90° *FlaK* 30; -20° to +90° *FlaK* 38; -10° to +100° *Flakvierling*
Traverse:	360°
Muzzle velocity:	900 m/s (2,953 fps) HE tracer
Maximum effective ceiling:	3,800 metres (12,467 feet)
Rate of fire (practical):	120 rpm *FlaK* 30; 180-220 rpm *FlaK* 38; 880 rpm for four guns combined *Flakvierling*
Ammunition types:	HE tracer
Shell weight:	0.119 kg (0.262 lb)

37/45 anti-tank gun (3.7 cm *PaK* 35/36)

Development of the very popular German Rheinmetall-Borsig *3.7 cm Pak 35/36 L45* anti-tank gun, of which some 15,000 copies were built, dates to 1933 with its initial combat use being in Spain in 1936. The gun was exported to several countries and was also copied, the best example of this perhaps being the US 37mm M3 anti-tank gun. The *PaK* 35/36 was a contemporary of the British 2-pdr anti-tank gun and the Bofors 37mm anti-tank gun and was somewhat inferior in performance, although in 1940 it was still one of the best anti-tank guns available. After only a few months into the war, as tank armour increased in thickness, it became inadequate for the role but it served throughout the war until 1945. The *PaK* 35/36 had a split trail carriage and was fitted with steel wheels, pneumatic tires and a small sloping shield; the gun itself was semi-automatic in the sense that the sliding wedge breech closed automatically. The gun could be towed by virtually any kind of tractor or truck, and it could also be moved by the gunners for short distances.

The crew of a 37/45 gun moving their piece in North Africa in the spring of 1942; a group of camels is resting in the background. (USSME)

Penetration capabilities varied by AP ammunition type and range, from 64mm at 100 metres falling off to 22.5mm at 600 metres. The Germans also supplied Italy with hollow charge ammunition (the *Stielgranate 41*) that could penetrate up to 180mm of armour, but the disadvantage to using this ammunition was that it was effective only at relatively close range (about 300 metres), and consequently was somewhat hazardous to the crew who would be exposed to enemy fire from longer ranges.

A 37/45 anti-tank gun in the desert in autumn 1941. (USSME)

Italy's first exposure to the gun was in 1935/36 in during the war against Ethiopia; the Ethiopians had 30 of these guns purchased from Germany, some of which were captured by the *Regio Esercito*. During the Spanish Civil War, in 1936, Germany supplied 40 examples of the gun to Italian forces in Spain. In 1937, during a visit to Germany the Italian Army Chief of Staff, General Pariani, was shown and possibly offered the weapon for purchase, but Pariani was of the correct opinion that performance of the Ansaldo/Böhler 47/32 anti-tank gun that had been adopted by Italy was superior to that of the *PaK* 35/36. However, apparently to supplement the 47/32, Italy acquired a batch of 100 *PaK* 35/36s in 1940, the first of which was sent as a sample sometime in 1940, with the remaining 99 arriving in Naples in December 1940. Of the 100, 87 were sent to Libya and the remainder

were held in Italy for possible shipment to Italian East Africa. The gun saw service in North Africa, particularly during the Axis offensive of spring 1941, when it was assigned as part of the anti-tank assets to the *Ariete* Armoured Division as well as to the *Bologna, Brescia* and *Pavia* divisions.

Following Italy's September 1943 surrender to the Allies, an undetermined number - possibly the 13 that had been held in Italy for possible service in Italian East Africa but were never sent - saw service in small numbers with the RSI's GNR. Guns of this type that were pressed into German service after 1943 were designated as the *3.7 cm PaK 162 (i)*.

Specifications:

Designation:	cannone controcarro da 37/45 – original designation 3.7 *PaK* 35/36 L45
Number acquired:	100
Originator:	Rheinmetall-Borsig AG, Düsseldorf
Producer:	Rheinmetall-Borsig AG, Düsseldorf
Caliber:	37mm (1.46 inches)
Length of tube:	1.665m (65.5 inches)
Overall width:	1.65m (65 inches)
Overall height:	1.22m (48 inches)
Weight in action:	444 kg (979 lb)
Carriage:	split trail
Wheel track:	1.54m (60.6 inches)
Wheel type/diameter:	steel with pneumatic tires
Breech type:	sliding wedge
Recuperator type:	hydro-spring
Elevation:	-8° to +25°
Traverse:	59° with trails open; 4° 30' with trails closed
Muzzle velocity:	745 m/s (2444 fps)
Maximum range:	6,800 metres (7,437 yards) maximum; 800 metres (875 yards) effective
Rate of fire:	12-15 rounds per minute
Ammunition types:	AP, HE, hollow charge, training
Shell weight:	AP 0.68 kg (1.5 lb)
Armour penetration:	34mm (1.3 inches) at 100 metres (109 yards) (3.7 cm *Pzgr Ptr.*); 64mm (2.5 inches) at 100 metres (3.7 cm *Pzgr Patr.* 40)

75/50 anti-aircraft gun (7.5 cm *Kanon PL* vz. 37)

In a somewhat curious turn of events, in 1940 Italy, which had received such a large number of Škoda guns as a result of WWI that they still formed a considerable part of the *Regio Esercito*'s artillery inventory on the eve of WWII, received yet another infusion of Škoda guns in 1940. Leading up to this arrangement was a request that Italy had made to Germany in June 1939 for fifty batteries of 88mm anti-aircraft guns in exchange for some credits for the supply of manufactured goods produced by Italian industry for its German ally. This move was necessary to enhance the anti-aircraft defences of Italian cities and ports against aerial attack in case of war, until Italian industry was able to produce a sufficient number of anti-aircraft guns to meet requirements. Germany, which needed the 88mm guns to meet its own requirements, instead offered Italy a number of Czech Škoda *7.5cm kanon PL vz37* anti-aircraft guns captured by the Germans in March 1939, as well as few *8,8 cm FlaK*, called in Italy the 88/55 (see separate entry). The German designation for the gun was the *7.5 cm FlaK M37 (t)*, which the Italians then rebaptized as the *cannone da 75/50*. The first batteries arrived in Italy in 1940, just a few days after Italy declared war on France and the United Kingdom.

The gun was quite modern, having entered Czech service only in 1937 and had a structure typical of the anti-aircraft pieces of that period, with the interesting feature of having a relatively low silhouette due to the fact that the barrel was mounted very low on the carriage without the usual central pivot. Its vertical sliding breech block automatically ejected the spent casing after firing, although loading was manual. An unusual feature for an anti-aircraft weapon was that it

had a muzzle brake, which made it instantly recognizable. The PL vz37 had been designed for mechanical towing and was mounted on a two-axle carriage with pneumatic tires, much like the iconic 40mm Bofors gun. The carriage itself was a standard and well tested cruciform platform, the side legs of which were folded for transport. The gun was fitted with a modern Škoda T7N fire control system, capable of directing fire against aircraft flying up to about 9,000 metres (29,528 feet) at a speed of 500 km/h (311 mph), which was quite remarkable in the early stages of the war. The 75/50 fired both Czech anti-aircraft ammunition and Italian made anti-tank ammunition, although the Czech ammunition could be used against ground targets as well. The only negative aspect of the gun was its relatively long emplacement time.

Organizationally and operationally the 75/50 guns underwent continuous changes throughout the course of the war. Initial use of the Škoda guns in Italian service was for homeland defence, with four fixed position battalions being created in June 1940, numbered from the 41st to 44th, assigned to the MACA. Later the 43rd battalion, consisting of two batteries, was re-roled as a field unit and sent to North Africa, attached to the *Trieste* Motorised Division, which deployed it until the battle of El Alamein, followed by the 42° *Gruppo*, assigned to the static defence of Tripoli and Bengasi. Although they suffered from combat loss and attrition, in 1943 in Tunisia a small number of the guns were still operational, assigned to the *Trieste* Division and to the *Spezia* Air Transportable Division. The 41st Battalion was assigned to the defence of Corinth in Greece.

The Škoda 75/50 guns were particularly appreciated by the Italians in North Africa for a number of reasons. The guns presented a low silhouette, which was an important factor in the desert; they were relatively light and maneuverable, and like the German 88 and the Italian 90/53 guns, were a dual-purpose gun that could be used effectively as an anti-tank weapon.

Deliveries continued throughout the war to units on mainland Italy; in March 1943 two new batteries were assigned to a MACA unit to defend the Cogne steel works, which produced military hardware, in the Val d'Aosta.

The surviving guns were taken back into German service after Italy's surrender in September 1943

Specifications:

Designation:	cannone da 75/50 – original designation 7.5 *kanon PL vz37*
Entry in Italian service:	1940
Number acquired:	Several dozen by the end of 1943
Originator:	Škoda, Plzen, Czecoslovakia
Producer:	Škoda
User countries:	Czechoslovakia, Italy, Finland, Germany
Caliber:	75mm (2.95 inches)
Length of tube:	3.65m (144.49 inches)
Height	1.82mm (71.65 inches)
Weight in action:	2,800 kg (6173 lb)
Carriage:	cruciform, mounted on 2-axle carriage
Breech type:	semi-automatic vertical sliding block
Recuperator type:	hydropneumatic
Elevation:	0° to +85°
Traverse:	360°
Muzzle velocity:	750-775 m/s (2,461-2,543 fps)
Maximum ceiling:	9,200 metres (30,184 feet) maximum; 4,000-6,000 metres (13,23 -19,685 feet) effective
Rate of fire:	10-15 rounds per minute
Ammunition types:	HE
Shell weight:	5.5 kg (12.13 lb)

75/97/38 anti-tank gun (*PaK* 1897/38)

This 75mm anti-tank gun, sometimes referred to also as 75/39, originated from the well-known *75mm modèle 1897 Schneider*, developed in France and produced in thousands of copies for the French army. The gun had been extensively used during WWI, and in 1940 was still in widespread use in both France and Poland; with the fall of Poland and France the *Wehrmacht* captured significant quantities of them, and distributed them to second line units. However, in summer 1941, during the initial phases of *Barbarossa*, the German Army found itself short of anti-tank guns capable of knocking out heavily armoured Russian tanks, notably the T34. Therefore, as a temporary solution, the Germans came up with the idea of adapting the French field piece to the anti-tank role by mounting its barrel, fitted with strengthening bands and a muzzle brake, on the carriage of the German *PaK* 38, instead of its original 50 mm barrel, because the original French carriage had only limited traverse and was not well-suited to mechanical towing. The result was rather successful

and enabled the Germans to have a reliable anti-tank gun until the industry of the Reich provided better material. When the new 75mm *PaK*40 reached the front line in late 1941, the 75/37/38 was passed to allied armies, among them to the expeditionary corps of the *Regio Esercito*.

As mentioned above, the gun was a hybrid of a *PaK*38 carriage and a 75mm Schneider barrel. It had a tubular split trail carriage, two rubber tired wheels and was fitted with a sloped shield, which, along with the appreciably low silhouette, gave the gunners a certain degree of protection against light fire. It was designed for mechanical traction. The French gun barrel was considered well-suited for the anti-tank role thanks to a good muzzle velocity and a high rate of fire.

In 1942 the *Regio Esercito* obtained nine batteries of six pieces each, issued to the artillery regiments of nine divisions of the ARMIR on the Russian front. They were wiped out with the rest of the army by the Red Army offensive of winter 1942/1943[1].

Specifications:

Designation:	cannone da 75/97/38
Number acquired:	54
Originator:	Déport, Sainte-Claire and Rimailho
Producer:	French arsenals, modified in German arsenals
Caliber:	75mm (2.95 inches)
Length of barrel:	2.58mm (101.58 inches)
Overall length:	4.65m (183.07 inches)

---

1 According to F. Cappellano, *Le artiglierie del Regio Esercito…, page 266*, some pieces of this type were deployed in Sicily as static anti-tank artillery in summer 1943 at the time of the Allied landing on the Island.

Weight in action:	1,190 kg (2,624 lb)
Carriage:	split trail
Wheel typer:	steel with solid rubber tires
Breech type:	interrupted screw
Recuperator type:	hydropneumatic
Elevation:	-10 to +18°
Traverse:	60°
Muzzle velocity:	450 m/sec (1476 fps)
Maximum range:	1,500 metres (1,640 yards)
Rate of fire:	12-14 rounds per minute
Ammunition types:	HEAT
Shell weight:	4.4 to 4.57 kg (9.7 to 10.08 lb) depending on specific type of German HEAT round

88/27 howitzer (Ordnance QF 25-pdr Mk II)

The 25-pdr Mk II Gun on Carriage 25-pdr Mark I was the standard British field gun of WWII. It was designed to replace the WWI vintage 18-pdr field gun and 4.5 inch howitzer, and is considered by some to be the best field artillery piece of the war. It entered into British service in 1940, and in addition to being used by Commonwealth forces, it was used by a number of other Allied nations. In 1942 the *Regio Esercito* captured a number of 25-pdr howitzers during the second Axis offensive, as a consequence of the fall of Tobruk, along with their tractors and a substantial supply of ammunition. The Italian designation for the well-known gun was *obice da 88/27 PB* (PB standing for *Preda Bellica* –war booty).

This piece had several interesting characteristics, one being the firing platform. In fact, while in firing position the carriage, a standard box trail, rested on a circular platform, which in itself was positioned on the ground. That arrangement allowed a traverse of 360° with very little effort as by lifting the trails the entire piece could be easily pivoted. Furthermore, the piece was designed for both direct fire, as a gun, and high angle fire, as a howitzer, and was also effective in the anti-tank role should the need arise. The carriage was fitted with rubber-tired wheels, and was designed exclusively for mechanical traction. With a properly trained crew, the gun could be brought into

A British 25-pdr (Ordnance QF 25 pdr) abandoned at El Mechili in February 1942. Note the detail of the circular firing platform in the foreground. (USSME)

A British 25-pdr abandoned at El Mechili in February 1942. (USSME)

action in two minutes. The ammunition for the 25-pdr was unfixed (separate loading), the shell itself was first loaded and rammed, and then the brass cartridge casing with the propellant charge was loaded and the breech closed for firing.

According to Italian records the *Trento* Division formed a battalion with 12 pieces, which fought at El Alamein. A further two pieces are attributed to the *Littorio* Armoured Division in the same battle. A few pieces followed the Italian army all the way to Tunisia, where eight 88/27 PB were assigned to the *16° Raggruppamento di artiglieria di corpo d'armata*, of the XXX Army Corps, in spring 1943.

Specifications:

Designation:	Obice da 88/27 PB – original designation ordnance QF 25-pr Mk II
Number in Italian service:	approximately 20
Manufacturer:	Royal Ordnance Factories
Caliber:	87.6mm (3.45 inches)
Barrel length:	2.476m (97.45 inches)
Length:	4.602m (181 inches)
Width:	2.134m (84 inches)
Height:	1.65m (65 inches)
Weight:	1,800 kg (3,968 lb)
Carriage:	Box trail
Breech:	Vertical sliding block
Recuperator:	Hydropneumatic
Elevation:	-5° to +45°
Traverse:	360° on platform; 4° left or right on carriage
Muzzle velocity:	Basic charge: 198 m/sec (650 fps), Charge 2: 307 m/sec (1,007 fps); Charge 3: 457 m/sec (1,499 fps); Charge super: 541 m/sec (1,775)
Range	Basic charge: 3,300 metres (3,609 yards); Charge 2: 6,000 metres (6,562 yards); Charge 3: 10,000 metres (10,936 yards); Charge super: 12,000 metres (13,123 yards)
Rate of fire:	6-8 rounds per minute
Ammunition types:	HE, HESH, smoke, illuminating, shot (blank)
Shell weight:	11.4 kg (25 lb) HE; 5.8 kg (12.8 lb) smoke
Weight, complete round:	14 kg (30.9 lb) HE; 9 kg (19.8 lb) smoke

88/55 dual-purpose gun (Krupp 8,8 cm *FlaK*)

Perhaps the most famous artillery piece of WWII was the German "eighty-eight" that was especially feared and respected by Allied armour crews because of its devastating capabilities. The 88mm *FlaK* 18 was initially conceived and clandestinely developed as an anti-aircraft gun by a Krupp design team working at Bofors in Sweden in 1931. By 1933 the gun was being produced in Germany and was an immediate success as an anti-aircraft gun due to its range and mobility. Its modern design enabled it to cope with any contemporary aerial targets. The barrel was a single-tube, enclosed within a jacket, with a semi-automatic sliding wedge breech mechanism that made loading much more efficient. Mobility was provided by its *Sonder Anhänger* 201 four-wheeled trailer, towed by the *SdKfz* halftrack tractor; a cruciform platform with folding side legs enabled it to be put in battery easily, as well as providing stability for the weapon. The pedestal mount had leveling jacks. The gun could be fired from its trailer, but for better stability was removed from the trailer and rested on the cruciform platform. The *FlaK* 18 first saw action during the Spanish Civil War by the Germans, where it was found to be highly effective in the anti-tank role.

The *FlaK* 18 was followed in 1936 by the *FlaK* 36, which differed mainly in the barrel construction, that was built in three separate pieces, protected by external rings that allowed individual segments to be replaced as they wore out instead of replacing the whole barrel, and in the type of trailer used, the *Sonder Anhänger* 202, which differed mainly in having dual sets of tires rather than single tires and, while in transit, permitted the barrel to be pointed forwards or backwards, enabling the gun to be put in firing position quickly. The mod. 37 was similar to the mod. 36, with a different fire control data transmission system that was better suited to static conditions. The guns were fitted with two types of sights: the Rbl F.32 was used in the anti-aircraft role, while the *Ziehlfernrohr* ZF 20 E was used in the anti-tank role. Many components of all three guns were interchangeable. The major drawback to the *FlaK* 18, 36 and the later 37, was its bulk and high silhouette, which made it difficult to conceal in the desert; this however, was largely offset by its ability to engage hostile targets at long ranges.

By 1945 Krupp had produced about 10,000 examples of the three models. A further improved model, the *FlaK* 41, was developed by Rheinmetall beginning in 1941, and was put into production in 1943, but only somewhat fewer than 600 were produced as it was an expensive system to produce and complex to maintain. It could achieve a higher ceiling than the earlier models and was used almost exclusively in fixed positions in Germany; none were supplied to Italy.

In addition to the 75/50 anti-aircraft gun (see separate entry above), the 88/55 was supplied to Italy from 1940 onwards. As a condition associated with furnishing the guns to Italy, Germany

An 88/55 anti-aircraft gun manned by an Italian crew in action in North Africa. (USSME)

requested Italian companies to produce some items for German artillery pieces under license. Accordingly, in May 1942 Ansaldo began production of components of both the 88mm and 7.5 cm *PaK* anti-tank guns, including cradles, gun tubes and barrel liners, and in 1943 OTO joined Ansaldo in production of tubes for the *FlaK* 18 and *FlaK* 36 to replace those needed in Italian service. After September 1943 these foundries continued to supply components to the Germans.

The first batteries reached Italy shortly after Italy's attack on France in June 1940. The supply continued during the entire war, because the production rate of the Italian anti-aircraft piece, the 90/53 (see separate entry above), was always too slow to face the mounting needs. By December 1940 there were 44 of the German guns in Italy, and a year later, in late 1941 there were 21 batteries equipped with a total of 84 of the 88mm *FlaK* guns. By the end of 1942 there were already 100 batteries in delivery and in July 1943, with at least 136 batteries, the 88/55 was the gun deployed in greatest quantity by Italian territorial air defence units. The majority of the batteries obtained were deployed around Italian cities and ports, but some were assigned to front line units.

Two battalions, the XVIII and the XXIX, originally sent to Libya in October and November 1940 to defend Libyan ports, later underwent name and subordination changes: in January 1942 the *XVIII Gruppo* became the *V Gruppo CC/CA* (V Anti-aircraft/Anti-tank Group) and was assigned to the *Brescia* Division, and later transferred to the *132° Reggimento artiglieria corazzata* (132nd Armoured Artillery Regiment) of the *Ariete* Armoured Division. In late May 1942 the group saw its first use in the anti-tank role during the battle of Gazala, inflicting heavy losses on tanks of the British 22nd Armoured Brigade, but in turn lost five of its guns on 30 May. On 10 June one of the group's remaining guns accounted for the destruction of ten British tanks. The following summer, the *133° Reggimento* of the *Littorio* Armoured Division also received a battalion, the XXIX.

In October 1942 another battalion, the *XXXI Gruppo*, was assigned to the *Ariete* Division's *132° Reggimento artiglieria corazzata*. This regiment, along with the rest of the division, was destroyed at El Alamein. Employment of the 88/55 in Italian service in North Africa ended with the battle of Enfidaville, Tunisia in April 1943. These guns, along with the equally powerful Italian 90/53 issued to the armoured divisions, were the only artillery that could inflict serious damage to British armoured units, although they came in too scarce a number to be able to balance the odds of battle. On the other hand a shortage of suitable tractors often posed problems; while in the

Loading an 88/55 anti-aircraft gun in North Africa. (USSME)

An Italian-manned 88/55 FlaK battery in North Africa, October 1942. (USSME)

Wehrmacht the gun was towed by the *SdKfz* halftrack tractor, the *Regio Esercito* adapted the Lancia 3Ro heavy truck to this role, but it was not really up to the job.

In April 1943, in Italy the Fascist National Party formed an armoured division, the *1ª Divisione Corazzata Camicie Nere "M"* (1st Black Shirt Armoured Division "M", the "M" signifying "Mussolini"), with personnel selected from the MVSN. Following arrangements with the German *SS*, this unit was to be equipped with German material, including 24 88/55 guns with the precious *SdKfz* halftracks. The division was still in training and had received only part of the equipment when Italy surrendered, and the Germans took back what had been delivered. After the surrender of Italy, the Germans captured the hundreds of pieces that had been delivered to Italy in the previous years. They remained on Italian soil, incorporated in the *FlaK* units and were often manned by Italian personnel.

Specifications:

Designation:	cannone da 88/55 – original designation 8.8 cm *Flugzeug abwehrkanone* 18, abbreviated as the *FlaK* 18, *FlaK* 36 and *FlaK* 37
Number acquired:	about 600
Originator:	Krupp, Essen
Producer:	Krupp; in Italy some barrels were produced by various firms including Ansaldo and OTO
User countries:	Germany, Italy, Spain,China
Caliber:	88mm (3.46 inches)
Length of tube:	4.93m (194.1 inches)
Overall length:	7.62m (300 inches) on trailer; 5.795m (228.2 inches) on platform
Overall width:	2.305m (90.7 inches) on trailer; 5.145m (202.6 inches) on platform
Overall height:	2.418m (95.2 inches) on trailer; 2.104m (82.8 inches) on platform
Weight in action:	4,983 kg (10,986 lb) to 5,150 kg (11,354 lb) depending on model
Carriage:	pedestal mount on cruciform platform carried by 4-wheel trailer
Wheel track:	2.00m (78.7 inches)
Breech type:	semi-automatic
Recuperator type:	hydropneumatic
Recoil length:	1200mm (47.2 inches) maximum; 900 mm (35.4 inches) minimum
Elevation:	-3° to +85°
Traverse:	360°
Muzzle velocity:	820 m/s (2690 fps)
Ceiling:	8,000 metres (26,247 feet) effective; 10,000 metres (32,808 feet) maximum
Rate of fire:	20 rounds per minute
Ammunition types:	HE, AP
Shell weight:	9.24 kg (20.4 lb) HE
Armour penetration:	105mm (4.13 inches) of armour at a 30° angle at 1,000 metres.

100/22 howitzer (Skoda 10 cm vz 14/19 and 16/19)

The 100/22 howitzer was another of the many Škoda artillery pieces utilized by the Italians during WWII, but unlike all of the other Škoda guns in the Italian inventory, was not left over from WWI. It was, instead, a more modern gun based on the WWI Škoda M 14, with a longer 24 caliber (L 24) barrel. However, the Italian system of measuring barrel lengths resulted in a designation of *obice da 100/22* rather than 100/24. Due to the collapse of the Austro-Hungarian Empire after WWI and the drawing of new national boundaries, the Škoda works were located in the new nation of Czechoslovakia and became the major armament producer in that country. Shortly after the war, in 1919, Škoda engineers set to work to modernize the 100/17 Model 14 howitzer, resulting in the modernized piece designated the *10 cm houfnice vz.14/19* in Czech service; upgraded howitzers built on the M16 carriage were designated as the *vz. 16/19*. In addition to the longer barrel, the gun also fired newly developed ammunition; the combination led to an increase in range over the Model 14. The updated gun enjoyed a modest degree of export sales, being acquired by Greece, Hungary, Poland and Yugoslavia.

In 1928 the Italians carried out experiments with a 100/22 gun, using two different types of ammunition (the M 15 and M 28 rounds) to increase the range of the gun, but it was decided not to upgrade the 100/17 guns in Italian service to 100/22 at that time. Italy ultimately came to possess 406 pieces of this type, most of which were ceded to them by the Germans, who had captured them from Poland and Czechoslovakia; one source states that Germany offered a total of 100 batteries of guns along with 266,000 HE and 240,000 shrapnel rounds, although it seems that only 320 guns actually were transferred by Germany. A further lot of 38 was captured by the Italians in Yugoslavia, as well as a number captured in Greece. In late September 1942 the *Regio Esercito* had 358 horse-drawn 100/22 howitzers and 48 fitted with steel wheels and semi-pneumatic tires (designated the 100/22 T.M.), suitable for mechanical towing

The 100/22 normally was issued to the artillery regiments of infantry divisions, but was also issued to the *Ariete II* Armoured Cavalry Division's artillery regiment. Some of the 100/22 howitzers were also used in the coast defence role in Sicily and Sardinia; in Sicily several mobile battalions were formed with three batteries each whose function was to react quickly as anti-landing units. In June 1943, thirteen divisional artillery groups were equipped with the 100/22. Because of its similarity to the 100/17 howitzer, 34 of the mod. 16/19 howitzers captured from Yugoslavia were used in the artillery school to train new artillery recruits who would be assigned as crews for the 100/17 howitzer.

A 100/22 howitzer displayed at the Sacrario dei Caduti d'Oltremare (Shrine to Those Killed Overseas) in Bari. (Enrico Finazzer)

Following the events of 8 September 1943 in Italy, some 100/22 howitzers (likely assigned to the *Ariete II* Division) were used by Italian forces in their unsuccessful attempt to defend Rome against the Germans, who seized – in the following days – quite a number of them. The 100/22 later served with both the Italian co-belligerent forces as well as with RSI forces after 8 September; one battalion supported the *I Raggruppamento Motorizzato* fighting alongside the Allies at Montelungo, while two batteries served with the *Condottieri* artillery regiment of the RSI's *X^a MAS* Division. In the post-war years a number of 100/17 and 100/22 howitzers were converted by the Naples Arsenal into howitzers designated *da 105/22 Mod. 14/61* and issued to the artillery groups of the motorised brigades. This materiel, considered better than the US M2 105mm howitzer, was not phased out until after the dissolution of the Warsaw Pact. It could be drawn by the Lancia TL 51 tractor at a speed of 50 km/h.

Specifications:

Designation:	obice da 100/22 - original designation 10 cm *houfnice vz.*14/19
Number acquired:	406
Originator:	Škoda, Plzeň
Producer:	Škoda
User countries:	Czechoslovakia, Italy, Greece, Hungary, Poland, Yugoslavia, Germany (after September 1943)
Caliber:	100mm (3.94 inches)
Length of tube:	2.175m (85.6 inches)
Length of rifling:	1.899m (74.8 inches)
Overall length:	2.400m (94.5 inches)
Weight in action:	1,505 kg (3,318 lb) (1430?)
Carriage:	box trail
Wheel type/diameter:	12 spoke wood with metal rim; some fitted with steel wheels and semi-pneumatic tires/1.30m (51.2 inches)
Breech type:	horizontal wedge
Recuperator type:	spring
Elevation:	-7º30' to +48º
Traverse:	5º38'
Muzzle velocity:	415 m/s (1362 fps)
Maximum range:	9,970 metres (10,903 yards
Rate of fire:	4-6 rounds per minute
Ammunition types:	HE
Shell weight:	14 kg (30.9 lb)

105/11 howitzer (Schneider 105M modèle 1919)

The *obice da 105/11*, or the *Canon Court de 105 M (montagne) modèle 19 Schneider* as it was designated in French, was a post-WWI French mountain howitzer that had been exported to a number of countries, including Greece, Spain, and Yugoslavia. A somewhat updated version was designated the *105mm modèle 28*. All in all, the howitzer did not have really remarkable characteristics, but was a simple and down-to-business piece of artillery. The carriage was a box trail with variable recoil, which was fitted with two wooden wheels and a shield. The barrel was in steel with a reinforcing ring in the rear part. The breech mechanism was an interrupted screw. Conceived for mountain warfare, it could be split in eight loads for animal transport, but it could also be towed in one piece; the barrel itself could be broken down into two sections.

As a result of its campaign against Greece in 1940, Italy captured a number of 105/11 howitzers that were subsequently integrated into the artillery inventory. Fortunately for the Italians, the French 105/11 howitzers could fire the 105mm Italian mod. 32 and mod. 36 rounds, obviating

A 105/11 howitzer displayed at the Musée de l'Artillerie, Draguignan, France. (Enrico Finazzer)

Breech detail of the 105/11 howitzer. (Enrico Finazzer)

the need for yet another ammunition type in the supply system. Although most of the captured pieces were assigned to static defence, in spring 1942 the artillery regiments of the three alpine divisions, the *Julia*, *Tridentina* and *Cuneense*, that were sent to the Eastern Front each received a third battalion consisting of two four-gun batteries equipped with the 105/11; those battalions took part in the fighting along the Don River and were lost during the retreat of the Alpine Army Corps in January 1943. In early 1942 the *Regio Esercito* had 96 of these howitzers in the inventory, and by May 1943 the GaF had deployed some of those in six batteries in fixed defensive positions along the Ligurian coastline.

The Germans do not appear to have assigned a specific designation for any of these guns that may have been taken from the Italians after September 1943, although they did designate those that they captured directly from the French as the *10.5cm leGebH 322(f)* for the mle. 1919 guns, and *10.5cm leGebH 323 (f)* for the mle. 1928 guns; the howitzers that they captured in Yugoslavia were designated as the *10.5cm leGebH 329 (j)*.

Specifications:

Designation:	obice da 105/11 - original designation *canon court de* 105 M *(montagne) modèle* 19 Schneider
Number acquired:	96
Originator:	Schneider, Le Creusot (France)
Producer:	Schneider
User countries:	France, Italy, Greece, Spain, Yugoslavia, Germany
Caliber:	105mm (4.1 inches)
Length of tube:	1.26m (49.46 inches)
Weight in action:	742 kg (1,636 lb)
Carriage:	box trail
Wheel type:	12 spoke wood wheels with metal rims
Breech type:	interrupted screw
Recuperator type:	hydropneumatic
Elevation:	-3° to +40°
Traverse:	9°
Muzzle velocity:	350 m/s (1148 fps)
Maximum range:	7,850 metres (8,585 yards)
Rate of fire:	3-4 rounds per minute
Ammunition types:	HE
Shell weight:	12 kg (26.5 lb)

149/28 howitzer (15 cm sFH 18)

The *obice da 149/28* was the Italian designation for the standard howitzer of the German Army, the *15 cm schwere Feldhaubitze* or *sFH18*. Manufactured from the mid-1930s to 1945 it was a compromise between two designs submitted by both major German armaments producers, Rheinmetall and Krupp. The German Army decided to adopt the Krupp carriage and the Rheinmetall barrel. It was supplied in several thousand pieces throughout the war and was appreciated by the gunners as a reliable howitzer, although starting with the invasion of Russia it began to be outranged by Soviet artillery. The *Regio Esercito* became aware of the positive characteristics of this piece while used by the Germans in North Africa, and, being constantly in search of modern artillery, arranged for the purchase of a limited quantity of this howitzer from its German ally.

This Italian crew seems to be removing a camouflage net from a 149/28 howitzer in North Africa. (Andrea and Antonio Tallillo)

The Rheinmetall barrel was in steel, with a reinforcing sleeve in the rear half, while the Krupp carriage was a split trail, ending with spades that enhanced the stability of the piece during fire. The wheels were made of steel as well, with solid rubber tires. The original version of the howitzer was designed for animal towing, divided into two loads, but very soon a specific request from the German Army caused the producers to design a new version which allowed mechanical traction in a single load, although at a limited speed. For movement, the ends of the split trail were lifted onto a two-wheeled limber and the gun was disconnected from the recoil system, pulled back in its cradle, and locked to

The 149/28 gun was an imposing piece, as illustrated by this photo taken with its Italian crew in North Africa. (Andrea and Antonio Tallillo)

the trails in order to distribute the weight evenly. The *sFH* 18 fired cased separate-loading ammunition and also had the distinction of being the first gun ever to be issued with a rocket-assisted shell, which, however, did not prove to be practical.

The *Regio Esercito* formed four battalions with the 38 pieces that were purchased from Germany. The *CXXXI Gruppo* and the *CXLVII Gruppo*, with 14 pieces, were sent to North Africa, assigned to the *8° Raggruppamento di artiglieria d'armata*. They took part in the operations in Libya and Egypt and, later, in Tunisia, assigned to the *1ª Armata*. The *XXIV Gruppo* and *L Gruppo*, with the remaining 24 pieces went to Russia, assigned to the *9° Raggruppamento di artiglieria d'armata*, of the ARMIR. These howitzers were deployed behind the divisions that defended the Don River line and were lost during the Red Army offensive of winter 1942/1943.

A 149/28 howitzer manned by Italians in position in North Africa, ready to fire. (Andrea and Antonio Tallillo)

Specifications:

Designation:	obice da 149/28 – original designation 15 cm *schwere Feldhaubitze* or *sFH*18
Number acquired:	38
Originator:	Krupp, Rheinmetall
Producer:	Krupp, Rheinmetall, Spreewerke, M.A.N., Škoda
User countries:	Germany, Italy, Finland
Caliber:	150mm (5.91 inches)
Length of tube:	4.44m (174.8 inches)
Weight in action:	5,512 kg (12,154 lb)
Carriage:	split trail
Breech type:	horizontal sliding block
Recuperator type:	hydropneumatic
Elevation:	-3° to +45°
Traverse:	64°
Muzzle velocity:	210 m/sec (689 fps) using Charge 1; 495 m/sec (1,624 fps) using Charge 8
Maximum range:	4,000 metres (4,374 yards) using Charge 1; 13,250 metres (14,490 yards) using Charge 8
Rate of fire:	4 rounds per minute
Ammunition types:	HE
Shell weight:	43.5 kg (95.9 lb)

SELF-PROPELLED GUNS

47/32 L40 self-propelled gun

Although plans for development of a 47/32 self-propelled gun on the L.3 light tank chassis were dropped, the Italian Army Staff was still interested in equipping the *bersaglieri* regiments with a self-propelled anti-tank gun in lieu of the towed 47/32 gun. In fact, during the course of development of the L.6 light tank, Ansaldo had examined the possibility of building an SP gun based on the L.6 chassis and in 1939 had built a wooden mockup of a vehicle that mounted a 75mm gun in a rotating turret. The Italian Army, however, preferred an SP mounting the 47/32 gun. Ansaldo obliged, and in the spring of 1941 a prototype was presented. The vehicle used all of the mechanical and

The prototype of the self-propelled gun which never entered service; the system consisted of a 47/32 gun mounted on the hull of an L.3 light tank and was built in 1939. (Fondazione Ansaldo)

A factory-fresh 47/32 self-propelled gun. (FIAT)

suspension components of the L.6, and mounted the 47/32 gun in a closed-topped casemate; the top, through which the crew entered and exited the vehicle, was soon eliminated because of ventilation problems. The casemate was rather poorly protected, and not even sloped against direct hits. The size of the crew varied from two to three; the prototype carried a crew of three, reduced to two in early production models, but increased to three in mid- and late production models. The ammunition, 70 rounds in total, was positioned behind the driver's seat and to the right of the gunner.

In June 1941, an order for 583 L.6 tanks was reduced to 283 tanks, with the remaining 300 chassis being diverted to produce the self-propelled 47/32 anti-tank gun. It was hoped that eventually all of the *Regio Esercito's* 47mm anti-tank guns would be mounted on this chassis. The vehicle was conceived as a light assault and support vehicle to equip the motorised and armoured divisions with a system that could provide close fire support to front-line units, to be used in conjunction with light tanks and reconnaissance vehicles, as well as being used to eliminate strong points. Doctrinally, it was not envisaged as a tank destroyer, although it was often pressed into service in that role when more suitable systems were not available. Platoon and company command vehicles, externally identical to the self-propelled gun, were also produced; the main gun in the command vehicles, however, was replaced by an 8mm Breda Model

An open formation of 47/32 self-propelled guns advancing in Tunisia in March 1943. (USSME)

A column of 47/32 self-propelled guns on the move in Tunisia, spring 1943. (USSME)

The 47/32 self-propelled gun seen from above, showing the rather small fighting compartment. (FIAT)

38 machine-gun disguised as a main gun, allowing more room in the interior of the vehicle for radio equipment. A significantly different variant of the vehicle, whose superstructure profile was similar to that of the SP gun, was the ammunition carrier developed for use with the 90/53 self-propelled gun; 33 carriers were built (see specific entry).

The first unit to see service was the *XIII Gruppo semoventi* of the *Cavalleggeri di Novara* Cavalry Regiment that joined the ARMIR with its 19 self-propelled guns on the Russian front in August 1942. They were wiped out by the Red Army offensive of the following winter. Other battalions were deployed in Tunisia, notably the I Battalion, within the *Superga* Division and the *CXXXVI Battaglione controcarri*. Most of the 47/32 *semoventi* fought in Sicily, against the Allied landings, in summer 1943. The *IV Battaglione* was assigned to the *Livorno* Division while the *CXXX, CXXXII, CXXXIII* and *CCXXXIII Battaglione controcarri* were deployed as independent anti-tank units. Two more battalions were in Corsica, i.e. the *XX*, within the *Friuli* Division, and the *CXXXI Battaglione controcarri*. The *IV Gruppo semoventi* of the *Cavalleggeri del Monferrato* Cavalry Regiment was sent to Albania. They did not see action and disbanded after the surrender of Italy. The final combat activity of the 47/32 self-propelled gun was in September 1943, just after the surrender of Italy, against the former German allies around Rome. Confused fighting took place with these *semoventi* of the *Raggruppamento Esplorante Corazzato* (armoured reconnaissance unit) *Lancieri di Montebello*, of the *Ariete II* Armoured Division, along with the *Squadrone semoventi* of the 4th Armoured Regiment.[1]

---

1   In the confused last phases of the Italian participation in the war, between spring and autumn 1943, the sources are often in disagreement as to the number and name of the units and their deployment. For example, according to Cappellano, *Gli autoveicoli da combattimento dell'Esercito Italiano*, in Rome in September 1943 the *squadrone semoventi* of the *X Battaglione esplorante* (reconnaissance unit) assigned to the *Piave* Motorised Division was involved in the fighting. On the other hand, according to Tallillo, Tallillo and Guglielmi, *Carro L6*, in Sicily there were two more battalions, i.e. the CXXXI and the CCXXX.

After the surrender of Italy the Germans captured 78 47/32 self-propelled guns and also took delivery of a further 120 new vehicles (74 gun versions, and 46 command versions), that, being of little use in the fighting against the Allies in the mountains of the peninsula, were for the most part assigned to second line units in the Balkans, which used them against the partisans. Others were modified by removing the gun and adapted to various uses. The final version produced under German control featured a modified fighting compartment that had slightly higher sides and no side access hatch. The German designation for the SP gun was *Sturmgeschutz L6 mit 47/32 630 (i)*, and for the command version was *Panzerbefehlswagen 47/32 770 (i)*. The armed forces of the RSI had a few *semoventi*, assigned to the *Gruppo Corazzato Leonessa* and to the *Gruppo Squadroni Corazzati San Giusto*.

The only surviving example is located at Fort Lee, Virginia.

Specifications:

Manufacturer:	FIAT/Ansaldo Fossati
Year adopted:	1942
Number produced:	357 (283 prior to September 1943 armistice; 74 after armistice for German forces).
Crew:	2 (commander/gunner, driver) early production; 3 (commander/gunner, loader, driver) mid- and late production
Weight:	6,825 kg (15,047 lb)
Main gun:	Ansaldo (Böhler license) Mod. 39 47/32 gun
Elevation:	-12° to +20°
Traverse:	27° *
Ammunition:	70 rounds in gun vehicles; 1,608 rounds of 8mm machine-gun ammunition in the command version
Engine:	SPA 18 VT, 4-cylinder in-line, 4053 cc
Horsepower:	68
Power-to-weight ratio:	9.96 hp/ton
Fuel capacity:	165 litres (43.59 US gallons; 36.29 Imperial gallons), including 20 litres (5.3 US gallons, 4.4 Imperial gallons) reserve
Maximum speed:	42.3 km/h road; 15.5 km/h cross-country
Operating radius (road):	200 km (124 miles)
Armour:	30mm frontal; 15mm sides; 6mm floor and roof
Length:	3.82m (12'6")
Width:	1.86m (6'1")
Height:	1.69m (5'6")

Track width:	260mm (10")
Ground clearance:	400mm (3'4")
Trench crossing:	1.70m (5'7")
Vertical obstacle:	700mm (2'4")
Fording depth:	1.00m (3'3")
Ground pressure:	0.44 kg/cm² (6.26 psi)
Radio:	In command version only: Marelli RF1 CA and RF2 CA
Dates of service:	1941-1945
Where employed:	North Africa, Russia, Italy, Corsica

* The traverse refers to the horizontal arc that can be covered by the gun while the vehicle is in a stationary position; as is true for all self-propelled guns, traverse could be increased by the simple expedient of traversing the entire vehicle in either direction.

75/18 M 40, M41 and M42 self-propelled howitzer

This excellent self-propelled gun/howitzer was the first Italian self-propelled gun to be produced in series and to serve with the *Regio Esercito* in WWII. There is some question as to whether this vehicle was inspired by the German *Sturmgeschutz III* assault gun, or if the idea of mating a 75/18 howitzer with an M.13 chassis was conceived by the Italians themselves prior to the debut of the *Sturmgeschutz III*. The *Regio Esercito*, in winter 1940, asked Ansaldo to study the possibility of mounting a 75/18 howitzer (see separate entry above) on the chassis of an M13/40 tank. The conversion from the tank to the self-propelled gun was made by mounting an armoured box-shaped superstructure on the regular chassis of the standard medium tank. The first series of the vehicle, designated the M40, was built on the chassis of the M 13/40, and successive series were built using the chassis of the M 14/41 (M41) and the M 15/42 (M42), with series production being halted in September 1943. The access for the three-man crew was from the top, which was closed with armoured plates. As already mentioned, the armament was a 75/18 howitzer, mounted on the front plate, moved slightly off-centre to the right, and, as secondary armament, there was a machine gun, generally an 8mm Breda model 38.

Development was carried out during the winter 1940, a wooden mockup was presented in January 1941, and the prototype was tested in February 1941. Several modifications were made

An M42 75/18 self-propelled gun; its low silhouette helped to render this a very effective weapon system. (FIAT)

to the 75/18 Model 1935 howitzer to render it compatible for use as a self-propelled system. Modifications included addition of the characteristic perforated muzzle brake (the first of its kind used on any self-propelled gun), which assisted in limiting the recoil travel of the gun to 350mm (13.8 inches). Although the armour was not very thick, varying from 25mm to 50mm on the front and sides, the protection of the crew, enhanced by the low silhouette of the *semovente*, was considered satisfactory, especially in comparison with the M series tanks. A series of orders soon followed (for 60 units in May 1941, 144 in December, and 200 in May 1942). Production models were assigned to operational units in early 1942. Since the self-propelled gun proved rather effective, production was carried on well beyond the initial number ordered, and as noted above, continued until late 1943.

Originally designed to supply close support fire to the armoured divisions, later these guns were employed in much the same fashion as the German *Jagdpanzer* in an anti-tank role and were included in the formation of the tank battalions, with one company out of three. The SP proved so effective that the *Regio Esercito* decided to reverse the proportion in favour of the self-propelled guns, forming battalions with two companies of *semoventi* and one of tanks. This new formation, however, remained mostly on paper since the production of self-propelled guns was always short of the needs. At the time of their introduction in North Africa, their armament (despite the rather short barrel length, low muzzle velocity, and consequent relatively

A 75/18 self-propelled gun photographed at the Fossati plant at Sestri Ponente. (Fondazione Ansaldo)

Egypt, autumn 1942. A column of 75/18 self--propelled guns advancing in the desert. (USSME)

119

A battery of 75/18 self-propelled guns at a halt in Egypt. Note the sand bags and spare track links secured to the front of the hull for added protection. (USSME)

short effective range) was formidable in comparison to both British and German tank guns. The effectiveness of their gun was further enhanced, as previously noted, by the use of shaped-charge EP ammunition. Crews of these vehicles were very confident of their capabilities and found the 75/18 gun to be an extremely reliable weapon. Crews in at least one *gruppo* (the *DLIV*) increased ammunition stowage capacity to about 100 rounds by removing the crew seats and simply sitting on the extra ammunition.

The first vehicles of this type to participate in combat in North Africa were the *DLI* and the *DLII Gruppo* attached to the *132° Reggimento artiglieria corazzata* of the *Ariete* Armoured Division, and received their baptism of fire in May 1942. The following summer two more battalions, the *DLIV* and the *DLVI Gruppo*, arrived in North Africa and were assigned to the *133° Reggimento artiglieria corazzata* of the *Littorio* Armoured Division. These battalions fought well throughout the Axis advance in Egypt and took part in the battle of El Alamein, where they suffered heavy losses. Three more battalions, the *DLVII*, the *DLVIII* and the *DLIX Gruppo,* attached to the *Centauro* Armoured Division, fought in the last phase of the North African campaign during the defence of the bridgehead of Tunisia in spring 1943. In Sicily there were some of these *semoventi*, without crews, probably scheduled to be sent to the Tunisian front for replacement, but they remained on the island after the surrender of the Axis forces there and did not see action against the Allied landings. The DLXI Battalion was deployed in Corsica, assigned to the *Friuli* Division, while some other self-propelled guns were in Greece with the *Brennero* Division. Many battalions of *semoventi* equipped both regiments of the *Ariete II* Armoured Division, the *Lancieri di Vittorio Emanuele II* and the *Cavalleggeri di Lucca*, as well as the *RECo* (divisional reconnaissance unit) *Lancieri di Montebello,* deployed to the north of Rome in September 1943. Two more companies had been assigned to the *Sassari* Infantry Division. These self-propelled guns took part in the fighting against the Germans in the aftermath of the Italian surrender.

After the Italian army disbanded following the surrender of Italy, the Germans captured many *semoventi*, that they valued to the point of making Ansaldo continue the production for the *Wehrmacht*, obtaining some 50 more pieces until 1945. Vehicles in German use were designated

The 75/18 self-propelled gun as it appeared upon its arrival at Aberdeen Proving Ground, Maryland, in December 1946. (USA Ord A43791)

Sturmgeschutz M40 850 (i) or *Sturmgeschutz M42 850 (i)*. A dozen pieces reached, via the Germans, the armed forces of the RSI; *semoventi da 75/18* equipped in particular the *Gruppo Squadroni corazzati S. Giusto*, the *Raggruppamento Anti Partigiani* (anti-guerrilla battalion) and the *Raggruppamento Cacciatori degli Appenini*.

During the post-war period, the Italians salvaged an unspecified number of 75/18 vehicles and incorporated them into the newly organized army for a brief period of time.

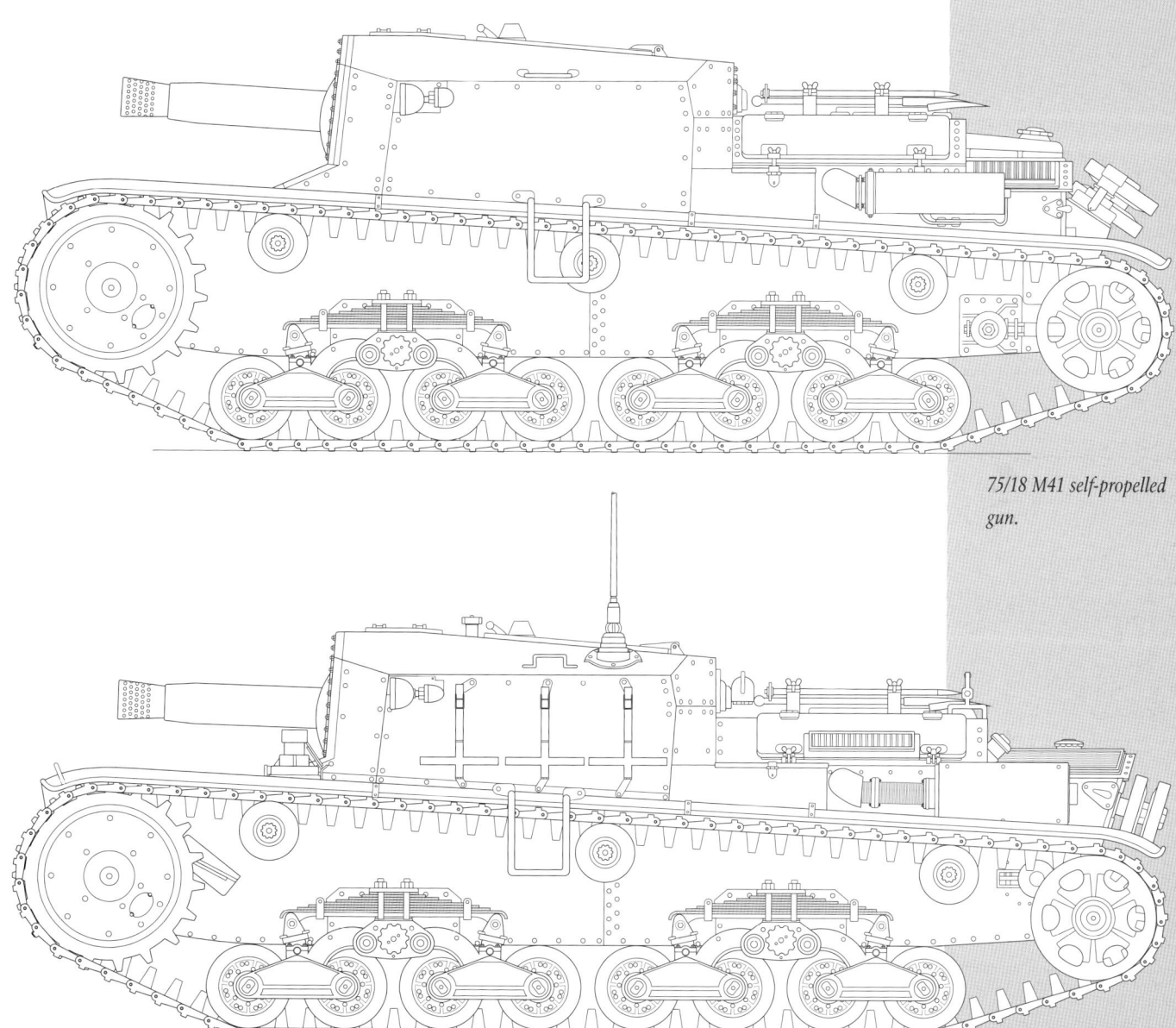

75/18 M41 self-propelled gun.

75/18 M42 self-propelled gun.

Specifications:

Manufacturer:	FIAT/Ansaldo-Fossati
Year adopted:	1941 (on M.13 and M.14 chassis; 1942 on M.15 chassis)
Number produced:	467 (60 on M.13, 162 on M.14, 245 on M.15). Of these, 53 were produced for the Germans on the M.15 chassis after 8 September 1943.
Crew:	3 (commander/gunner, loader, driver)
Weight:	13,100 kg (28,880 lb) (M.13 and M.14); 15,000 kg (33,069 lb) (M42)
Main gun:	Ansaldo Mod. 35 75/18 gun/howitzer (modified)
Elevation:	-12° to +22°
Traverse:	40°
Ammunition capacity:	44-50

Secondary armament:	One 8mm machine-gun with 1,104 rounds
Engine:	SPA 15 TM 41, V-8 Diesel, 11,980cc (M.13 and M.14); SPA 15 TB M42, V-8 gasoline, 11,980cc (M.15)
Horsepower:	145 (M.13 and M.14); 190 (M.15)
Power-to-weight ratio:	11.1 hp/ton (M.13 and M.14); 12.7 hp/ton (M.15)
Fuel capacity:	182 litres(48.08 US gallons; 40 Imperial gallons) (M.13 and M.14); 338 litres (89.29 US gallons; 74.35 Imperial gallons) (M.15)
Maximum speed (road):	35 km/h (22 mph) (M.13 and M.14); 38.4 km/h (24 mph) (M.15)
Maximum speed (cross-country):	15 km/h (9 mph)
Operating radius (road):	210 km (130 miles) (M.13 and M.14); 150 km (93 miles) (M.15)
Armour (hull):	50mm frontal; 25mm sides and rear; 9-15mm top; 6mm floor
Length:	4.915m (16'1") (M.13 and M.14); 5.043m (16'6") (M.15)
Width:	2.20m (7'2") (M.13 and M.14); 2.23m (7'4") (M.15)
Height:	1.85m (6')
Track width:	260mm (10")
Ground clearance:	380mm (1'3") (M.13 and M.14); 410mm (1'4")
Trench crossing:	2.10m (6'10")
Vertical obstacle:	800mm (2'7")
Fording depth:	1.00m (3'3")
Ground pressure:	0.96 kg/cm^2 (13.65 psi)
Radio:	Marelli RF1 CA
Dates of service:	1941-1945
Where employed:	Egypt, Libya, Tunisia, Greece, Sardinia, Sicily, Italy

75/34 M 42 self-propelled gun

The *semovente M 42 da 75/34* (also referred to as the M 42M) was designed as a tank destroyer to be used in conjunction with the P.40 tank, and was to use the P.40 chassis as well as its 75/34 gun in order to equip Italian armoured divisions with a more effective anti-tank system. However, due to delays in production of the P.40, the vehicle utilized the M 15/42 chassis, in effect making it a development of the 75/18 self-propelled gun (see separate entry above). The prototype of the M 42 was tested on 15 March 1943, and immediately afterward the *Regio Esercito* placed a rush order for 500 pieces. However, only a small number of the *semoventi*, about 60, were able to be delivered before the surrender of Italy, and even fewer reached front line units.

A 75/34 self-propelled gun photographed at the Fossati plant at Sestri Ponenete. (Fondazione Ansaldo)

A 75/34 self-propelled gun captured by partisan forces in Torino in April 1945 (Istituto Piemontese per la Storia della Resistenza Torino)

A 75/34 self-propelled gun in insurgent hands in April 1945 (Istituto Piemontese per la Storia della Resistenza Torino)

These *semoventi* came out of the production lines too late to take part in any action against the Allies, and only a few units were able to receive them before the surrender of Italy. The first unit equipped with 75/34 self-propelled guns was the *XIX Battaglione carri*, that had two companies assigned. Later, two more companies formed the *XXX Battaglione controcarri*, deployed in Sardinia with the *Sabauda* Division. The *Ariete II* Armoured Division had the *CXXXV Battaglione controcarri semoventi*, with three companies, which did not see action. A few other pieces of this type went

75/34 M42 self-propelled gun.

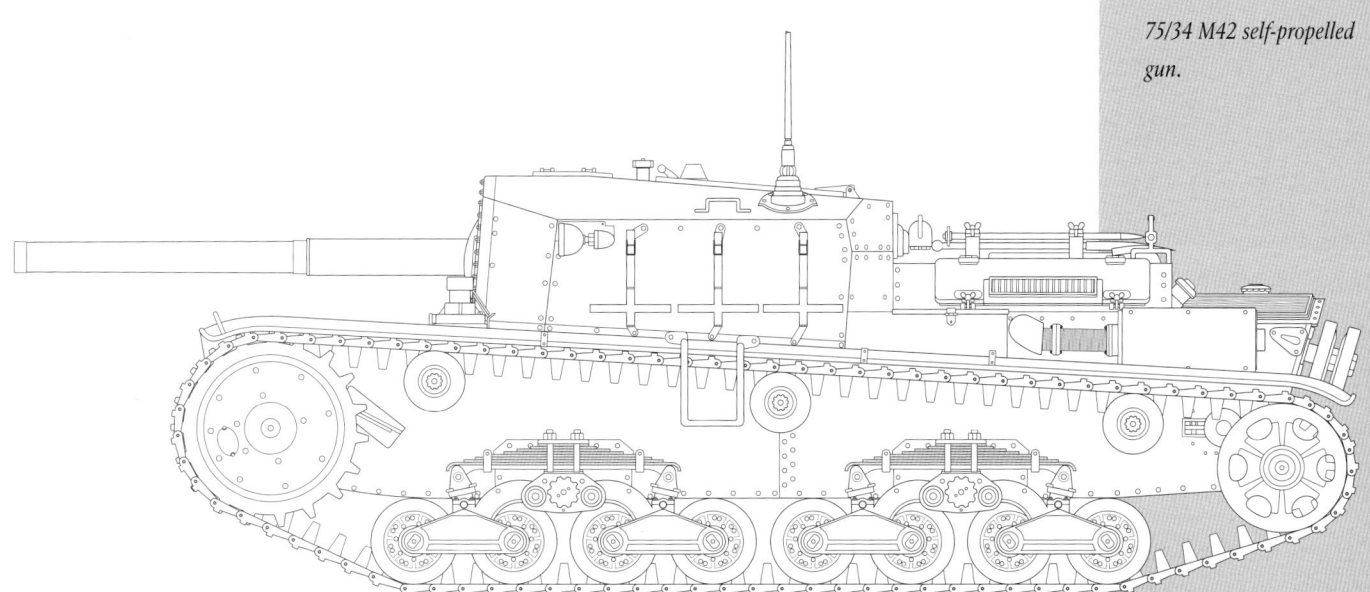

to the *31° Reggimento carristi*, based in Siena, and to the *32° Reggimento carristi*, based in Verona, as well as to the *Cavalleggeri di Alessandria* Cavalry Regiment, based in the Balkans.

After the surrender of Italy, the Germans captured 36 *semoventi M42* and, furthermore, had Ansaldo continue their production. Until 1945 the Italian factory delivered 80 guns on the M42 chassis, while 29 more were produced on the new M43 chassis, which was slightly larger. The M42 and M43 versions were designated by the Germans, respectively, *StuG M42 mit 75/34 (850) (i)* and *StuG M43 mit 75/34 (851) (i)*. One piece was assigned to the *Gruppo squadroni corazzati S. Giusto* of the RSI.

Specifications:

Manufacturer:	FIAT/Ansaldo-Fossati
Year adopted:	1943
Number produced:	169 (109 of which were produced for the Germans after 8 September 1943)
Crew:	3 (commander/gunner, loader, driver)
Weight:	15,000 kg (33,069 lb)
Main gun:	Ansaldo 75/34 gun
Elevation:	-12° to +22°
Traverse:	40°
Ammunition capacity:	46 rounds
Secondary armament:	One 8mm Breda Model 38 machine-gun for anti-aircraft defence with 1,104 rounds
Engine:	SPA 15 TB M42, V-8, gasoline, 11,980 cc
Horsepower:	192
Power-to-weight ratio:	12.4 hp/ton
Fuel capacity:	327 litres (86 US gallons; 71.93 Imperial gallons)
Maximum speed (road):	40 km/h (25 mph)
Maximum speed (cross country):	15 km/h (9.3 mph)
Operating radius:	200 km (124 miles)
Operating radius (cross-country):	6 hours
Armour:	30mm frontal; 25mm sides; 14.5mm top and floor
Length:	5.06m (16'7")
Width:	2.25m (7'4")
Height:	1.85m (7')
Ground clearance:	380mm (1'3")
Trench crossing:	2.10m (6'10")
Vertical obstacle:	900mm (3')
Fording depth:	1.00m (3'3")
Dates of service:	1943-1945
Where employed:	Italy

90/53 M 41M self-propelled gun

The M 41M self-propelled gun was a very effective, impressive piece of equipment, consisting of the Model 39/41 90/53 dual-purpose gun mounted on a modified M 14/41 tank chassis. The use of the 90mm anti-aircraft gun as an anti-tank weapon was not new, it had already served well enough in that role in North Africa as an *autocannone* (see separate entry above). What was new was to mount it on an armoured self-propelled chassis that seemed particularly suited for the Eastern Front, where the unfavourable terrain conditions and the few roads impaired the use of wheeled trucks. Although the system was designed specifically as an anti-tank weapon to counter the Soviet T-34 tank, none of the vehicles were in fact ever sent to the Eastern Front. Even though a formal order to develop a tracked 90mm system was not issued by the *Regio Esercito* until late December 1941, the Ansaldo firm, which produced both the gun and the armoured hull for the system, already had built a wooden mockup a month earlier, in November. On 5 March 1942 the prototype underwent firing trials, no mean feat considering the extensive modifications that had to be made to both the chassis and the hull (based on those of the M.14 medium tank) and to the gun itself. Chassis and hull modifications included lengthening the hull by about seven inches, repositioning the engine from the rear to the front of the vehicle, altering the suspension system to achieve better weight distribution, and reworking the oil and water circulation systems. The engine was the same as that of the tank upon which the M41 M was based, but as the *semovente* was heavier, it made the vehicle very slow. Major changes were also made to the gun cradle, the gun mount, the traverse and elevation mechanisms, and sights of the 90/53 gun. The gun was simply mounted on this modified chassis, without a superstructure, but with a basic shield to protect the gunners. The gunners themselves did not travel on the self-propelled gun, the actual vehicle crew consisting of only the driver and the commander, while the gunners rode in a separate vehicle. On the *semovente* itself there was room for only 8 rounds, while concurrent with the development of the M 41M, an accompanying tracked armoured ammunition carrier was developed by modifying the L.6 tank. The carrier had a 26-round capacity and also towed a two-wheeled caisson that had a 40-round capacity. The self-propelled gun was not equipped with a secondary weapon for close defence, probably because it was considered that it would have fired from a convenient distance from the front line. The system was capable only of direct fire, and could not be used in an anti-aircraft role.

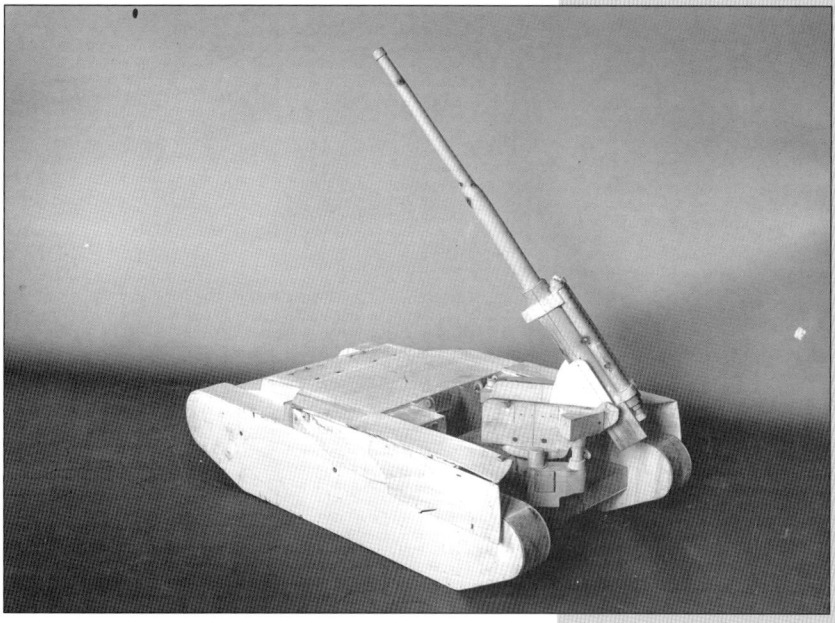

Wooden scale model of the 90/53 self-propelled gun. (Fondazione Ansaldo)

Reflecting a noteworthy effort by Italy's exhausted industry, in April Ansaldo delivered the 30 SP ordered by the *Regio Esercito*. With them, the *Regio Esercito* formed the *10° Reggimento artiglieria controcarro* (10th Anti-tank Artillery Regiment), also at times referred to as the *X Raggruppamento Semoventi*, consisting of three battalions, i.e. *CLXI, CLXII* and *CLXIII*, with 8 guns each. The six remaining pieces were left at Nettuno, near Rome, as a reserve. Because of the

Frontal view of a 90/53 self-propelled gun photographed at Genoa in 1942. (Fondazione Ansaldo)

Rear view of a 90/53 self-propelled gun taken at Ansaldo's Cornigliano works in 1942. (Fondazione Ansaldo)

A 90/53 self-propelled gun captured by US forces in Sicily in September 1943. (U.S. Army SC 328126)

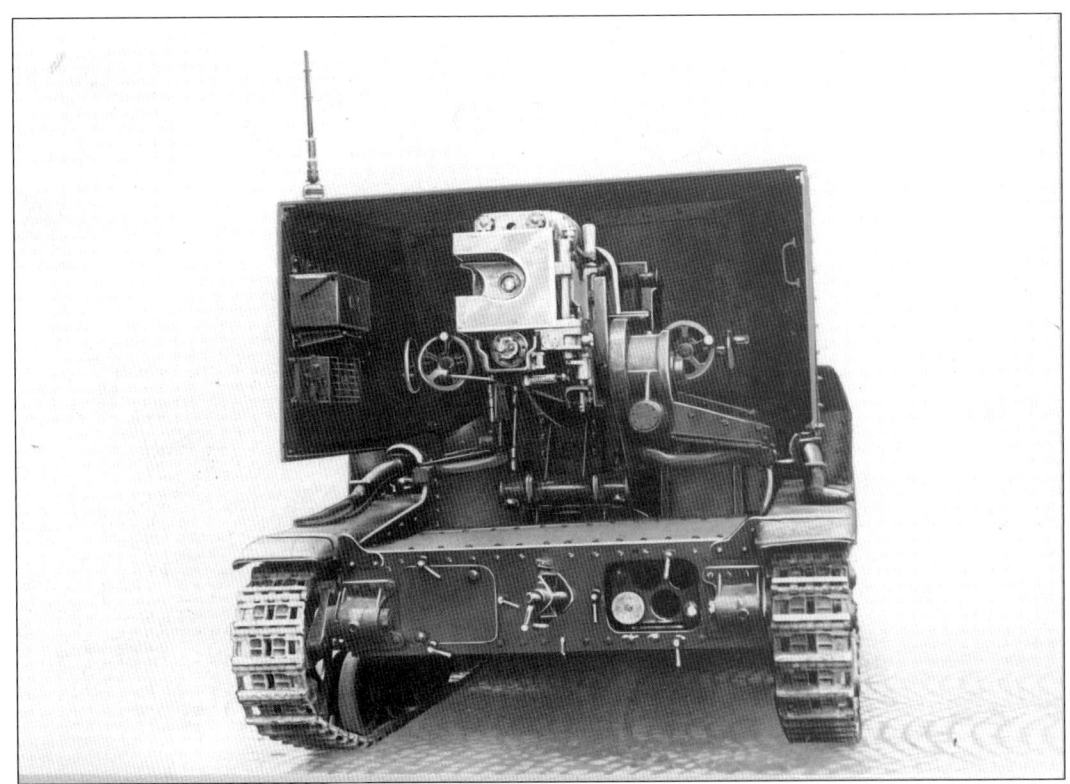

problems of reliability with the engine and of the very low speed, the army decided that the pieces were not really suited for the Eastern Front, and instead in December 1942 they were sent to Sicily, with the intention of transferring them to Tunisia, recently occupied by Axis troops. In fact, they remained on the island, deployed near Canicattì, where they remained until the Allied landings of July 1943. The first battalion to see action was the *CLXI Gruppo*, that was sent on 10 July to reinforce the 207th Coastal Division, which was fighting against the forces that had landed, managing

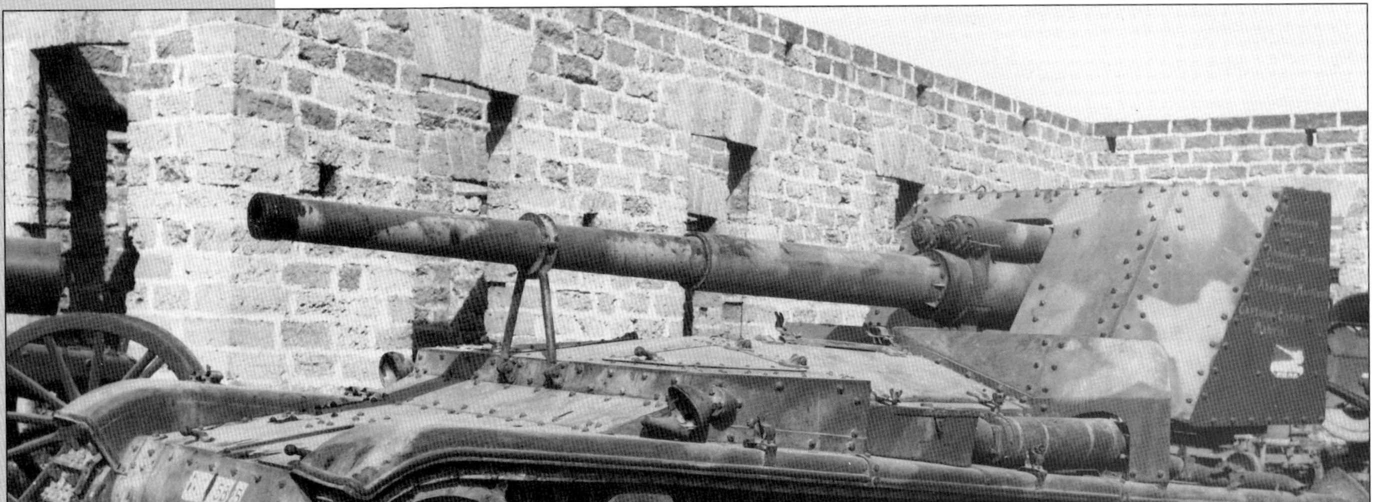

The captured 90/53 self-propelled gun at Aberdeen Proving Ground, Maryland, in December 1946. (USA Ord A43788)

to stabilize a defensive line at Campobello di Licata. The following day, the three battalions were reunited and assigned to the tactical group commanded by the Italian General Ottorino Schreiber, that fought for the next eight days while retreating to the interior of the island. Attesting to their effectiveness, in the words of one officer who served with the *X Raggruppamento*, "*Once a tank was in our sights, it was dead*"[1]. On 19 July only four *semoventi* remained and were reassigned to the *Aosta* Division. Two of M 41M guns were lost in the following days, while the last two reached Messina, where they were abandoned when Sicily was finally evacuated. The six remaining self-propelled guns were captured by the Germans after the surrender of Italy, and renamed *Gepanzerte Selbfahrleffte 90/53 (i) 801*, but there is no record of their use in combat by the Germans. The sole surviving example, captured in Sicily, was brought to the United States where it was displayed at Aberdeen Proving Ground, Maryland until 2010 when it was transferred to the Army Artillery Museum at Fort Sill, Oklahoma.

1   Co-author interview with Vittorio de Castiglioni, Colonel, Italian Army, in 1971.

The nicely restored 90/53 self-propelled, which is now part of the collection of the US Army Artillery Museum, Fort Sill, Oklahoma. (U.S. Army Artillery Museum)

This view of the restored 90/53 self-propelled shows the correct white silhouette which was associated with the vehicle's unit. (U.S. Army Artillery Museum)

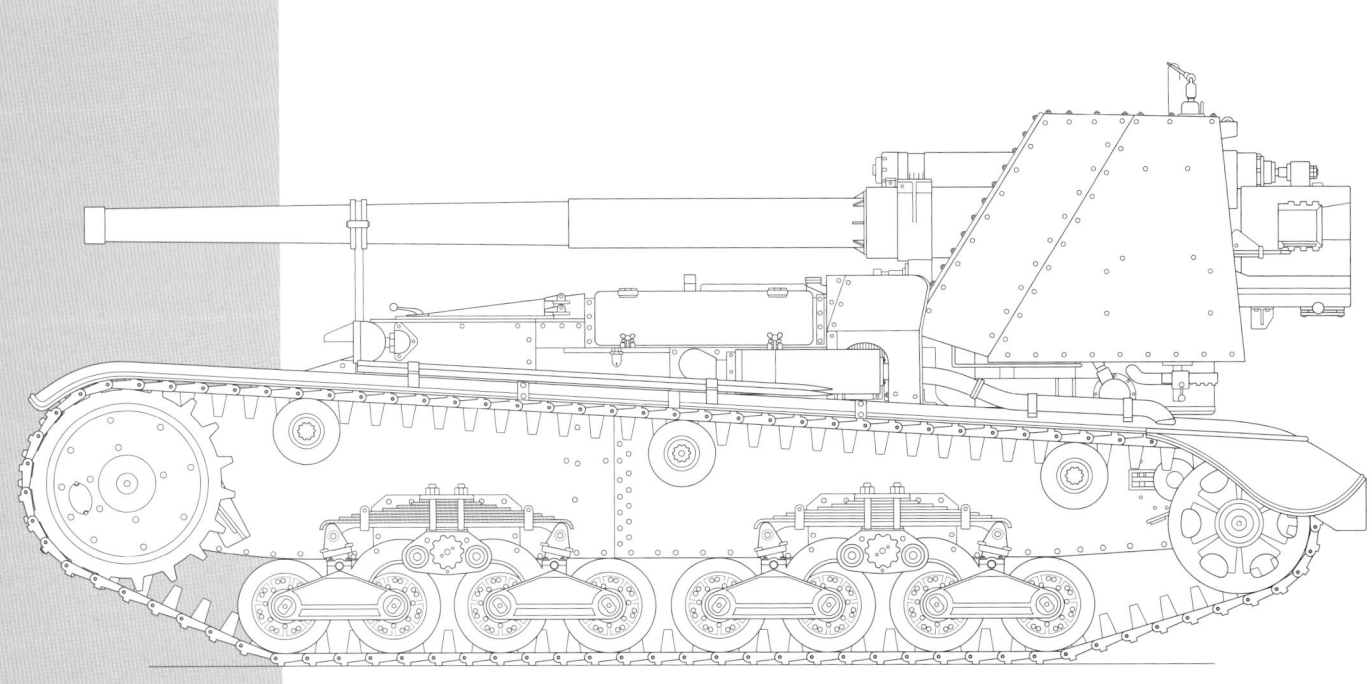

90/53 M41M self-propel-led gun.

Specifications:

Manufacturer:	SPA/FIAT-Ansaldo
Year adopted:	1942
Number produced:	30 (some sources quote 48, but evidence does not support this)
Crew:	4 (commander/gunner, loader, radioman, driver)
Weight:	15,700 kg (34,613 lb)
Main gun:	Ansaldo Model 39/41 dual-purpose gun (90/53)
Elevation:	-5° to + 19°
Traverse:	90°
Ammunition capacity:	8 rounds stowed on board, 26 carried by accompanying ammunition carrier, and 40 carried in a caisson towed by the carrier, for a total of 74 rounds.
Secondary armament:	None
Engine:	SPA15 TM41, V-8 Diesel, 11,980cc
Horsepower:	145
Power/weight ratio:	9.2 hp/ton
Fuel capacity:	182 litres (48.08 US gallons; 40 Imperial gallons)
Maximum speed (road):	25 km/h (15.5 mph)
Maximum speed (cross country):	15 km/h (9.3 mph)
Operating radius (road):	200 km (124 miles)
Armour (gun shield):	40mm frontal; 10mm sides
Armour (hull):	30mm frontal; 10mm sides; 25mm rear; 6mm floor
Length:	5.08m (16"8")
Width:	2.28m (7'5")
Height:	2.30m (7'6")
Track width:	260 mm (10")
Ground pressure:	0.98 kg/cm² (13.95 psi)
Ground clearance:	410mm (1'4")
Trench crossing:	2.10m (6'11")
Vertical obstacle:	800 mm (2'8")
Fording depth:	1.00m (3'3")
Radio:	Marelli RF 1 CA
Dates of service:	Late April 1942 to August 1943
Where employed:	Sicily, June-August 1943

105/25 M 42L self-propelled gun

This self-propelled artillery piece had its origin in plans developed by the *Regio Esercito* in 1942 to mount a 105mm howitzer in the turret of the P.40 medium tank which was being developed during that period. Accordingly, it asked Ansaldo to design a new howitzer, the 105/25. The M 42L, like the M 42M, was planned to be built on the P.40 chassis, but since development of the new tank progressed very slowly, it was instead built upon a slightly enlarged M 15/42 chassis (the L, *larga*, or wide variant, sometimes referred to as the M.43 chassis as it was built and approved for service in 1943). The tests were carried out in February 1943 followed by immediate adoption by the Army.

A 105/25 self-propelled gun in the yard of the Fossati works at Sestri Ponente. (Fondazione Ansaldo)

A batch of 105/25 self-propelled guns ready for delivery to the Regio Esercito, lined up in a shed at Fossati's Sestri Ponente works. (Fondazione Ansaldo)

A 75/18 self-propelled gun alongside a 105/25 self--propelled gun. Notice the slightly wider and lower hull of the latter vehicle, giving rise to the nickname of "The Dachshund" by which the vehicle was popularly known. (Fondazione Ansaldo)

The prototype of the 105/25 self-propelled system, in a factory photograph. (FIAT)

A factory-fresh 105/25 self-propelled gun, prior to application of the camouflage paint scheme. (FIAT)

The 105/25 self-propelled gun represented the heaviest armoured vehicle used operationally by the Italians during the 1940-1943 period, with respect to both its armament and its armour, and is unanimously considered to be the best armoured vehicle produced in Italy during the war. The new M43 chassis differed from the original M42 by being 190mm (about 7.5 inches) wider to enable the rather large gun to be mounted and, more importantly, was 110mm (4.33 inches) lower, a feature that gave it a very low silhouette, which along with its thicker armour was greatly appreciated by the crew, which consisted of three men. Its width and low silhouette earned it the name of *il bassotto* ("the Dachshund") from Italian armoured artillerymen. It is worthwhile to note that as a departure from the bolted plate construction that had been used on all Italian armoured vehicles since the L 3/33, the major portion of the superstructure of the M 42L was welded (the front still utilized bolted construction). The engine was basically that of the M15/42 tank, with minor modifications. It also carried a Breda model 38 machine gun as secondary armament for close-in defence.

Between March and July 1943, orders totaling 464 M 42Ls were placed, but records indicate that only 30 were produced before the Armistice; other records indicate that a total of 105 were produced in 1943 and a further 55 in 1944. German sources reflect production of the M 42L under their control in late 1943 and throughout 1944 to total 87 units, while according to Ansaldo this number was 91. It thus appears that between 117 and 160 M 42Ls were produced, but the most reliable number appears to be 121 (30 prior to the armistice, and 91 following the armistice).

The first *semoventi M 42L da 105/25* came out of the factory in late spring 1943 and were first assigned to units in June. The first unit to receive the *bassotto* was the newly formed *DCI Gruppo*, with twelve self-propelled guns, assigned to the *Ariete II* Armoured Cavalry Division. Another battalion, the *DCII Gruppo* was still under formation at the time Italy surrendered in September. Ironically, the *bassotto* engaged in its first action against the Germans, during the fighting around Rome, just after the armistice. The Germans captured 26 intact *semoventi*, that they renamed *StuG M43 mit 105/25 853(i)*. Only one *bassotto* was assigned to a unit of the RSI armed forces, namely to the *Gruppo Squadroni Corazzato Leoncello*. Two were recaptured in 1945 by Italian co-belligerent forces of the *Corpo Italiano di Liberazione* fighting alongside the Allies against the Germans. In the post-war period some of the 105/25 guns were modified to fire US 105mm howitzer ammunition and were used as part of the fixed defensive fortifications along the Italian border.

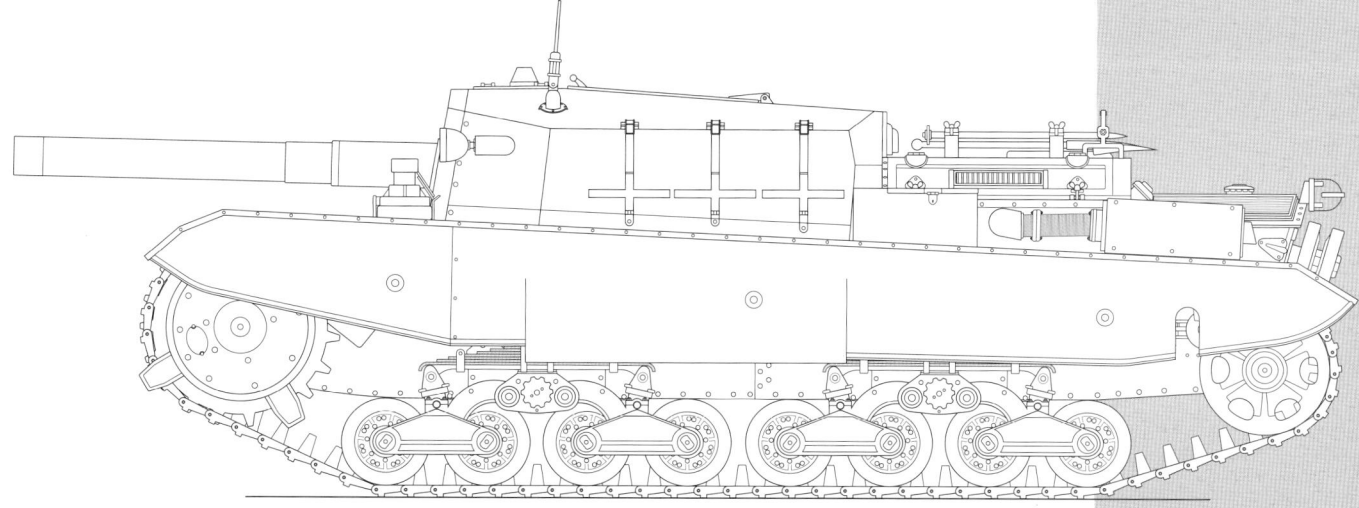

105/25 M42L self-propelled gun.

Specifications:

Manufacturer:	FIAT/Ansaldo-Fossati
Year adopted:	1943
Number produced:	121 (precise total uncertain; see text above)
Crew:	3 (driver, gunner, loader/radio operator)
Weight:	15,700 kg (34,612 lb)
Main gun:	Ansaldo 105/25 gun
Elevation:	-10° to +18°
Traverse:	18° to either side
Ammunition capacity:	48 rounds
Secondary armament:	One 8mm Breda Model 38 machine-gun with 864 rounds
Engine:	SPA 15 TB, V-8 gasoline, 11,980cc

Horsepower:	192
Power-to-weight ratio:	12.2 hp/ton
Fuel capacity:	316 litres (83.5 US gallons; 69.51 Imperial gallons)
Maximum speed (road):	38.4 km/h (23.8 mph)
Operating radius (road):	170 km (106 miles)
Operating radius (cross-country):	10 hours
Armour:	50-70mm frontal; 45mm upper sides; 25mm lower sides and rear; 15mm deck and floor
Length:	5.07m (16'8")
Width:	2.40m (7'11")
Height:	1.74m (5'8")
Track width:	260mm (10.2")
Ground clearance:	350mm (1'2")
Trench crossing:	2.10m (6'10")
Vertical obstacle:	800mm (2'7")
Fording depth:	1.00m (3'3")
Ground pressure:	0.98 kg/cm^2 (13.94 psi)
Radio:	Marelli RF1 CA
Dates of service:	1943-1945
Where employed:	Italy

75/46 M 42T self-propelled gun

Subsequent to the armistice in September 1943, control of the Ansaldo works was assumed by the Germans, who ordered production of a modified version of the *semovente* M 42L (see separate entry above). A modified Ansaldo 75/46 anti-aircraft gun, which was quite effective as an anti-tank weapon, replaced the 105/25 gun and German-pattern spaced armour side skirts were added to the sides. This self-propelled gun, that could also be classified as a tank destroyer, was produced beginning in 1944, under German control, by Ansaldo for the German army and was called *StuG M43 mit 75/46 852(i)* by the Germans and *semovente* M 42T *da 75/46*, the T signifying

A 75/46 self-propelled gun as used by the German Army. (FIAT)

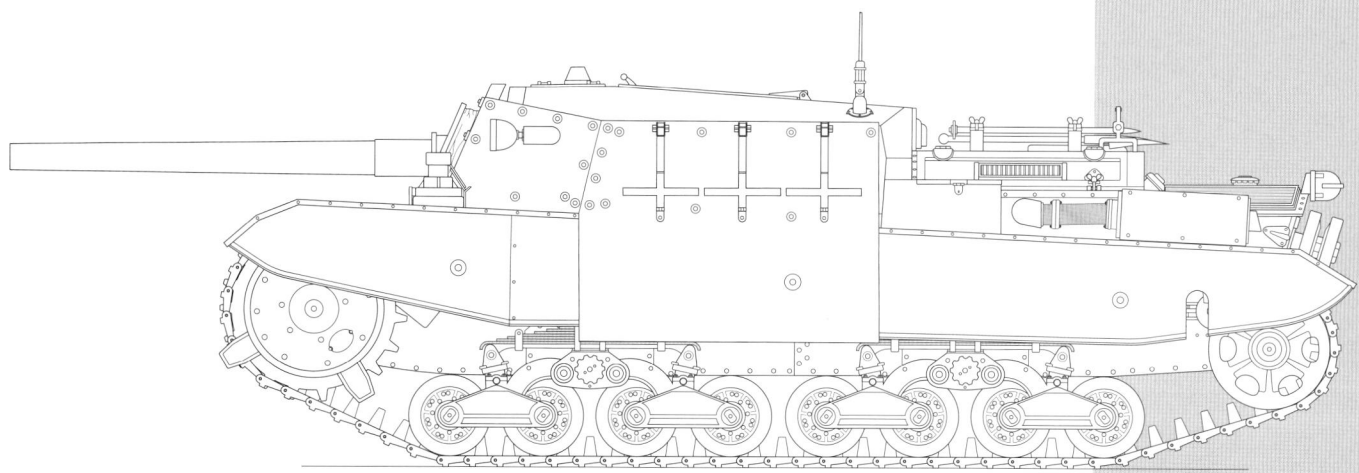

75/46 M42T self-propelled gun.

tedesco (German), in Italian. Production of this vehicle reached a total of 11 pieces, all of which were used exclusively by German forces in Italy.

Except as noted below, characteristics and specifications are identical to those of the *semovente* M 42L *da* 105/25.

Specifications:

Manufacturer:	FIAT/Ansaldo-Fossati
Year adopted:	1944 (ordered by German authorities)
Number produced:	11
Weight:	16,000 kg (35,274 lb)
Power-to-weight ratio:	12 hp/ton
Main gun:	Ansaldo Mod. 34 75/46 anti-aircraft gun (modified)
Dates of service:	1944-1945
Where employed:	Italy

149/40 self-propelled gun

The 149mm self-propelled gun was a large vehicle by Italian standards, weighing some 24 tons (52,910 lb). The proposal to the *Regio Esercito* for this powerful self-propelled gun was a private initiative by the Ansaldo firm which had started to develop this design in winter 1941 with a view to mounting the 149/40 gun (see separate entry above) on a special Ansaldo chassis that used a strengthened P.40 tank suspension system. The prototype was ready during the course of 1943 and in August of that year some tests were carried out on it.

Only one vehicle of this type was built in August 1943, although 20 were to have been ready by the end of the year. Series production was not undertaken, however, due to the September armistice between Italy and the Allies.

The vehicle was quite similar in concept and layout to the US 155mm M12 GMC (Gun Motor Carriage), which was built on the M3 *Lee* tank chassis and mounted a World War I vintage 155mm gun. The stability of the weapon was enhanced by two spades that had to be hammered in the ground preparatory to firing. The system did not mount any kind of protection for the gunners, who were completely exposed, nor did it carry secondary weapons for close-in defence, as because of the considerable range of

Wooden model of the 149/40 self-propelled gun. (Fondazione Ansaldo)

The prototype of the 149/40 gun with camouflage livery. (Fondazione Ansaldo)

Prototype of the 149/40 self-propelled gun during trials held in Genoa in 1943. (Fondazione Ansaldo)

The 149/40 self-propelled at Aberdeen Proving Ground, December 1946. The German markings are spurious. (USA Ord A43806)

The sole example of the 149/40 self-propelled now rests at Fort Sill, Oklahoma. Unfortunately, the tracks are missing, having been removed and lost at Aberdeen Proving Ground sometime in the 1970s. (U.S. Army Artillery Museum)

The massive size of the 149/40 self-propelled gun is evident in this view. (U.S. Army Artillery Museum)

the gun it was to be deployed far to the rear of the front lines. The Italian self-propelled gun was to have replaced the towed Model 1935 149/40 guns in divisional artillery units. It would have had the advantage of overcoming the chronic shortage of heavy artillery tractors; furthermore, it was considerably lighter than the two loads and associated Breda tractors necessary for the towed version of the gun and it could be put into battery almost immediately.

The one prototype system that was produced was confiscated by the Germans and was designated as the *gepanzerte Selbstfahrlafette M 43 854 (i)*. There is some doubt as to just when and where the system was captured by the Allies. Records at the US Army Ordnance Museum in Aberdeen, Maryland indicated that the system was captured near Rome and shipped to Aberdeen in 1944, but this is suspect as usually authoritative American sources at the time indicated that the Germans moved the gun to Germany where it was found by Allied forces in 1945 at Hillersleben and subsequently shipped to the US where it remained on display at Aberdeen Proving Ground, Maryland until 2010, when it was moved to the Artillery Museum at Fort Sill, in Oklahoma.

Specifications:

Manufacturer:	Ansaldo-Fossati
Prototype:	1943
Number produced:	1 (prototype)
Crew:	2 (gun crew rode in separate vehicle)
Weight:	24,000 kg (52,910 lb) approximate
Main gun:	149/40 gun (based on Mod. 35 towed gun)
Elevation:	45°
Traverse:	53°
Ammunition capacity:	6 rounds carried on board
Secondary armament:	None
Engine:	SPA 228 gasoline
Horsepower:	250
Maximum speed (road):	35 km/h (22 mph)
Armour:	25mm frontal; 14mm sides; 6mm top deck
Length:	6.63m (21'9")
Width:	3.05m (9'10")
Height:	2.03m (6'8")
Track width:	400mm (1'4")
Ground clearance:	400mm (1'4")
Where employed:	There is no record of this gun having been operationally employed.

149/40 self-propelled gun.

ARTILLERY TRACTORS

Pavesi mod. 26, mod. 30 and mod. 30A heavy field artillery tractor

The Pavesi series of heavy artillery tractors were unique and somewhat ungainly looking machines developed by Ugo Pavesi, based on an agricultural tractor, the P4, which was developed immediately after WWI. Therefore, when in 1923 the Italian Army put forward a request for a tractor for its army corps artillery, the *Motomeccanica Pavesi* firm was the only factory able to submit a prototype. The tests carried out in the same year were considered highly satisfactory and a pre-series of 45 tractors was ordered in 1924, delivered in 1925, and accordingly designated as the mod. 25. Following the pre-series production run, several modifications were made to the tractor resulting in the Pavesi mod. 26 which was series produced over a period of four years. In the meantime, production of the tractors had been undertaken by FIAT in lieu of Pavesi itself. In 1930 a model incorporating further modifications, including the ability to disengage power to the rear wheels , designated the Pavesi mod. 30, was introduced. A total of 1000 mod. 26 and mod. 30 tractors was produced, and in 1934 a third model incorporating further improvements was introduced as the Pavesi mod. 30A. By 1937 a total of 2,300 were on hand, with a further 270 on order.

The tractor was instantly recognizable due to its articulated layout and its very large diameter wire spoke wheels that provided very high ground clearance. All four wheels, independently sprung, were powered. The tractor consisted of two separate frames that were articulated, allowing

A very nicely restored Pavesi mod. 30 tractor; this machine was restored in 2009. (Fabio Temeroli)

A 149/35 being towed by
a Pavesi tractor during
the final phase of the
Greek campaign; note
the grousers extended on
the wheels of the tractor.
(Antonio and Andrea
Tallillo)

a very tight turning radius for a machine of its size; essentially, when the front half of the tractor (the front frame) was steered in a given direction, the rear half (the rear frame) followed, much as a trailer follows. The front frame held the engine (which in the mod. 26 could use different kinds of fuel ranging from gasoline to diesel, while the mod. 30 used gasoline only), the driving compartment, fuel tanks, and front frame transmission elements, while the rear frame hosted the transmission elements for the rear frame and a platform for the gun crew. The body was stamped steel; the forward body had seats for the driver on the right and a mechanic on the left and had a waterproof canvas cover that could be erected on bows that could be folded or completely removed. The rear body had six seats that could be folded to allow a 1,000 kg cargo load to be carried; a number of storage boxes were also incorporated, and the rear body had a separate canvas cover that could

A group of 105/28 guns in a parade, being towed by Pavesi tractors.
(Antonio and Andrea Tallillo)

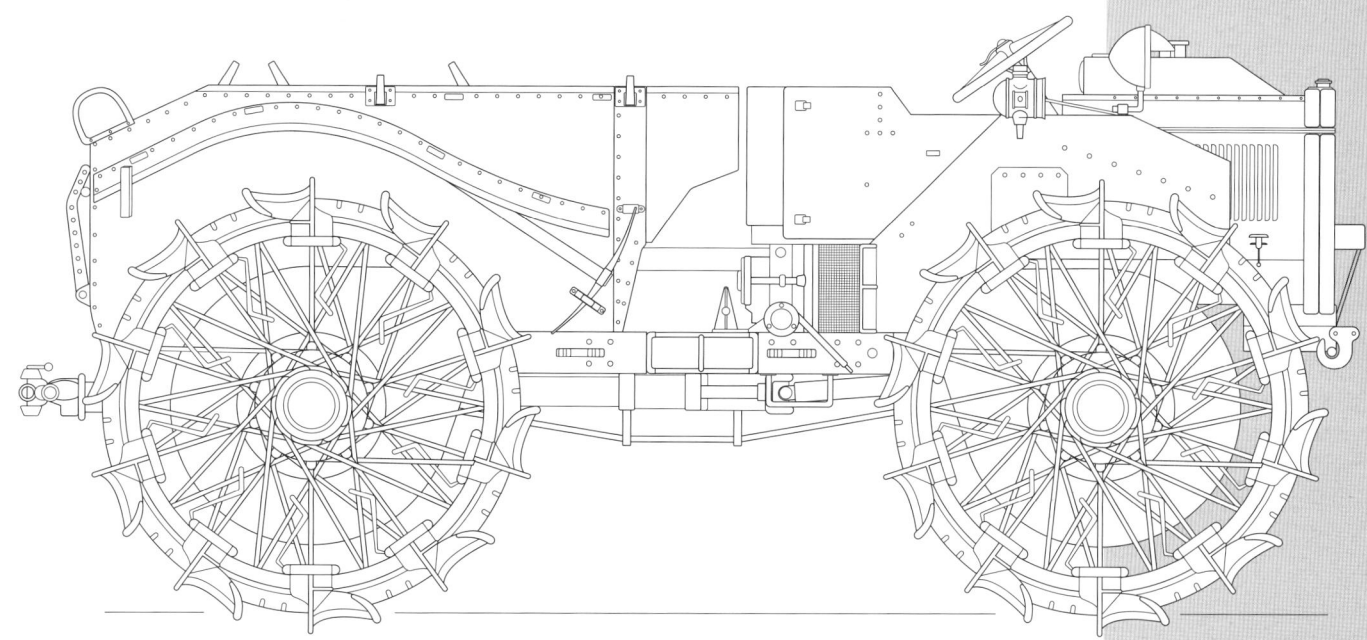

Pavesi mod. 30 heavy field artillery tractor.

be erected as well. The wheels measured 1.30m (51 inches) in diameter and were quite wide at 250mm (9.8 inches). The wheels were fitted with semi-pneumatic *Celerflex* tires and also had ten grousers on the outer side of the rims that normally folded inward towards the wheel hub, but that could be folded outward and kept open by spring clips, providing extra ground contact and traction. During the latter half of the 1930s the Pavesis began to be fitted with pneumatic tires, and following experience gained in Libya in 1938, the Pirelli *Sigillo Verde* type tire, mounted on eight-spoke cast steel wheels, was adopted for the Pavesis. A very interesting feature of all versions of the Pavesi was the ability to join 2 or more tractors to add power and tow very heavy loads even on narrow mountain roads.

Operationally, the Pavesi tractors first saw service in Ethiopia, followed by service with the Italian troops in the Spanish Civil War. They saw widespread use throughout the war in virtually every theater in which the Italians were committed. Although originally designed to tow heavy field artillery, their use was later extended to towing the lighter 100/17 howitzer and the 75/46 anti-aircraft gun. Despite their rather archaic appearance, slow speed, and high fuel consumption, the Pavesi tractors were very sturdy and capable and served not only with the *Regio Esercito* for the duration of the war, but were also used by the Germans, who redesignated it the *Radschlepper Pavesi Typ P 4-100 (I)*, until their surrender in 1945.

Many other countries had also tested and adopted the Pavesi artillery tractors. Between 1930 and 1938 a total of about 100 tractors were delivered to Bulgaria – undisclosed numbers of the mod. 26 in 1930, mod. 30 in 1935, and 50 mod 30A in 1938; Greece bought a substantial number[1] that were later used against Italy. Other countries that used the Pavesi were Finland and Spain; in addition, the Pavesi was produced under license in the UK (Armstrong Siddeley), Sweden (*Artilleritraktor m/28 typ Pavesi*) and Hungary (Weiss-Manfred Pavesi P4/100).

Specifications:

Designation:	trattore Pavesi mod. 26 and mod. 30
Manufacturer:	FIAT
Weight (unloaded)	4,680 kg (10,318 lb) mod 26; 4,780 kg (10,538 lb) mod 30
Carrying capacity:	1,000 kg (2205 lb) mod 26
Towing capacity:	12,000 kg (26,455 lb) on road; 3,500 kg (7,.716 lb) off road
Length:	4.10m(1561.4 inches) mod 26; 4.115m (162 inches) mod 30
Width:	2.05m (80.7 inches)

1   Greece bought an initial lot of 130 tractors, followed by a further order, possibly for another 94 machines, but the status of delivery of the second order is not certain.

Height:	2.40m (94.5 inches) with canvas top erected
Engine:	P 4-100 4 cylinder 4,720 cc (288 cu. in.)
Horsepower:	52 @ 1,500 rpm mod26; 57 @ 1,800 rpm mod 30
Transmission:	manual 4 speed, 1 reverse; differential lock
Fuel capacity:	105 litres (27.74 US gallons; 23.09 Imperial gallons) mod 26; 100 litres (26.42 US gallons; 22 Imperial gallons) mod. 30
Wheelbase:	2.42m (95.3 inches)
Track:	1.565m ((61.6 inches)
Turning radius:	4.75m (187 inches)
Tire size:	150x1160 *Celerflex* or 11.25x30 tires (mod. 30)
Maximum speed (road):	22 km/h (13.8 mph)
Maximum range:	180 km (112 miles)
Maximum gradient:	75%
Ground clearance:	490mm (19.3 inches)
Fording depth:	800 mm (31.5 inches)
Special notes:	3,800 kg (8,378 lb) capacity winch; capacity could be increased to 5,000 kg (11,023 lb) by use of a pulley

Breda mod. 32, mod. 33 and mod. 40/41 heavy tractor

The Breda mod. 32 heavy tractor was the first of a series of Breda heavy artillery tractors used by the *Regio Esercito*. The Breda firm manufactured a wide range of machinery ranging from locomotives and railroad cars to heavy trucks, as well as being involved in the manufacture of artillery. The Breda 32 itself was based on the earlier 1927 *autocarro trattore Breda* 4 x 4, was adopted in 1932 and began being issued to units in 1933. The Breda 32 replaced a number of older prime movers such as the FIAT *tipo 20* and Pavesi-Tolotti *tipo B* tractors and trucks such as the FIAT 18 BLR to tow army-level heavy artillery. It was quite a powerful machine, with a gasoline engine and six wheels, two in front and a dual tire arrangement in the rear, that performed well off-road and over broken terrain as well as on paved roads. The frame was stamped steel, with a metal cab and half doors.

A classic factory photograph of a Breda 32 heavy artillery tractor. (Claudio Pergher Archive)

Factory testing of the frame and front suspension elements of the Breda 32 tractor. (Claudio Pergher Archive)

The Breda mod 32 was first used in Spain, to tow the Spanish Nationalist Army's heavy artillery, and by the outbreak of WWII all of the Italian heavy artillery regiments had been equipped with this tractor. The Hungarian Army also used the Breda mod. 32, mainly to tow the 210/22 howitzers that were also of Italian origin. During the post-war period some of the Breda mod. 32

A Breda 32 in camouflage livery participating in a military parade. (Claudio Pergher Archive)

This Breda 32 is towing a 149/35 gun and limber in a mountainous environment; the engine side panel is raised for increased cooling. (Claudio Pergher Archive)

A Breda 32 heavy tractor towing a 149/40 gun and limber of the XXIII Gruppo in North Africa. (Claudio Pergher Archive)

The Breda 33 for engineer use had an elongated bed. (Claudio Pergher Archive)

A Breda 40 heavy tractor; the short wheelbase is rather striking. (Claudio Pergher Archive)

A Breda 40 with chains on its tire undergoing snow mobility tests. (Claudio Pergher Archive)

A factory-new Breda 41 tractor shown at the Breda works. (Claudio Pergher Archive)

143

The Breda 41 in mottled camouflage livery, probably dark green over sand. (Claudio Pergher Archive)

The Breda 41 with its retractable boom in the extended position. (Claudio Pergher Archive)

were modernized and used by the Italian Army; others were in service with the Italian railway system well into the 1980s.

A modified version of the Breda mod 32, designated the Breda mod 33, was developed for the engineers, differing from the mod. 32 in its greater length; the dual rear tire arrangement was common to both models.

The Breda mod. 40 was a development, much modernized, of the mod. 32 for use in Italy's African colonies. Although a prototype was ready in 1940, it was not until 1942 that series production actually began, with the first examples arriving in North Africa during the summer of 1942. The prototype had an all metal body, while production models had a metal cab and a wood cargo body. With respect to the earlier Breda mod. 32, the Breda mod. 40 had a more modern type of cabin with full doors, and a much more powerful diesel engine in place of the mod. 32's gasoline

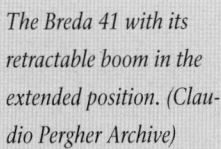

144

Breda 32.

Breda 40.

engine. The Breda mod. 40 was also fitted with modern 8 spoke cast steel wheels with *Artiglio* tires and differed dimensionally from the mod. 32. A modified version of the Breda mod. 40, with higher sideboards on the bed and mounting a retractable crane on the front of the vehicle, to be used as a retrieval vehicle, was designated the Breda mod. 41.

Production of the Breda mod. 40/41 continued under German auspices after September 1943, with 100 delivered in 1944 alone. The tractor continued to be manufactured for a brief period during the post-war years.

Specifications:

Designation:	trattrice pesante Breda 32 and trattrice pesante Breda 33
Manufacturer:	Breda Meccannica Bresciana
Weight (unloaded)	8,400 kg (18,519 lb) mod. 32; 8,500 kg (18,739 lb) mod. 33
Carrying capacity:	3,500 kg (7,716 lb) on road; 2,500 kg (5,512 lb) off road; 2,000 kg (4,409 lb) mod. 33
Towing capacity:	up to 25 tonnes on road at 8% grade; 10 tonnes off road
Length:	5.15m (202.8 inches) mod. 32; 6.32m (245.7 inches) mod. 33
Width:	2.08m (81.9 inches) mod. 32; 2.10m (82.7 inches) mod. 33
Height:	3.00m(118.1 inches) mod.32; 2.91m (114.6 inches) mod. 33
Engine:	SPA Model T5, 4 cylinder gasoline, 8,150 cc (497 cu. in)
Horsepower:	84 @ 1450 rpm
Transmission:	5 speeds forward, 1 reverse; 4-wheel drive
Fuel capacity:	200 litres (52.8 US gallons; 44 Imperial gallons) mod. 32; 125 litres (33 US gallons; 27.5 Imperial gallons) mod. 33
Wheelbase:	2.65m (104.3 inches) mod 32; 3.80m (149.6 inches) mod. 33
Track:	1.68m (66.1 inches) front and 1.615m (63.6 inches) rear
Turning radius:	5.75 mm (226.4 inches); 8.00m (315 inches) mod. 33
Tire size:	*Celerflex* semi-pneumatic 205 x 980
Maximum speed (road):	30 km/h (18.6 mph)
Maximum range:	240 km (149 miles) unladen on road; 150 km (93.2 miles) with towed load on road; 10 hours unladen off-road; 6 hours with towed load off-road (mod. 32)
Maximum gradient:	35%
Ground clearance:	390mm (15.4 inches)
Fording depth:	NA
Special notes:	7,500 kg (16,535 lb) capacity winch

Specifications:

Designation:	trattrice pesante Breda 40
Manufacturer:	Breda Meccanica Bresciana
Weight (unloaded)	10,100 kg (22,267 lb)
Carrying capacity:	3,500 kg (7,716.2 lb) on road; 2,500 kg (5512 lb) off road
Towing capacity:	10,000 kg (2204.6 lb)
Length:	5.40m (212.6 inches)
Width:	2.40m (94.5 inches)
Height:	2.61m to top of cab; 2.92m with canvas cover on rear
Engine:	Breda D 11, 6 cylinder diesel, 8,850 cc (540 cu. in)
Horsepower:	115 @ 1800 rpm
Transmission:	5 forward speed. 1 reverse
Fuel capacity:	200 litres (52.8 US gallons; 44 Imperial gallons)
Wheelbase:	2.90m (114.2 inches)
Track:	1.81m (71.3 inches) front and 1.795m (70.7 inches) rear
Turning radius:	8.55m (336.6 inches)
Tire size:	9 x 50
Maximum speed (road):	41 km/h (25.5 mph)
Maximum range:	260 km (161.6 miles)
Maximum gradient:	48%
Ground clearance:	460mm (18.1 inches)
Fording depth:	NA

FIAT OCI 708 CM tracked artillery tractor

The adoption of the 75/18 howitzer for mountain troops by Italy in 1934 (see specific entry) led to a need for a light artillery tractor capable of towing the piece in mountainous terrain. The solution was found in a tracked agricultural tractor of simple design, powered by a gasoline engine and designated the mod. 708 C, manufactured by OCI (*Officine Costruzioni Industriali*), which was a FIAT subsidiary located in Modena. A modified OCI 708 C tractor was presented as a military prototype in late 1934, designated the OCI 708 CM, with the letter M signifying *militare* (military). In 1935 200 examples of the tractor, officially designated as the *trattore da montagna* 708 CM, were ordered.

A factory photograph of a FIAT OCI 708 CM light tractor. The OCI used a steering wheel rather than lateral levers for steering. Claudio Pergher Archive)

FIAT OCI tractors towing a 75/18 howitzer and ammunition trailer. (Claudio Pergher Archive)

The OCI 708 CM was a very small crawler tractor, somewhat similar to the US Clark CA -1 airborne tractor. It was well suited to its intended role in mountainous terrain, although it was somewhat fragile mechanically in the military role. It was successfully tested as a prime mover for the 47/32 anti-tank gun and for the 100/17 mod. 16 howitzer, but was never assigned that role; its use remained limited to towing the 75/18 in the mountains, and in this role it took part in the military maneuvers of 1936 in Irpinia, with the 10th Artillery Regiment, being judged satisfactory. It was also assigned to infantry units in Libya as a supply tractor, but in this latter role its utility was limited because although it moved efficiently off roads, on road it had a limited range and had to be loaded on trucks for long transfers. The *Regia Aeronautica* used a number of the 708 CM as airfield tow vehicles.

The 708 CM made its operational debut in Eritrea in 1935, where it was used to tow the 77/28 guns of two groups. In 1936 the tractor was assigned to units in Somalia and Libya, and later saw service in the Spanish Civil War (54 tractors). Upon Italy's entry in WWII in June 1940 there were 381 OCI 708 CM tractors assigned to the Italian Fifth Army in Libya; by October 1941 only 113 remained operational. Production of the OCI 708 CM continued until 1943.

Specifications:

Designation:	FIAT OCI 708 CM
Manufacturer:	Officine Costruzioni Industriali (OCI), Modena (FIAT subsidiary)
Weight (unloaded/loaded)	2,540 kg (5600 lb)
Towing capacity:	2,200 kg (4850 lb)
Length:	3.05mm 120.1 inches)
Width:	1.23m (48.4 inches)
Height:	1.47m (57.9 inches)
Engine:	OCI 708 C, 4 cylinder gasoline, 2,520cc (154 cu. in.)
Horsepower:	30 @ 2300 rpm
Transmission:	manual 4 speed forward, 1 reverse

The OCI was used extensively by the Regia Aeronautica, as shown here towing what appears to be a Cant Z1007bis tri--motor bomber. (Claudio Pergher Archive)

A FIAT OCI lies abandoned in a North African port. (Claudio Pergher Archive)

Fuel capacity:	84 litres (22.2 US gallons; 18.48 Imperial gallons)
Track contact on ground:	2.278m (89.7 inches)
Track:	1.00m (39.4 inches)
Turning radius:	1.50m (59 inches)
Maximum speed (road):	16 km/h (9.9 mph)
Maximum range:	7 hours endurance without refueling
Maximum gradient:	50%
Ground clearance:	260 mm (10.2 inches)

SPA TL 37 field artillery tractor

In 1935 the Italian Army issued a requirement for a light artillery tractor to tow the suitably modified 75mm and 100mm guns in the inventory. Vehicle requirements included 4-wheel drive, with wheels capable of being fitted with either solid or pneumatic tires, ability to carry a six-man artillery crew, and the ability to tow both 75mm and 100mm pieces at a speed of 40 km/h (24 mph) on paved roads. In 1936 SPA engineers, in competition with Breda, set to work, developing a prototype called the *trattore di Fanteria* (infantry tractor) which was further developed into the standard pattern adopted by the *Regio Esercito* in 1937 and designated the SPA TL 37, the TL signifying *trattore leggero*, or light tractor.

The TL 37 reflected much of the genius historically exhibited by the Italian automotive industry: its design was both sound and innovative, and tailored as it was for its military application, was a reliable vehicle despite the mechanical complexity of its four-wheel drive and four-wheel steering. The vehicle was built on a solid steel frame; suspension was independent, and in addition to being powered, all four of the wheels steered, giving the vehicle a tight turning radius. The all-metal body had seating for six, and had a total of nine storage compartments, as well as an ammunition storage locker in the rear. It had right-hand drive that was standard on Italian military trucks. The TL 37 could be and was fitted with a number of different wheel and tire combinations: wheels could be solid stamped steel discs, stamped steel with eight holes, or cast wheels with six spokes; tires could be solid, semi-pneumatic *Celerflex*, or fully pneumatic. Each vehicle was also fitted with a 2,000 kg (4,409 lb) capacity winch.

In October 1937, 250 examples were ordered, and a test group of 24 TL 37s was sent to Libya in 1938, where it was used to tow the 75/27 mod. 06 guns mounted on the *carrello elastico*, as well as towing ammunition trailers for the guns. The results proved to be entirely satisfactory, setting the stage for mechanization of Italian artillery in the desert. At the time it was thought that the TL 37 could also fill the need for a light reconnaissance vehicle. Although series production of the TL 37 was initiated, monthly production fell far short of requirements and never amounted to more than 150 vehicles per month, hardly adequate to replace losses and to convert the horse-drawn artillery to mechanical towing.

Although it never assumed the role as a reconnaissance vehicle as such, the TL 37 was built in a number of versions and variants, including the TL 37 *pontiere* engineer vehicle; the TL 37 *Coloniale* which was fitted with 9.75 x 24 Pirelli *tipo Libia* tires specifically for use in North Africa, a higher capacity (2,500 kg/5,512 lb) winch, and other refinements; the TL 37 *Libia*, very similar to the *Coloniale*, but with extended range capability thanks to supplementary fuel tanks, and the TL 37 *protetto*, which was an armoured personnel carrier, produced in 150 examples and used in Yugoslavia. The AS 37 was a light truck based on the TL 37 chassis, while both the *camionetta AS43* and the *camionetta desertica* mod. 43 light desert trucks, intended for use as a command and reconnaissance vehicle, were in turn a development based on the AS 37. A local modification of the TL 37 tractor in North Africa mounted a 75/27 mod. 11 field gun on the tractor chassis; three batteries of this unique vehicle were built.

The TL 37 artillery tractor was issued to the motorised artillery batteries of infantry, cavalry, motorised, and armoured divisions and saw service in all Italian combat theaters, including Yugoslavia, Greece, Russia, and North Africa where it saw its greatest use. Prior to the Axis defeat in Tunisia, on 30 April 1943, there were between 2,150 and 2,267 TL 37s of the various versions (excluding the AS

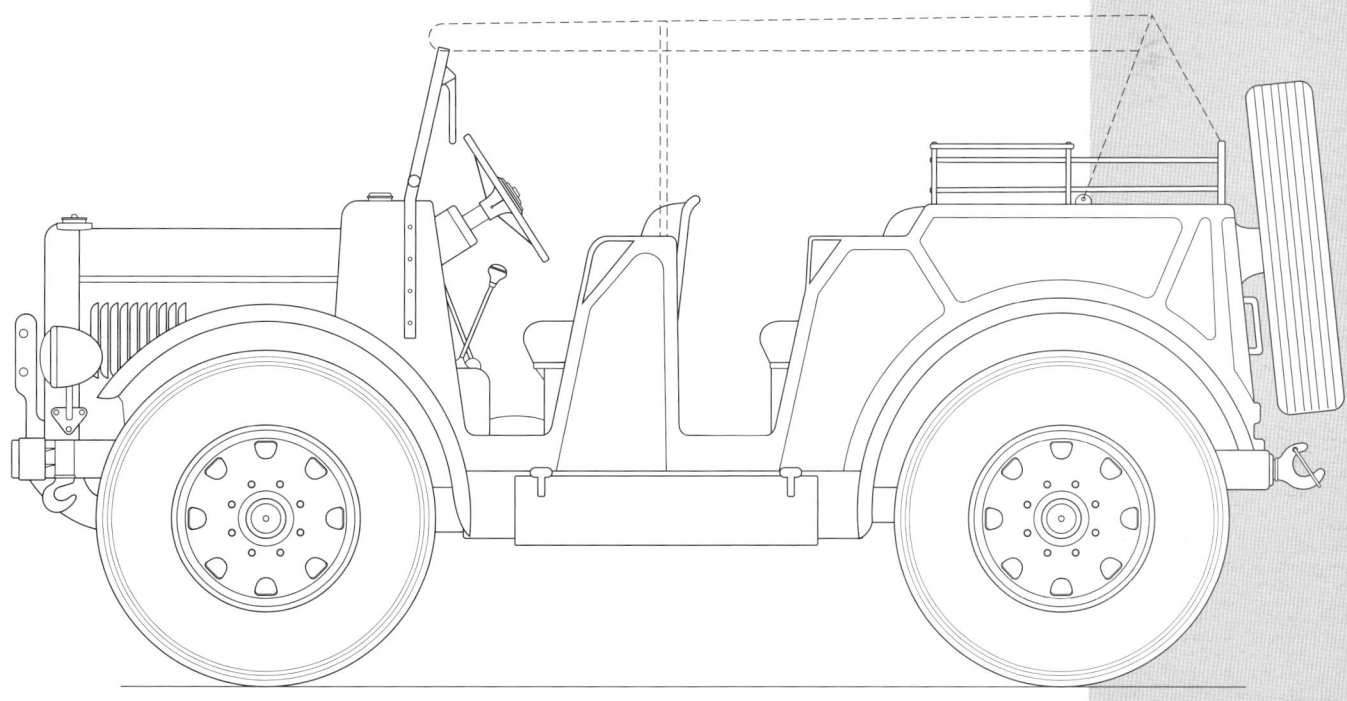

SPA TL 37 field artillery tractor.

37) in service, according to different sources. That the TL 37 was a modern, high-quality vehicle well suited for its task as an artillery tractor is attested to by a report by an Australian commission in 1941 which, after having tested the TL 37, judged it to be the best artillery tractor available on either side in North Africa. After September 1943 the Germans took possession of large numbers of the TL 37, which were designated *Radschlepper TL 37 (i)*, and ordered its continued production by SPA for their own use. As might be expected, small numbers of the TL 37 were used by both RSI forces in northern Italy and by the Italian co-belligerent forces in the south. During the post-war period, between 1946 and 1948, the TL 37 remained in service with alpine artillery units.

Specifications:

Designation:	TL 37 (*trattore leggero* 37)
Manufacturer:	FIAT/SPA
Weight (unloaded)	3,181 kg (9,076 lb) with pneumatic tires; 3,560 kg (7,848.5 lb) with semi-pneumatic tires
Carrying capacity:	800 kg (1764 lb)
Towing capacity:	2,000 kg (4409 lb)
Length:	4.13m (162.6 inches)
Width:	1.83m (72 inches)
Height:	2.18m with canvas roof (85.8 inches)
Engine:	SPA Model 18 TL, 4 cylinder gasoline, 4,053cc (247 cu. in.)
Horsepower:	52 @ 2000 rpm
Transmission:	manual transmission with 5 forward speed and reverse; four-wheel drive with lockable differential
Fuel capacity:	100 litres (26.5 US gallons; 22 Imperial gallons)
Wheelbase:	2.50m (98.4 inches)
Track:	1.518m (59.8 inches)with pneumatic tires; 1.44m (56.7 inches) with semi-pneumatic tires
Turning radius:	4.50m (177.2 inches)
Tire size:	*Artiglio* pneumatic 9.00 x 24 and 9.75 x 24; *tipo Libia* pneumatic 11.25 x 24; *Celerflex* semi-pneumatic 160 x 881
Maximum speed (road):	38.2 km/h (23.7 mph) fully loaded
Maximum range:	355 km (221 miles) with two supplemental 20-litre (5.3 gallon) jerrycans
Maximum gradient:	80% in 1st gear at 2.4 km/h (1.5 mph)
Ground clearance:	345mm (13.6 inches)
Fording depth:	700mm (27.6 inches)

A well restored TL 37 displayed at Cuneo during a commemorative event in honor of the Cuneense Alpine Division. (Enrico Finazzer)

SPA TM 40 heavy field artillery tractor

The TM 40 (*trattore medio*, or medium tractor) artillery tractor resulted from a request put forward by the *Regio Esercito* in 1938 for a tractor to replace the old Pavesi tractors (see specific entry above). SPA presented its prototype in competition with Breda and Lancia, and after extensive tests it was adopted in 1941. Due to the high degree of satisfaction registered with the earlier TL 37, the TM 40 followed the same general construction principles as the TL 37. Although adopted in 1941,

A TM 40 as it appeared in a vintage newspaper photograph. (Claudio Pergher Archive)

Frontal view of a factory new TM 40. (Claudio Pergher Archive)

the TM 40 was not actually introduced into service until 1942 due to production delays caused primarily by lack of raw materials. In the interim, the Pavesi tractors continued to serve in the role, and the 4 x 2 Lancia 3Ro heavy truck was also pressed into service as a prime mover.

Like the earlier TL 37, the TL 40 was a four-wheel drive tractor, with all four wheels steerable. Also like the TL 37, it could be fitted with either semi-pneumatic or pneumatic tires. Unlike the TL 37, the TM 40 was a cab-over-engine machine. The larger size of the TM 40 with respect to the TL 37 enabled it to carry a total of eight men (driver and passenger in the front, and six crew in the back seated face to face), as well as ammunition for guns up to 149mm.

Early deliveries of the TM 40 were sent to the Russian front, but deliveries continued at a snail's pace. By December 1942 only 107 had been delivered to units, and only an additional 90 could be delivered during the first quarter of 1943. The TM 40 was also used by the *Regia Marina*, and a closed-cab version was used by the *Regia Aeronautica*. After the Italian surrender in September 1943 SPA continued to produce the TM 40 for the German forces in northern Italy. The German designation for the TM 40 was *Radschlepper 110 PS Spa (i)*; ironically,

Rear view of the TM 40, clearly showing the impressive size of the spare tire and the stowage compartment. (Claudio Pergher Archive)

SPA TM 40 heavy field artillery tractor.

A camouflaged TM 40 on the move in North Africa towing a 105/28 gun. (Claudio Pergher Archive)

The TM 40 was used in Russia; here one is shown towing a German 7.5 cm PaK 40 anti-tank gun. (Claudio Pergher Archive)

A TM 40 fitted with tire chains to help cope with the severe conditions on the Russian front. (Claudio Pergher Archive)

production of the tractor seems to have proceeded rather well under German patronage, as 153 examples were built in 1944. During the early months of 1945 some examples of the TM 40 were built using a German-style *Einheits* body, some of which survived and were used by the reconstituted Italian Army for a time during the post-war period.

Specifications:

Designation:	TM 40
Manufacturer:	FIAT/SPA
Weight (unloaded):	6,575 kg (14,495 lb)
Carrying capacity:	1,285 kg (2833 lb)
Towing capacity:	5,000 kg (11,023 lb)
Length:	4.68m (184.3 inches)
Width:	2.20m (86.6 inches)
Height:	2.80m (110.2 inches)
Engine:	Type 366, 6 cylinder diesel, 9,365cc (572 cu. in.)
Horsepower:	105 @ 2000rpm
Transmission:	manual transmission with 5 forward speed and reverse; four-wheel drive with lockable differential
Fuel capacity:	140 litres (37 US gallons; 30.8 Imperial gallons)
Wheelbase:	2.50m (98.4 inches)
Track:	1.63m (64.2 inches) with pneumatic tires; 1.665m (65.6 inches) with semi-pneumatic tires
Turning radius:	5.60m (220.5 inches)
Tire size:	*Artiglio* pneumatic 50x9 or 12.75x37; semi pneumatic 265x980
Maximum speed (road):	43.35 km/h (29.96 mph)
Maximum range:	300 km (186.4 miles)
Maximum gradient:	45% with 5000 kg load
Ground clearance:	330 mm (13 inches)
Fording depth:	900 mm (35.4 inches)

Breda 61 half-tracked tractor

As allies of the Germans the Italians were influenced by German practice and in late 1941 the *Regio Esercito* developed an interest in half-tracked vehicles, widely used by the German armed forces both as troop transports and artillery tractors. Negotiations started with Germany in order to obtain the designs of some of the *SdKfz* models, and in in late spring 1943 Italian industry was able to present two prototypes, the 3 ton FIAT 727 which closely resembled the Hanomag HL K 6, and the 8 ton Breda 61, which essentially was a license-produced version of the German Krauss-Maffei KM m 11 (*SdKfz* 7) half-track, fitted with right-hand drive and powered by a Breda engine, specifically designed for towing of artillery, with 12 seats for driver and crew. Both of these initiatives were too late and the *Regio Esercito* did not see a single vehicle for its own use; however the Breda 61 was appreciated by the Germans who after the Armistice had Breda produce at least 199 pieces for the *Wehrmacht*.

A Breda 61 half-track; this vehicle was a very close copy of the German Krauss-Maffei 8-ton half-track for which it can be easily mistaken. (Bruno Benvenuti Archive)

Breda 61 continued to be produced under German control and issued to German units after the September 1943 Italian armistice. (Claudio Pergher Archive)

A Breda 61 half-track and the 149/19 howitzer it was towing destroyed somewhere in Italy. (Claudio Pergher Archive)

Specifications

Designation:	Breda 61
Manufacturer:	Breda Meccanica Bresciana
Weight:	11,200 kg (24,692 lb) empty; 13,000 kg (28,660 lb) fully laden
Carrying capacity:	1,800 kg (3968 lb)
Towing capacity:	8,000 kg (17,637 lb)
Length:	6.90m (271.7 inches)
Width:	2.45m (96.5 inches)
Height:	2.75m (108.3 inches)
Engine:	Breda Type T14 gasoline, 6 cylinders, 7,412 cc (452 cu. in.)
Horsepower:	130 @ 2400rpm
Transmission:	Data uncertain. Presumably a manual transmission similar to that of the *SdKfz* 7 with four forward and one reverse, doubled by means of a reduction gear.
Fuel capacity:	170 + 35 litres (45 US gallons + 9.29 gallons reserve; 37.4 Imperial gallons + 7.7 gallons reserve)
Front tread:	2.02m (79.5 inches)
Turning radius:	8.00m (315 inches)
Maximum speed (road):	50 km/h (31 mph)
Operating radius:	170-200 km (106-124 miles)
Maximum gradient:	24%
Ground clearance:	390mm (15.4 inches)

BIBLIOGRAPHY

Balocco, Col. R. *Fanti e artiglieri*. Manualetti di Tecnica Militare, Fascicolo XXI, dicembre 1934.

Benussi, Giulio. *Armi portatili, artiglierie e semoventi del Regio Esercito Italiano 1900-1943*. Milano: Intergest, 1975.

Benussi, Giulio. *Semicingolati, motoveicoli e veicoli speciali del Regio Esercito Italiano 1919-1943*. Milano: Intergest, 1976.

Benussi, Giulio. *Veicoli Speciali del Regio Esercito Italiano nella Seconda Guerra Mondiale*. Milano: Intergest, undated.

Bishop, Chris. *The Encyclopedia of Weapons of World War II*. Barnes & Noble Books, 1998.

Cappellano, Filippo. *Le artiglierie del Regio Esercito nella seconda guerra mondiale*. Parma: Albertelli Edizioni Speciali, 1998.

Cappellano, Filippo. *Il treno C/20*. Notiziario Modellistico, Gruppo Modellistico Trentino di Studio e Ricerca Storica 1/13, aprile 2013, pages 22-27.

Cappellano, Filippo, and Formiconi, Paolo. *Il cannone da 149/40 Mod. 35*. Storia Militare, N. 216, September 2011, pages 4-17.

Ceva, Lucio. *Storie delle Forze Armate in Italia*. UTET, 1999.

Ceva, Lucio. *La condotta italiana della guerra*. Feltrinelli, 1975.

Ceva, Lucio, and Curami, Andrea. *La meccanizzazione dell'esercito italiano dalle origini al 1943*. Roma: Stato Maggiore Esercito, Ufficio Storico, 1994.

Chamberlain, Peter, and Gander, Terry. *Anti-Aircraft Guns*. WW2 Fact Files. London: MacDonald and Janes's, 1975.

Chamberlain, Peter, and Gander, Terry. *Anti-Tank Weapons*. WW2 Fact Files. London: MacDonald and Janes's, 1974.

Chamberlain, Peter, and Gander, Terry. *Infantry, Mountain, and Airborne Guns*. WW2 Fact Files. London: MacDonald and Janes's, 1973.

Chamberlain, Peter, and Gander, Terry. *Light and Medium Field Artillery*. WW2 Fact Files. London: MacDonald and Janes's, 1975.

Cucut, Carlo *Le forze armate del RSI*. Trento: Gruppo Modellistico Trentino, 2005.

Favagrossa, Carlo. *Perché perdemmo la guerra*. Milano: Rizzoli Editore, 1946.

Finazzer, Enrico. *Le artiglierie del Regio Esercito nella seconda guerra mondiale*. Genova: Italia Storica, 2012.

Gander, Terry. *Heavy Artillery of WWII*. Vital Guide. Ramsbury, Marlborough, Wiltshire: Airlife (The CrowoodPress), 2004.

Guglielmi, Daniele. *Sd.Kfz. 7, mittlerer Zugkraftwagen 8 t*. Genova: Auriga Publishing International srl, 2009.

Haskew, Michael E. *Artillery From the Civil War to the Present Day*. New York: Metro Books (for Amber Books), 2008.

Hogg, Ian. *Twentieth Century Artillery*. London: Amber Books Ltd., 2000.

Madeja, W. Victor. *Italian Army Order of Battle: 1940-44*. Allentown, Pennsylvania: Valor Publishing Company, 1990.

Montanari, Mario. *L'esercito italiano alla vigilia della 2ª Guerra Mondiale*. Rome: Stato Maggiore Esercito, Ufficio Storico, 1975.

Montanari, Mario. *Le operazioni in Africa Settentrionale*. Rome: Stato Maggiore Esercito, Ufficio Storico, 1985-1993..

Ortner, M. Christian. *The Austro-Hungarian Artillery from 1867 to 1918. Technology, Organization and Tactics*. Vienna: Verlag Militaria, 2007.

Pergher, Claudio. *Le macchine di Pavesi*. Trento: Gruppo Modellistico Trentino, 2002.

Pignato, Nicola. *Artiglierie e automezzi dell'Esercito Italiano nella seconda Guerra mondiale*. Parma: Ermanno Albertelli Editore, 1972.

Pignato, Nicola. *L'obice da 149/19 OTO 1937*, in Storia Militare No. 150, March 2006.

Pignato, Nicola. *Il 105/28 del Regio Esercito*, in Storia Militare No. 182, November 2008.

Pignato, Nicola. *L'ultimo "75" dell'artiglieria italiana*, in Storia Militare No. 188, May 2009.

Pignato, Nicola. *Un "pezzo da 90"*, in Storia Militare No. 201, June 2010

Pignato, Nicola. *Motoriii!!! Le truppe corazzate italiane 1919/1994*. Trento: Gruppo Modellistico Trentino di Studio e Ricerca Storica, 1995.

Pignato, Nicola, and Cappellano, Filippo. *Dal TL37 al A.S. 43*. Trento: Gruppo Modellistico Trentino di Studio e Ricerca Storica, 1997.

Pignato, Nicola, and Cappellano, Filippo. *Gli autoveicoli da combattimento dell'Esercito Italiano – Vol. II, dal 1940 al 1945*. Roma: Stato Maggiore Esercito, Ufficio Storico, 2002..

Pignato, Nicola, and Cappellano, Filippo. *L'obice da 210/22 mod. 35.*, in Storia Militare No. 171, January 2008.

Pignato, Nicola, and Cappellano, Filippo. *La produzione di artiglierie in Italia durante la seconda guerra mondiale*, Parte 1ª in Storia Militare No. 74, 1999, pages 33-41.

Pignato, Nicola, and Cappellano, Filippo. *La produzione di artiglierie in Italia durante la seconda guerra mondiale*, Parte 2ª in Storia Militare No. 75, 1999, pages 24-32.

Pignato, Nicola, and Geibel, Adam. *A Forgotten Gun: The 75mm Déport*. Journal of Military Ordnance, September 1996.

Pràšil, Michal. *Skoda Heavy Guns. 24cm Cannon, 38cm Howitzer, 42cm Howitzer and Gasoline-electrical Trains*. Atglen, Pennsylvania: Schiffer Publishing Ltd., 1997.

Raudino, S. and Stefanni, E. (edited by). *Storia dell'artiglieria italiana, parte V, vol. XV and XVI*. Rivista d'artiglieria e genio 1953-1955.

Riccio, Ralph. *Italian Tanks and Combat Vehicles of World War II*. Fidenza: Roadrunner/Mattioli 1885 spa, 2010.

Riccio, Ralph, and Pignato, Nicola. *Italian Truck-Mounted Artillery*. Carrollton, Texas: Squadron/Signal Publications, 2010.

Rochat, Giorgio. *Le guerre italiane 1935-1943*. Torino: Einaudi Editore, 2005.

Santoni, Alberto. *Le operazioni in Sicilia e Calabria*. Rome: Stato Maggiore Esercito, Ufficio Storico, 1983.

Vanderveen, Bart H. *The Observer's Fighting Vehicles Directory World War II*. London: Frederick Warne & Co Ltd., 1972.

Zanlucchi, Paolo. *E qui, quando fiorirà la terra? Lettere del cappellano militare don Onorio Spada – Marzo 1942 – settembre 1943*. Rovereto: Egon Editore, 2011.

Tactical and Technical Trends, No. 46, May 1, 1944